Global Non-Proliferation
and Counter-Terrorism

Global Non-Proliferation and Counter-Terrorism

The Impact of UNSCR 1540

OLIVIA BOSCH
PETER VAN HAM
editors

CLINGENDAEL INSTITUTE
The Hague

CHATHAM HOUSE
London

BROOKINGS INSTITUTION PRESS
Washington, D.C.

10247343

Copyright © 2007
ROYAL INSTITUTE OF INTERNATIONAL AFFAIRS

Chatham House (the Royal Institute of International Affairs) is an independent body which promotes the rigorous study of international questions and does not express opinions of its own. The opinions expressed in this publication are the responsibility of the authors.

Chatham House, 10 St. James's Square, London SW1Y 4 LE
(www.chathamhouse.org.uk); charity registration no. 208223

Global Non-Proliferation and Counter-Terrorism: The Impact of United Nations Security Council Resolution 1540 may be ordered from:
BROOKINGS INSTITUTION PRESS
c/o HFS, P.O. Box 50370, Baltimore, MD 21211-4370
Tel.: 800/537-5487; 410/516-6956; Fax: 410/516-6998
Internet: www.brookings.edu

Library of Congress Cataloging-in-Publication data
Global non-proliferation and counter-terrorism : the impact of UNSCR 1540 / Olivia Bosch and Peter van Ham, editors.
    p.   cm.
Summary: "Brings together scholars and policymakers to examine the impact of UN Security Council Resolution 1540 on the bioscientific community, the Chemical Weapons Convention, the IAEA, trade and customs, and counterproliferation initiatives. Provides an overview of a wide range of new policy-related questions arising from UNSCR 1540's future implementation and enforcement"—Provided by publisher.
    Includes bibliographical references and index.
    ISBN-13: 978-0-8157-1017-2 (pbk. : alk. paper)
    ISBN-10: 0-8157-1017-8 (pbk. : alk. paper)
    1. Arms control.   2. Weapons of mass destruction.   3. Terrorism-Prevention.   4. United Nations. Security Council-Resolutions.   I. Bosch, Olivia.   II. Ham, Peter van, 1963–   III. Title.
    JZ5625.G56 2006
    327.1'745-dc22   2006100297

9 8 7 6 5 4 3 2 1

The paper used in this publication meets minimum requirements of the American National Standard for Information Sciences—Permanence of Paper for Printed Library Materials: ANSI Z39.48-1992.

Typeset in Minion

Composition by R. Lynn Rivenbark
Macon, Georgia

Printed by R. R. Donnelley
Harrisonburg, Virginia

Contents

Foreword

I was honored to be invited to contribute the foreword to this volume. To my knowledge, it is the first-ever scientific undertaking of such breadth on this topic. Inputs from the specialized academic and scientific community have been enormously helpful and inspirational throughout the early and most difficult stages of the implementation process. They still are now, when the Security Council, indeed the United Nations as a whole, ponders how to take the process regarding the 1540 regime further.

UNSCR 1540 is an exceptional multilateral response to an exceptional multifaceted security challenge. By adopting it, the Security Council took the rare step of pronouncing on a threat of global significance, instead of a country- or region-specific menace. And by so doing, it undertook to fill an important gap in existing non-proliferation treaties and multilateral arrangements, which do not currently capture the role of non-state actors in matters related to weapons of mass destruction (WMD).

In this regard, it may be worth noting that subsequent to the eventual unanimous adoption of this landmark resolution, the main line of criticism of the action taken by the Security Council was directed not at the substance of the resolution, but rather at form and procedure. The Security Council was thus seen as having conducted itself as a world legislator of sorts. In fact, what it did was give binding meaning to the unanimous and unreserved declaration by the summit-level meeting of the Security Council back in 1992 that nuclear, chemical, and biological weapons proliferation is a threat to international peace and security. Security Council action was taken twelve years afterward—twelve years during which little, if any, progress had been made in the more traditional modes of addressing WMD proliferation, but also a period that witnessed 9/11 and many other terrorist attacks of an increasingly ominous nature. Moreover, the Security Council did no more than set out in a very generic manner a series of parameters, leaving their domestic articulation entirely to the discretion of national parliaments.

The adoption of UNSCR 1540 responded to an exceptional security challenge. At a time of increased potential access to WMD and related technology, when terrorist activity itself proliferates, the nexus between the two topples every other item on everyone's security agenda, irrespective of regional contexts. It would therefore have been irresponsible for the United Nations and its Security Council not to consider generating global defenses against this ultimate nightmare scenario.

I have always been struck by the fact that this resolution, in conjunction with the work of the committee established to assist the Security Council in monitoring its implementation, goes by a number that is also a tennis score. Not just any tennis score, but one that reflects a particularly dire situation for the player who serves, in which one has to serve and play hard and well to redress the game.

The 1540 regime plays accordingly in both the non-proliferation and counter-terrorism areas. It provides the international community with a sound basis and a flexible reference for addressing WMD proliferation and terrorism from whichever direction is considered to be more effective at a given juncture.

Its most valuable feature is that the concerns it addresses are brought forward at the UN's universal level. The implementation processes at the UN may be slow, involving heavier managerial parameters and cultivating consensus while largely precluding "intrusion." They certainly carry valuable legitimacy, however, while ensuring badly needed uniformity of applicable standards in the area of preventing access to WMD and related materials and technologies. UN action in preventing terrorists from acquiring WMD, or otherwise preventing the latter from becoming accessible to the former, is by no means to be seen as a stand-alone; not only does it not preclude, but it actually fosters and is enhanced by measures and actions in the same vein, taken at regional, sub-regional and national levels.

The April 2006 UNSCR 1673 carries on, without notable changes, the regime set forth by the original 1540 resolution. There is unquestionable merit in exhausting the potential of fully implementing the latter, in terms of mapping out the global situation of legal, administrative, and physical safeguards put in place to deny non-state actors access to WMD, and of extending the broadest international assistance and cooperation in support of achieving a uniform, though perhaps still minimal, safety net.

It remains to be seen whether delivering further on the tremendous potential encapsulated in the 1540 regime will translate into taking its legal ambit and depth a step forward, into consolidating it as part of a joint, stronger counter-terrorism undertaking within the UN system, or else using it concurrently as a basis for action outside the United Nations.

Last but not least, I am proud to have been a part of the early stages of implementing this long-awaited response by the United Nations to a nexus between the two utmost security challenges of our times, the proliferation of both WMD and terrorism—a nexus capable of rendering futile all of our collective dreams, aspirations, even all of our other concerns. Nothing happened during "my watch." I hope we will achieve the point of protection in this field where nothing will ever happen under anyone else's watch as well.

AMBASSADOR MIHNEA MOTOC
Chairman, 1540 Committee, 2004–05, and
Permanent Representative of Romania to the United Nations

December 2006

List of Abbreviations

AG	Australia Group
ARF	ASEAN Regional Forum
ASEAN	Association of Southeast Asian Nations
BW	Biological Weapons
BTWC	Biological and (Toxin) Weapons Convention (also known as BWC)
CTC	Counter-Terrorism Committee
CTED	Counter-Terrorism Committee Executive Directorate
CWC	Chemical Weapons Convention
CSI	Container Security Initiative
DPRK	Democratic People's Republic of Korea
FAO	Food and Agriculture Organization
GMO	Genetically Modified Organism
GPC	General Purpose Criterion of the CWC
HCOC	Hague Code of Conduct (against ballistic missile proliferation)
HLSG	High Level Strategic Group of Directors General
IAEA	International Atomic Energy Agency
IATA	International Air Transport Association
ICRC	International Committee of the Red Cross
IMO	International Maritime Organization
Interpol	International Criminal Police Organization
ISTC	International Science and Technology Center
JI	Jemaah Islamiyah
MANPADS	Man Portable Air Defense Systems

MTCR	Missile Technology Control Regime
NIH	National Institutes of Health (USA)
NBC	Nuclear, Biological, and Chemical
NSG	Nuclear Suppliers Group
OIE	World Organisation for Animal Health (created as the Office International des Epizooties)
OPCW	Organisation for the Prohibition of Chemical Weapons
PSI	Proliferation Security Initiative
RILO	Regional Intelligence Liaison Offices
SUA	(Convention for the) Suppression of Unlawful Acts against the Safety of Maritime Navigation
START	Strategic Arms Reduction Treaty
UAV	Unmanned Aerial Vehicle
UN	United Nations
UNDDA	UN Department of Disarmament Affairs
UNIDIR	UN Institute for Disarmament Research
UNODC	UN Office on Drugs and Crime
UNSC	UN Security Council
UNSCR	UN Security Council Resolution
UPU	Universal Postal Union
USDA	United States Department of Agriculture
WA	Wassenaar Arrangement
WCO	World Customs Organization
WHO	World Health Organization

PART I

UN Security Council Resolution 1540, Context and Non-State Actors

PETER VAN HAM *and* OLIVIA BOSCH

1

Global Non-Proliferation and Counter-Terrorism: The Role of Resolution 1540 and Its Implications

Scenarios in which terrorists use weapons of mass destruction (WMD) have been posited for decades, but the threat and the issues involved have received new attention in the early 2000s.[1] U.S. Secretary of Defense Donald Rumsfeld has reformulated what has been popularly called the "sum of all fears" as the "nexus between weapons of mass destruction and terrorist networks," arguing that we "really have to think very carefully about what we do as a people, and as a world, and as a society."[2] This nexus—part of a more complex and interrelated composite picture of threats and vulnerabilities— and the new interdisciplinary approaches to dealing with these problems are central to the theme of this volume.[3] It addresses them through the prism of a radically new initiative incorporated in United Nations Security Council Resolution (UNSCR) 1540, adopted on April 28, 2004, under the auspices of Chapter VII of the UN Charter.[4]

The proliferation of nuclear, chemical, and biological weapons was declared a threat to international peace and security at the heads of state summit of the Security Council on January 31, 1992, but this was presented in a statement, not a legally binding resolution. Both the United States and the members of the European Union see WMD proliferation as one of their main security challenges.[5] Consensus ends there, however, because there is little agreement on how this threat can best be dealt with, especially when there are the additional concerns of terrorism and also, as recently underscored by UNSCR 1540, illicit trafficking.[6]

The May 2003 U.S.-led Proliferation Security Initiative to establish an ad hoc counter-proliferation arrangement, the December 2003 revelations of the Khan global smuggling network for nuclear weapon–related technologies, which included end-users such as Iran, Libya, and North Korea, and growing worries about the fissures in the bio-weapons verification mechanisms have all reinforced the urgency of the need to keep WMD out of the "wrong hands." They have underlined the fact that existing non-proliferation treaties and regimes, although important, are inadequate and not universal in their coverage.

Against this background, UNSCR 1540 was passed in April 2004, to try to address the inadequacies of existing measures and the particular challenge of controlling WMD proliferation by non-state actors. The Resolution's primary requirements are that states:

—"refrain from providing any form of support to non-State actors that attempt to develop, acquire, manufacture, possess, transport, transfer or use nuclear, chemical or biological weapons and their means of delivery" (operative paragraph (OP) 1); [7]

—"adopt and enforce appropriate effective laws which prohibit any non-State actor to manufacture, acquire, possess, develop, transport, transfer or use nuclear, chemical or biological weapons and their means of delivery, in particular for terrorist purposes, as well as attempts to engage in any of the foregoing activities, participate in them as an accomplice, assist or finance them" (OP 2); and

—"take and enforce effective measures to establish domestic controls to prevent the proliferation of nuclear, chemical or biological weapons and their means of delivery, including by establishing appropriate controls over related materials . . . " by developing security, physical protection, border, and export controls (OP 3).

This chapter examines the strategic context of the Resolution, its origins and affiliation with UN resolutions on counter-terrorism, and its significance and features. It goes on to look at what constitutes a non-state actor in this context and the significance of the biological and life sciences community, for which, unlike the nuclear and chemical sectors, there is no one international organization associated with implementing treaties concerning limitations or bans on these sectors' materials for weapons purposes. The implementation of the Resolution is examined with respect to its reinforcement of the main non-proliferation treaties as well as to its additional requirements to deal with the new proliferation challenges. The chapter concludes with an initial exploratory examination of issues surrounding enforcement, not a focus of the traditional treaty regimes and for which there is a lack of global capacity given the current disparities between states in recognizing, let alone dealing with, the concerns raised by the Resolution.

The Strategic Context

One could argue that Resolution 1540 creates the foundation of a new system of global governance for dealing with the nexus of WMD proliferation, terrorism, and illicit trafficking. It is important to note that the Resolution has direct consequences for all states' domestic legal structures, imposing upon each country the requirement to criminalize WMD proliferation by and among non-state actors and to implement effective controls. This is a departure from the governance model whereby UN member states, through a long process of debate and negotiation, come to agree upon shared standards and norms. The strategic imperative of the post–9/11 security environment has dictated a swifter and less consensual model, which can be seen as among the outer tiers of a layered non-proliferation defense and which is in line with the United States' international security agenda.

The early, under-institutionalized nature of the UNSCR 1540 system (see below) was in line with what Washington wanted in the approach to the Resolution's adoption. The United States' initial approach was to avoid new bureaucracy while establishing swift and, hopefully, effective measures within a system where it could expect to have significant leverage. Lin Brooks, then the acting director of the U.S. National Nuclear Security Administration, argued in 2003 that the United States is "seeking to free [itself] from intellectual prohibitions against exploring a full range of technical options. . . . I have a bias in favor of things that might be usable."[8]

Resolution 1540 is testimony to the American view of "effective multilateralism." The Bush administration has taken a proactive approach by initiating the Proliferation Security Initiative and the Container Security Initiative as well as proposing to strengthen the role of the Nuclear Suppliers Group in monitoring nuclear exports. Washington's focus is on "coalitions of the willing," sometimes known as the "international community" or, even less concretely, the club of "civilized" nations. The *Wall Street Journal* has aptly characterized these groupings as follows: "There's no headquarters, no secretary-general, no talkfests—and, perhaps most important of all, no French or Russian veto."[9] The Bush administration exudes a general distrust of multilateral institutions and is keen to work around them. John Bolton, America's ambassador to the UN since 2005, has made it very clear that "the idea that we could have a UN Security Council resolution or a nice international treaty is fine if you have unlimited time. We don't, not with the threats out there . . . , want to engage in an endless legal seminar."[10] This means that Washington follows a policy of multilateralism "by invitation," asking others to work with the United States, follow its leadership, and trust its judgment.

During the May 2005 NPT (Nuclear Non-Proliferation Treaty) Review Conference in New York, proliferation analyst Joseph Cirincione argued that Washington's stance "reflects a deep disdain for the international agreements and institutions. Many neo-conservatives in Washington believe these multilateral meetings are worthless. Worse, they see them as a trap where global Lilliputians can tie down the American Gulliver. To move beyond these 'outmoded' instruments, President Bush pulled out of some treaties, ignored others, and gutted still others."[11] He further claimed that the "idea was to replace these international forums with US-centric initiatives, and to shift the focus from treaties to direct action that would eliminate certain regimes that had weapons. The war with Iraq was step one, intended to send a message to Iran and North Korea that they had better abandon their programs or face the consequences."[12]

The Origins of UNSCR 1540

Although Resolution 1540 may have come as a surprise to many, it did not come out of the blue. In September 2003, President Bush launched the idea of criminalizing WMD proliferation in his address to the UN General Assembly. He argued that

> because proliferators will use any route or channel that is open to them, we need the broadest possible cooperation to stop them. Today, I ask the UN Security Council to adopt a new anti-proliferation resolution. This resolution should call on all members of the UN to criminalize the proliferation of weapons—weapons of mass destruction, to enact strict export controls consistent with international standards, and to secure any and all sensitive materials within their own borders. The United States stands ready to help any nation draft these new laws, and to assist in their enforcement.[13]

Over the course of only seven months, the United States engaged in negotiations on the Resolution, and Russia produced an initial draft, supported by other members of the Security Council. During this period, intensive diplomatic discussions took place. Numerous countries expressed concern that the proposed resolution might serve as a basis for imposing economic, and even military, sanctions against states that were deemed in "non-compliance." China supported the Resolution only after several provisions had been negotiated, including deletion of the word *interdiction* from what is now operative paragraph 10 calling on international cooperation to stem illicit trafficking.[14] Another negotiating change was the insertion of "States Parties" in operative paragraph 5, enabling states not yet parties to a treaty to retain their national security prerogative. The draft resolution was in the end co-sponsored by France, Romania, Russia, Spain, the United Kingdom, and the United States.[15]

Several regional groupings within the UN contested whether it was really necessary to adopt Resolution 1540 under Chapter VII. The issues involved were discussed at an open Security Council meeting on April 22, 2004, where some thirty states debated the merits of the draft resolution.[16] Some members, such as Pakistan and India, questioned whether it was the role of the Security Council to prescribe legislative action by member states, and others, for example Cuba, argued that they had become subject to laws into whose drafting they had had no input. But other members, such as France, stated that the Resolution was about setting goals, leaving each state free to determine specific measures and penalties in accordance with national circumstances. The holding of an open meeting in which uncertainties and reservations were expressed was a rather unusual procedure. This indicated that the far-ranging legal implications of the Resolution required more support than might be engendered by the customary Security Council fiat.[17] At the same time, however, all states have agreed in UN Charter Article 24(1) that on issues of international peace and security, the Security Council acts on their behalf, and they have also agreed to be bound by its resolutions (articles 2(5), 25, and 49).[18]

UNSCR 1540 does not replace the traditional forums and processes for negotiating arms control and non-proliferation treaties. Instead, it is a mechanism that supplements these traditional forums. It reinforces the norms, obligations, and legal requirements of the three main WMD treaties—the 1968 Nuclear Non-Proliferation Treaty (NPT), the 1972 Biological and Toxin Weapons Convention (BTWC), and the 1993 Chemical Weapons Convention (CWC)—as well as requires effective enforcement, which is not yet prevalent much less universal in the treaty regimes. The Resolution, acting pursuant to Chapter VII, imposes obligations on all member states without the usual caveats, buy-offs, and deals that have accompanied treaties such as the NPT and the CWC. This is a major change, because it impinges upon the Westphalian concept of state sovereignty by forcing treaty-like obligations on all states without their explicit consent although, as mentioned above, UN member states agree to adhere to Security Council resolutions.

Institutional Affiliation with Counter-Terrorism

UNSCR 1540 is clearly a non- and counter-proliferation measure, but it arises out of a family of UN resolutions dealing with counter-terrorism, and by 2006 its administrative aspects had become bundled in with these resolutions. They began with UNSCR 1267 (October 15, 1999), a resolution dealing with individuals and groups that were financially, politically, or otherwise helping the Taliban or Al-Qaeda groups and their terrorist activities. Resolution 1267 gave rise to the Al-Qaeda and Taliban Sanctions Committee, a subsidiary body of the Security Council whose purpose is to maintain a list of individuals and entities against whom sanctions (assets freeze, travel ban, arms embargo) are applied; and promote the full application of the sanctions by States.

A subsequent resolution, UNSCR 1373 (September 28, 2001), had the most direct influence on UNSCR 1540. Quickly passed in the aftermath of the terrorist attacks on the World Trade Center and the Pentagon and the airliner's crash in Pennsylvania on September 11, 2001 (9/11), Resolution 1373 requires all UN member states to take steps to combat terrorism, with the UN serving as a focal point for building the networks and professional capacity to do so at the global level.

This was the first time since its inception in 1945 that the Security Council had invoked Chapter VII to legislate on a functional rather than usually state-specific threat to international peace and security. Its application is universal, setting global legislative requirements for all states, and functional, focusing on counter-terrorism rather than a specific threat. The scope of Resolution 1373 is more strategic than the initial shorter-term, tactical aims of Resolution 1267.[19] Also, the possibility of terrorists accessing WMD was already on the minds of its drafters: it includes two paragraphs (3(a) and 4) concerned with terrorist possession of WMD and trafficking in related materials.

UNSCR 1540 emerged from those two paragraphs because UNSCR 1373 already had a heavy agenda for implementing its counter-terrorism elements. It does not follow directly from any specific terrorist incident or threat involving nuclear, biological, or chemical weapons, although its origins lie in the wake of the March–April 2003 Iraq conflict and concerns about the acquisition of nuclear, chemical, or biological weapons and related materials by terrorists and tyrannical states. In the mold of Resolution 1373, Resolution 1540 is universal and generic, and adopts many of the former resolution's committee processes to facilitate states' implementation, set out below.

The next member of the family of resolutions dealing with counter-terrorism was Resolution 1566, passed on October 8, 2004, in the wake of the September 2004 gun attack on a school in Beslan, Russia. The Resolution does not refer specifically to this incident, but it is significant for introducing further new measures to counter-terrorism, condemning all terrorism irrespective of motivation or justification, and including the best attempt so far to define terrorism.[20] Additionally, its provisions require Resolution 1373's

Counter-Terrorism Committee (CTC) both to work with relevant organizations in order to develop best practices for implementing provisions on terrorist financing and to reinforce visits to states, as set out in UNSCR 1535, so as to monitor implementation and to facilitate the provision of assistance. Some of these activities may have applicability to the future role of the 1540 Committee. The Resolution also mandates a working group of Security Council members to examine practical measures that could be applied to terrorists not on the Al-Qaeda/Taliban Sanctions list and to consider the feasibility of an international compensation fund for the victims of terrorism.

When it became clear that these resolutions created a new and comprehensive UN agenda for countering terrorism and proliferation, there was scope for coordination between the several committees arising from the resolutions (see chapter 2 by Thomas Biersteker).[21] On April 25, 2005, the chairmen of the 1540 Committee, the CTC, and the Al-Qaeda/Taliban Sanctions Committee, though not their first meeting, for the first time had jointly briefed the Council.[22] The Security Council ultimately "called for strengthened cooperation among the Committees through enhanced information sharing, coordinated visits to countries and other issues of relevance." Given the significant overlap of their areas of interest, the three committees perceived the need for closer cooperation among them. Together they could give rise to a new system of global governance at the UN level; and although it is important to identify Resolution 1540 as a specifically non-proliferation measure, the implication is that its full and effective implementation could be expected to result in or contribute to preventing the use of WMD by terrorists.

Resolution 1540: Its Significance

Resolution 1540 aims to fill several voids in the international system for controlling WMD proliferation. First, there is its focus on non-state actors. Existing treaties and regimes assume that only states have the intention and capabilities to develop WMD. The NPT, the BTWC, and the CWC, as the three main non-proliferation treaties, establish standards and norms of non-proliferation applicable, first and foremost, to states. Their references to non-state entities are secondary.

Because international law does not apply to individuals, non-state actors are subject only to prohibitions laid down in an often ambiguous patchwork of domestic law. Whereas some countries have a sophisticated and effective legal framework of laws, regulations, and controls, others have little in place that could deter terrorists and traffickers from acquiring and transporting WMD, related materials, and delivery means or that could prosecute them for doing so. In an effort to oblige all states to tighten their domestic legal framework, Resolution 1540 is a re-presentation of states parties' obligations under the main treaties.[23] But it goes further, requiring all states, even those not party to the treaties, to criminalize and enforce measures against WMD proliferation to and by non-state actors.

The second gap filled by Resolution 1540 is in dealing with the proliferation of biological agents and weapons. Unlike the International Atomic Energy Agency (IAEA) and the Organisation for the Prohibition of Chemical Weapons (OPCW), which are international organizations fostering states' implementation and compliance with the NPT and the CWC respectively, there is no such organization for the BTWC. Despite potential pandemics such as avian influenza and the worldwide promulgation of biological technologies and know-how for public health applications as championed by UN Secretary General Kofi Annan, the international approach to non-proliferation of biological weapons and materials is less structured.[24] Chapter 3 in this book, by Elizabeth M. Prescott, and chapter 9, by Jeffrey Almond, discuss the implications of this situation and good practice in the life sciences and chemical industries for addressing biological proliferation issues.

Third, Resolution 1540 is the only measure that explicitly integrates proliferation concerns about delivery means with those about nuclear, chemical, and biological agents. Chapter 8, by Ted Whiteside, presents the issues and challenges involved in delivery systems, which are not the subject of legally binding non-proliferation treaties such as the NPT, the BTWC, and the CWC because of their applicability to the development of civil space capabilities and conventional weapons systems. Thus international control in this area goes little beyond the politically binding international export control guidelines that countries implement through their national export regulations.

Fourth, the resolution is significant in requiring measures beyond the obligations laid out in the three treaties. These are specified in its operative paragraphs 2 and 3, and concern financial, security and accountability, physical protection, border, and export controls. Although these issues are central to the Resolution, the 1540 Committee did little work on them in its first two years. Chapters 10 and 12, by Will Robinson and Gerald Epstein respectively, highlight some of the envisaged challenges presented by these new types of controls.

Lastly, the Resolution requires enforcement. It emphasizes enforcement in operative paragraphs 2 and 3; and its adoption under the UN Charter's Chapter VII, in which threats to international peace and security are addressed and whose obligations are mandatory, opens up for consideration the possibility of a range of sanctions in case of non-compliance. This aims not only to address the enforcement weakness in the treaty and export control regimes but also to emphasize the role states are expected to play in developing capacity and working together to pre-empt proliferation (OP 10). Chapter 11, by Siew Gay Ong, examines the role of the Proliferation Security Initiative as an arrangement for preventing the proliferation of nuclear, chemical, and biological weapons, materials, and delivery means, and in chapter 13 Roelof Jan Manschot highlights through case studies, including that of Pakistani Abdul Qadeer Khan in the 1980s, the difficulties of balancing the different objectives of the law enforcement and intelligence communities when non-state actors are subject to prosecution.

Resolution 1540: Its Features

Just as UNSCR 1373 mandated the creation of the Counter-Terrorism Committee, so the 1540 Committee was set up to report on states' fulfillment of their obligations under Resolution 1540. The 1540 Committee, initially mandated for a maximum of two years but renewed on April 27, 2006, with UNSCR 1673, comprises representatives of all fifteen Security Council members, the ten non-permanent members of which rotate every two years. It was initially chaired by the Romanian ambassador, Mihnea Motoc.[25] When Romania's two-year membership in the Security Council ended at the end of December 2005, he was succeeded by Peter Burian, the UN ambassador of Slovakia, upon its joining the Security Council in January 2006.

The Security Council, learning from the experience of previous committees (especially those monitoring mandatory arms embargoes), called for outside technical assistance in order to ensure that the review and monitoring process proceeded professionally and without delay. The 1540 Committee, in conducting its work, could "call . . . as appropriate on other expertise" (OP 5), and thus an experts group, initially of four members but expanded to eight, was set up by the end of July 2005.[26]

The 1540 Committee was also mandated to call upon all states to produce reports, within six months of the passing of the Resolution, "on steps they have taken or intend to take to implement this resolution" (OP 5). By the deadline for submissions on October 28, 2004, the number of reports submitted (excluding one by the EU) was 59; by April 20, 2006, it had risen to 129. One of the main roles of the renewed 1540 Committee will be to encourage and assist those states, primarily from Africa, the Caribbean, and the South Pacific, that still have to provide first reports.[27]

The Resolution's drafters were aware that states have differing capacities for dealing with legislative and administrative issues, and Resolution 1540, like

UNSCR 1373, recommends that states either request or offer legal and technical assistance with implementation. With respect to the CTC, assistance was needed particularly for drafting anti-terrorism laws and developing banking and financial laws and regulations. The World Bank, as a UN body, is reported to have received more than 100 requests from countries to assist them in building capacity to deal with money laundering and terrorist financing. While some observers have expressed worry that this "assistance clause" was expressly put into 1540 by the United States so that it could dictate to others how to deal in the proper way with WMD proliferation with respect to non-state actors,[28] the 1540 Committee's Work Guidelines explicitly state that it can undertake cooperation with relevant international organizations as needed for its work (appendix C, 2(d)).

Non-State Actors

UNSCR 1540 is a non- and counter-proliferation rather than a disarmament mechanism, with an emphasis on prevention. It aims to prevent individuals and other non-state entities from conducting activities related to the proliferation and use of nuclear, chemical, and biological weapons, related materials, and delivery means, and it criminalizes these activities through legislation arising from or reinforced by the Resolution's implementation. The Resolution defines a non-state actor in a footnote as an "individual or entity, not acting under the lawful authority of any State in conducting activities which come within the scope of this resolution." The definition is not prescriptive as to the nature, sector, or type of non-state actor: they may be, for example, individuals or entities with malign, criminal, or anti-state interests, non-governmental organizations, or multinational corporations.[29] Instead, the Resolution refers to anyone acting unlawfully in the light of its objectives, and thus implies a wide scope for the legislative provisions states could put into place, reflecting the different sectors that have the potential for proliferation.

This section will look briefly at the terrorist and the trafficker, explicitly referred to in the Resolution and expected to engage in the unlawful activities covered by it. Attention is drawn to a particular type of non-state actor who may fall foul of the new laws: individuals in the science and technology communities around the world upon whom the trafficker and terrorist can be expected to rely. The chapters in this volume by Elizabeth Prescott and Jeffrey Almond elaborate the scientific community's distinct capabilities and characteristics and its potential to provide the information, know-how, and materials sought by terrorists or traffickers interested in acquiring nuclear, chemical, and biological weapon capabilities. The Resolution's operative paragraph 8(d) is clear in its call on all states "to develop appropriate ways to work with and inform industry and the public [academia] regarding their obligations under such laws" as implemented for Resolution 1540, thereby implicitly drawing attention to the need to deal with the potential of industrial and academic, scientific, and engineering personnel to abet terrorists and traffickers. When scientists and technicians possess or handle nuclear, chemical, and biological materials under ambiguous circumstances, their prosecution, depending on the status of a country's legislation or regulations, poses complex challenges. These are elaborated in chapter 4 by Sarah Meek and Chandré Gould and in the chapters by Gerald Epstein and Roelof Manschot.

Terrorists and Traffickers

The stated central concern of UNSCR 1540 is to prevent the use by non-state actors, such as terrorists, of nuclear, chemical, and biological weapons. For decades the security literature has examined the possibility that this "sum of all fears" could become a reality, and a number of incidents exemplifying what might be involved have already been well reported. These events include the arrest in 1972 of members of the far-right Order of the Rising Sun, who possessed typhoid bacteria cultures with which they planned to poison water supplies in Chicago and other U.S. cities; the Rajneesh cult's use in 1984 of food poisoning in ten restaurants in Wasco County, Oregon, in an attempt to influence local elections; and, probably most notorious, the Japanese Aum Shinrikyo sect's acquisition of dual-use technologies and actual use of the nerve agent sarin in 1994 and 1995, most notably against the Tokyo subway system.

The attacks of 9/11 greatly heightened concern about terrorists using means other than a conventional gun, bomb, or mortar attack to achieve mass casualties and large-scale destruction or disruption and for ends that may not be clear and have little or no possibility of being settled by negotiation. Following 9/11, the U.S. postal system was heavily disrupted by the release of anthrax-filled packages, the source of which remains undetermined. There followed similar but hoax activity. Also, Osama bin Laden's terrorist network and affiliated Islamic groups have expressed an aspiration to obtain some form of nuclear capability.

These commonly cited examples indicate that despite the potential, individuals or non-state groups with terrorist intent have yet to develop their own fully fledged nuclear, chemical, or biological weapons programs. The main obstacles remain the large infrastructure of resources and know-how needed to make deliverable nuclear weapons and the less demanding but still complex requirements for chemical and biological weapons. Instead, within the realm of their individual or small-group capability, they are believed more likely to resort to means such as the theft of states' old or unprotected WMD stocks; to devise innovative ways of using easily available materials, component parts, or radiological waste instead of nuclear materials; or to seek support from states that have or are alleged to have WMD programs.

The availability of sensitive materials that can be trafficked for potential terrorist use and the means by which they might be obtained are thus emphasized by the Resolution. Its preamble codifies illicit trafficking as an additional dimension of proliferation and presents it as a threat to international peace and security. Attention is thereby drawn to acquisition or to development activities at an early stage in a proliferation process, these perhaps serving as indirect indicators of a possible intention to use nuclear, chemical, or biological weapons.

Among examples of such indicators arising in the scientific community is the illicit trafficking activities of the Pakistani metallurgist A. Q. Khan and his network, whose prosecution in the early 1980s is covered in the chapter by Roelof Manschot. The chapter by Sarah Meek and Chandré Gould is a case study of the issues involved in unraveling the alleged criminal conduct of Wouter Basson, a respected South African cardiologist working on apartheid South Africa's WMD programs, called Project Coast.[30] Both Khan and Basson are instances of scientists who are corrupted by considerations of privilege, prestige, and money and who are in a position to facilitate the development of clandestine state WMD programs or potential WMD use by terrorists. The vetting of personnel in sensitive positions continues to be important, but more attention is given to physical controls on nuclear, chemical, and biological materials. The G-8's Action Plan on Non-Proliferation of June 2004 encourages schemes for the redirection of the employment of personnel who have worked on the former WMD programs of Libya and Iraq. These schemes could contribute to fulfilling the Resolution's operative paragraph 8(d), and are discussed further in this volume's final chapter.

Resolution 1540: Treaties and Additional Measures

Resolution 1540 requires states to "promote the universal adoption and full implementation, and, where necessary, strengthening of multilateral treaties to which they are parties, whose aim is to prevent the proliferation of nuclear, biological or chemical weapons" (OP 8(a)). It also requires them to "fulfil their commitment to multilateral cooperation, in particular within the framework of the International Atomic Energy Agency, the Organisation for the Prohibition of Chemical Weapons, and the Biological and Toxin Weapons Convention" (OP 8(c)).

Most states have already signed and ratified the three main WMD treaties, and thus have some form of relevant national legislation in place whose enforcement would go a long way toward compliance with Resolution 1540. In most cases, states will also have worked with the named organizations, particularly when adopting secondary legislation or regulations for creating the necessary national authorities to implement and enforce the treaties.

However, Resolution 1540 emphasizes not these treaties per se but the resulting national legislation and other regulations and controls that provide the basis upon which action can be taken against non-state actors. As much of the legislation to implement and comply with the Resolution is similar to that for the existing WMD treaties, a positive or complementary side effect is that states that are willing but have not yet had the time or resources to become a party can both implement and comply simultaneously.

The emphasis of the legislation is significant: Resolution 1540 encourages and promotes universal WMD treaty implementation, but states not yet a party retain their prerogative not to sign these treaties. During the open debate before adoption of the Resolution, Indian officials made it clear that "we shall not accept any interpretation of the draft resolution that imposes obligations arising from treaties that India has not signed or ratified. . . . "[31] There is less than universal adherence to the three WMD treaties (much less implementation of them). Some countries, such as India, Pakistan, and Israel, have not signed the NPT but have adopted national legislation in compliance with Resolution 1540. Others have not signed the CWC or the BTWC, and may perceive themselves to be confronted with de facto new legal obligations even though they, like all UN members, are bound to adhere to Security Council resolutions.

The Resolution stipulates that it does not alter the "rights and obligations" of states parties to the NPT, the CWC, and the BTWC or change the responsibilities of the IAEA and the OPCW. It should therefore be clear that UNSCR 1540 does not supersede existing international non-proliferation and arms control instruments but instead fills the gaps in their varying approaches. The history of treaty negotiations to ban or control the three types of WMD material—nuclear, chemical, and biological—is markedly different in each case, leading to a variety of mechanisms for treaty implementation as well as for dealing with treaty violations. Each of the three treaties raises different issues and challenges highlighted by the Resolution.

The Chemical Weapons Convention

The CWC relies on a "general purpose criterion" to ban the use of any chemical as a weapon except for purposes permitted under the terms of the convention, for example riot control, and has specifically mandated the Organisation for the Prohibition of Chemical Weapons to facilitate its implementation and verification regime. The treaty has established lists (in annexed schedules) of various types of chemicals that have been weaponized in the past and whose export is therefore subject to declaration and routine inspection. The schedules also specify the volumes of these chemicals permitted for commercial export. However, they are merely illustrative, to help inspectors and industry to manage the inspection and verification regime for the export of chemicals and the destruction of old CW stockpiles, because the treaty's "general purpose criterion" bans all chemicals, including those not yet invented, for use as weapons.

The CWC illustrates the challenges raised by Resolution 1540 when it comes to dealing with volumes of chemical agents that are significant in a terrorist, as opposed to military, context. The Resolution does not use the term *WMD* at all (except in the preamble, referring to the 1992 Statement). It refers instead to destructive materials separately, underlining the importance of distinguishing between the three as well as drawing the proliferation debate away from the notion of "mass destruction" as the sole (or prime) basis upon which prosecution or preventive action can be taken.

Chapter 5 of this book, by Ron G. Manley, illustrates how legislators as well as law enforcement officials are challenged by Resolution 1540 in trying to deal with the potentially smaller amounts of chemicals, perhaps measured only in kilograms, that might have terrorist significance, compared to the more easily measurable volumes of chemicals, usually in the order of tons, known to have military significance.[32] Although the "general purpose criterion" covers all chemicals, implementing the Resolution means that attention is drawn to chemicals not listed in a schedule. One example, as Manley points out, is sodium cyanide or potassium cyanide—in small amounts it can pose a threat in terrorist hands—and there are some riot-control agents that are not subject to inspection. It remains to be seen how states' legislators will work with industry in dealing with their obligations under prospective new legislation in accordance with Resolution 1540's operative paragraphs 3 and 8(d). This legislation could also be undertaken in tandem with the export control guidelines of the Australia Group.

The Nuclear Non-Proliferation Treaty

The NPT is commonly regarded as an arrangement between the nuclear weapons states, which agree to transfer nuclear technology and materials to non-nuclear weapons states for peaceful purposes, and the non-nuclear weapons states, which in return commit themselves not to divert this material to developing nuclear weapons.[33] This treaty has near-universal adherence.

India, Israel, and Pakistan are the only non-signatories, and North Korea withdrew from it in 2003, arguably. The importance of the NPT in relation to Resolution 1540 in the context of this book lies in the role of the IAEA as an international organization through which nuclear non-proliferation goals can be achieved.

In contrast to the CWC, which specifically mandated the creation of the OPCW, the NPT appointed the pre-existing IAEA (established in 1956) as the organization with which non-nuclear weapon states were to sign safeguard agreements and to implement non-proliferation measures. These agreements are "for the exclusive purpose of verification of the fulfilment of its obligations . . . with a view to preventing diversion of nuclear energy from peaceful uses to nuclear weapons or other nuclear explosive devices" (NPT, article 3-1). The IAEA was empowered to conduct inspections of declared civil nuclear power and research facilities in order to ensure that high-level source or special fissionable material usable for nuclear weapons, that is, enriched uranium or plutonium (an energy fuel cycle waste by-product), is adequately accounted for, handled, stored, and disposed of.

Although the NPT and Resolution 1540 both focus on nuclear materials and weapons, the IAEA has a broader remit (see chapter 6 by Tariq Rauf and Jan Lodding), also to cover the monitoring, safe handling, and disposal of lower-level radioactive waste, for example from hospitals and industry. The safe handling and transportation of all types of this material and waste is thus already covered by the IAEA, notably in its Code of Conduct on the Safety and Security of Radioactive Sources and the Convention on the Physical Protection of Nuclear Materials. Both measures are mentioned in the preamble to UNSCR 1540, and have subsequently been enhanced to take account of the more rigorous enforcement requirements of the Resolution. On April 13, 2005, the UN General Assembly added the International Convention on the Suppression of Acts of Nuclear Terrorism to this existing legal framework. Unlike Resolution 1540, it criminalizes the possession, use, or threatened use of radioactive devices by non-state actors.

In support of Resolution 1540, the Convention further requires all participating governments to prosecute terrorists under their domestic legal system and encourages exchanges of information and increased cooperation in order to avoid nuclear terrorism.[34] The IAEA's Illicit Trafficking Database is an additional source of information. It has documented more than 660 confirmed incidents of illicit trafficking and other related unauthorized activities involving nuclear and other radioactive materials from 1993 to 2004, even though only about 18 are confirmed incidents involving trafficking in highly enriched uranium or plutonium. All the cases are assessed for patterns or trends that could provide guidance for states framing further domestic legislation and enforcement mechanisms so as to comply with UNSCR 1540.[35]

Just as the OPCW has an assistance and protection program under the CWC's Article 10, so the International Atomic Energy Agency has a program of assistance on legislation, training, and materials accountancy. These are useful resources to which the 1540 Committee can refer in its role of brokering assistance to states in meeting the Resolution's requirements.

The Biological and Toxin Weapons Convention

The BTWC bans the development, acquisition, and use of biological and toxin agents as weapons, relying on the same general purpose criterion as used by the CWC.[36] Article 1 of the BTWC points out that this objective applies to all states, and thus it is the principal focus of the treaty, but Article 3 refers to states undertaking "not to transfer to any recipient whatsoever, directly or indirectly, . . . the agents, toxins, weapons, equipment or means of delivery specified in Article 1." It is noted that "means of delivery" is mentioned, as it is too, in UNSCR 1540.

As mentioned earlier, Resolution 1540 emphasizes the need to have national laws in place owing to the BTWC lacking an international organization for implementing the treaty comparable to the IAEA and the OPCW. The chapter in this study by Angela Woodward highlights this void and what states parties to the treaty have done over the years to try to cope with it through procedural rather than institutional channels. If all states ratified and enforced treaty legislation, then many of the objectives of UNSCR 1540 would also be met with respect to biological non-proliferation.

New and Additional Requirements

Resolution 1540 recognizes that most states have undertaken binding legal obligations under the main treaties or have made other commitments to stem the proliferation of nuclear, chemical, or biological weapons, but it is particularly notable and significant for "*Recognizing further* the urgent need for all States to take additional effective measures to prevent the proliferation of nuclear, chemical or biological weapons and their means of delivery" (preambular paragraph, italics in original). Thus even if all UN member states become parties to the main WMD treaties and fully implement the consequent national legislation, the Resolution still requires them to "take additional effective measures." This phrase draws attention to new measures beyond treaty requirements, in operative paragraphs 2 and 3, which need to be implemented and also to be enforced for effective compliance with the Resolution. These additional measures are intended to improve the financial, security, and physical protection of sensitive materials and also border and export controls. The aim is to address one of the new features of the Resolution—the naming in the preamble of illicit trafficking as a new dimension of proliferation and therefore a threat to international peace and security. However, the 1540 Committee did little work on these additional measures during its first two years of operation, other than noting the information that states had provided in their submissions on the measures they had undertaken or intended to undertake in these areas.

Although the physical protection of sensitive materials has been fairly well developed by the work of the IAEA and although export control regimes are well established, financial controls and border controls are not on the traditional arms control and non-proliferation agenda. The chapter by Will Robinson examines the new role of the World Customs Organization in addressing some of the latter two controls, and the chapter by Gerald Epstein highlights some of the challenges of addressing the security and accountability of sensitive biological materials.

Enforcement

Enforcing compliance with Security Council resolutions is a political process, and is only as strong as states' willingness to undertake it within the collective security framework of the UN system. Although Iraq's non-compliance with UNSCRs from April 1991 to March 2003 was notable, even more so was the controversy surrounding how UN member states would enforce those resolutions, which in the end resulted in the March–April 2003 conflict in Iraq.

UNSCR 1540 has not given rise so far to these types of enforcement challenge, which are mentioned here to place the Resolution in the wider context of national and international security issues. Yet in the context of the recent UN reforms, the processes by which UNSCRs 1373 and 1540 came about, the comprehensiveness of Resolution 1540's coverage, and its universal and mandatory requirements place it in a new and as yet undefined category of measures under which states can no longer allow proscribed activities with impunity in and across their borders. If in this age of global communications states continue to tolerate proscribed activities and remain unable to institute accountable and transparent governance mechanisms, they subject themselves to examination by others. Resolution 1540 provides a framework within which nations can question one another about activities that suggest illicit trafficking or other proscribed activity. Evasive answers cast doubt on a state's commitment to preventing the misuse of a dual-use technology or other activity proscribed by Resolution 1540. Even though the Resolution does not mandate specific enforcement measures or penalties for non-compliance—it requires states to do so instead—the Security Council can take such action as it deems necessary.

Conclusion

The lax enforcement and patchy coverage of the non-proliferation regimes became more conspicuous after 9/11, when concerns about potential terrorist use of WMD became more pressing, at least on America's security agenda. Resolution 1540 clearly indicates that the UN is taking a more vigorous approach to keeping nuclear, chemical, and biological weapons, related materials, and means of delivery from terrorists and traffickers. Although the UN has been exercising its authority in a clearer and more forceful way since the 1992 Security Council Statement, there has been a lack of consistency in addressing WMD proliferation threats, and this can be attributed to disagreements among the five permanent member states of the Security Council about the UN's role in this area of security. Although other states have also expressed concern about the possible implications of the Resolution's implementation, this has not surfaced during the first two years of the 1540 Committee's work.

Resolution 1540 gives the Security Council a more concrete mission and mandate in the area of non- and counter-proliferation, but they are still imprecise. It remains to be seen how the Resolution's provisions will be made operational and enforced. Imprecision was necessary, however, because states have widely varying capacities for implementing and enforcing the Resolution, and it is they, not the Security Council, that must take appropriate action in accordance with their national capabilities and legislative frameworks.

Notes

1. The phrase "weapons of mass destruction" (WMD) is conventionally used as shorthand for nuclear, chemical, and biological weapons, with their differences to be recognized. A Statement arising from the January 1992 UN Security Council summit refers to WMD, but UNSCR 1540 does not, other than in the preamble referring to the 1992 Statement.

2. U.S. Secretary of Defense Donald Rumsfeld, Interview with ABC "This Week," February 3, 2002, at www.defenselink.mil/transcripts/2002/t02032002_t0203abc.html.

3. This edited volume arises from a major international conference organized by Olivia Bosch and Peter van Ham on "Global Proliferation and Counter-Terrorism: The Role of UNSCR 1540," October 11–12, 2004, Chatham House, London. See also the reference in the Chairman's Report, "Report of the Committee Established Pursuant

to Resolution 1540 (2004)," United Nations Security Council, S/2006/257, April 25, 2006, p. 42, at http://disarmament2.un.org/Committee1540/chairreport.html.

4. UNSCR 1540, adopted at the 4956th meeting of the UN Security Council, April 28, 2004. A copy of the text appears as appendix A in this volume and at http://disarmament2.un.org/Committee1540/Res1540(E).pdf.

5. *The National Security Strategy of the United States of America* (Washington, D.C.: The White House, September 2002), at www.whitehouse.gov/nsc/nss.html; Javier Solana, *A Secure Europe in a Better World*, European Council, Thessaloniki (June 2003), at http://ue.eu.int/ueDocs/cms_Data/docs/pressdata/EN/reports/76255.pdf; and "The European Union Strategy against Proliferation of Weapons of Mass Destruction," The Council of the European Union, Brussels (December 2003), at http://ue.eu.int/uedocs/cmsUpload/st15708.en03.pdf.

6. Although there is no definitive definition of this term for the purposes of UNSCR 1540, *illicit trafficking* tends to refer to the usually accountable and legal movement of items but which are used for proscribed purposes; *smuggling* has a connotation of activity that intends to circumvent or breach customs regulations, usually for financial gain, for example falsifying cargo manifests in order to minimize customs duties.

7. The Resolution's operative paragraphs are numbered from 1 to 12, as distinct from the unnumbered paragraphs in the preamble. Paragraphs 1–5 and 12, beginning with "Decides," are deemed technically to carry more emphasis than those numbered 6 to 11. The Resolution also has a footnote, which, for only its purposes, provides definitions of means of delivery, non-state actors, and related materials.

8. Quoted in senators Carl Levin and Jack Reed, "Toward a More Responsible Nuclear Nonproliferation Strategy," *Arms Control Today*, Vol. 34, No. 2 (January/February 2004), pp. 9–14, at www.armscontrol.org/act/2004_01-02/LevinReed.asp.

9. "The New Multilateralism," *Wall Street Journal*, January 8, 2004.

10. Quoted in Carla Anne Roberts, "The U.N.: Searching For Relevance," *Wall Street Journal*, October 21, 2003.

11. Joseph Cirincione, "Nuclear Regime in Peril," *YaleGlobal Online Magazine*, May 17, 2005, at www.carnegieendowment.org/publications/index.cfm?fa=view&id=16946.

12. Ibid.

13. "President Bush Addresses United Nations General Assembly," New York, September 23, 2003, Office of the Press Secretary, the White House, at www.whitehouse.gov/news/releases/2003/09/20030923-4.html.

14. James Holmes, "Rough Waters Ahead," *Bulletin of the Atomic Scientists*, Vol. 61, No. 6 (November–December 2005), p. 24.

15. "Romania Co-authored the Security Council Resolution on Non-Proliferation of Weapons of Mass Destruction," Press Release, April 30, 2004, at www.roembus.org/english/security_council/April_30_Romania%20co-authored%20the%20Security%20Council%20resolution%20on%20non-proliferation%20of%20weapons%20of%20mass%20destruction.htm.

16. "Speakers in Security Council Debate on Weapons of Mass Destruction Express Doubts over Content of Proposed Non-Proliferation Text," Press Release SC/8070, Security Council, 4950th Meeting, April 22, 2004, at www.un.org/News/Press/docs/2004/sc8070.doc.htm.

17. Gabriel H. Oosthuizen and Elizabeth Wilmshurst, "Terrorism and Weapons of Mass Destruction: United Nations Security Council Resolution 1540," Chatham House Briefing Paper, September 2004, p. 3.

18. Curtis A. Ward, "Building Capacity to Combat International Terrorism: The Role of the United Nations Security Council," *Journal of Conflict & Security Law*, Vol. 8, No. 2 (2003), p. 294.

19. With the passing of UNSCR 1455 on January 17, 2003, the reporting and evaluation procedures of Resolution 1373's CTC were adopted for Resolution 1267.

20. Paragraph 3(d) provides what has been called the closest definition of terrorism to date: "criminal acts, including against civilians, committed with the intent to cause death or serious bodily injury, or taking of hostages, with the purpose to provoke a state of terror in the general public or in a group of persons or particular persons, intimidate a population or compel a government or an international organization to do or to abstain from doing any act, which constitute offences within the scope of and as defined in the international conventions and protocols relating to terrorism, are under no circumstances justifiable by considerations of a political, philosophical, ideological, racial, ethnic, religious or other similar nature."

21. Biersteker elaborates the evolution of the respective resolutions' committees and areas of common activity.

22. See "Security Council Briefed by Chairmen of Anti-Terrorism Committees; Calls for Strengthened Cooperation, Enhanced Information Sharing," 5168th Meeting, Press Release SC/8366, April 25, 2004, at www.un.org/News/Press/docs/2005/sc8366.doc.htm.

23. A "State Party" is one that has both signed and ratified (or acceded to) a treaty. The process of ratification (or accession, after an initial requisite number of States Parties has enabled the treaty to enter into force) means that a state makes the international treaty obligations part of its domestic law and national regulations.

24. Kofi Annan, "A Global Strategy for Fighting Terrorism," Keynote Address to the Closing Plenary of the International Summit on Democracy, Terrorism and Security, March 10, 2005, at http://english.safe-democracy.org/keynotes/a-global-strategy-for-fighting-terrorism.html#transcripcion; Kofi Annan, "Uniting against Terrorism: Recommendations for a Global Counter-Terrorism Strategy," Report of the Secretary General, United Nations General Assembly, April 27, 2006, at www.un.org/unitingagainstterrorism/sg-terrorism-2may06.pdf.

25. See foreword in this volume.

26. These experts, joining the group between February 6 and July 23, 2005, are B. Andemicael (Eritrea), V. Beck (Germany), R. Cupitt (United States), G. Heineken (Argentina), R. Monteleone-Neto (Brazil), P. Palanque (France), V. Slipchenko (Russian Federation), and I. Suseanu (Romania).

27. "Report of the Committee Established Pursuant to Resolution 1540 (2004)," United Nations Security Council, S/2006/257, April 25, 2006, at http://disarmament 2.un.org/Committee1540/chairreport.html, p. 7.

28. Alyn Ware, "International Ju-Jitsu: Using United Nations Security Council Resolution 1540 to Advance Nuclear Disarmament," www.wagingpeace.org/articles/2004/07/00_ware_ju-jitsu.htm, p. 3.

29. Citing Richard A. Falkenrath: "The term 'non-state actors' includes traditional, familiar terrorist organisations; paramilitary guerrilla groups fighting for control of territory; cults and other religious organisations; militias or other geographically fixed paramilitary groups; organised crime syndicates; mercenary groups; breakaway units of a state's military, intelligence or security services; corrupt multinational corporations; and lone individuals" in "Confronting Nuclear, Biological and Chemical Terrorism," *Survival*, Vol. 40, No. 3 (Autumn 1998), p. 62.

30. Chandré Gould and Peter Folb, *Project Coast: Apartheid's Chemical and Biological Warfare Programme* (Geneva: UNIDIR, December 2002).

31. See also the reference in "Report of the Committee Established Pursuant to Resolution 1540 (2004)," United Nations Security Council, S/2006/257, April 25, 2006, p. 42, at http://disarmament2.un.org/Committee1540/chairreport.html.

32. Ron Manley provides the following examples: the United States in the 1980s had 100,000 tons of chemical agents. Iraq had up to 10,000 tons of chemical nerve agent sarin at that time. Aum Shinrikyo (1995) used a few kilograms of sarin.

33. The 1968 Nuclear Non-Proliferation Treaty defines a nuclear-weapon state as "one which has manufactured and exploded a nuclear weapon or other nuclear explosive device prior to January 1, 1967" (article IX). Although not named, these states are China, France, Russia (originally the Soviet Union), the United Kingdom, and the United States. By historical accident, these states are also the five permanent members of the UN Security Council.

34. Claire Applegarth, "UN Adopts Nuclear Terrorism Convention; Treaty Seven Years in the Making," *Arms Control Today* (May 2005), p. 40, at www.armscontrol.org/act/2005_05/NuclearTerrorismConvention.asp.

35. See IAEA at www.iaea.org.

36. Toxins are poisonous chemicals of biological derivation. Technological advances mean that now many of them can be synthesized.

THOMAS J. BIERSTEKER

2

The UN's Counter-Terrorism Efforts: Lessons for UNSCR 1540

The United Nations is often criticized as an institution that is inefficient and unable to respond quickly and effectively in crisis situations and that generally lacks the capacity to adapt creatively to changing circumstances. While some have called for its fundamental reform or overhaul, others have urged its abolishment altogether. Criticisms of the UN's management of the Oil-for-Food Program, developed to ameliorate the negative humanitarian consequences produced by comprehensive sanctions against Iraq in the 1990s, raised the volume of criticism of the organization to new levels, particularly within the United States.

Although many of the criticisms are well founded, few appreciate fully the extent to which the UN can on occasion be a responsive, innovative, pragmatic, and adaptive institution able to recognize its deficiencies and capable of internal reform and institutional learning. Nowhere is this set of characteristics more evident than in the series of measures undertaken by the world body since the terrorist attacks of September 11, 2001. Cynics argue that the organization had no choice but to appear to be relevant in the changed security context as it was defined by the United States after the attacks on the World Trade Center and the Pentagon. On closer examination, however, the UN has managed to respond reasonably well to the ongoing need for institutional innovation. It has been driven by a combination of institutional self-interest, pragmatism, and a degree of creative individual policy entrepreneurship.

The passage of UN Security Council Resolution 1540 on April 28, 2004, is recent evidence of the responsive, adaptive, and innovative nature of the organization. The resolution addresses a pressing global security concern: the potential acquisition by non-state actors of weapons of mass destruction (or disruption) or of materials that could be used in their manufacture. It contains mandatory reporting and monitoring provisions for all UN member states, but it is best understood in the context of the UN's innovative actions taken to criminalize acts of terrorism after September 2001. In particular, UN Security Council Resolution 1373 (September 28, 2001) and, to a lesser extent, the supplementary measures contained in resolutions 1377 (November 12, 2001) and 1455 (January 17, 2003) need to be examined, both to appreciate the significance of the approach taken in UNSCR 1540 and to understand its potential drawbacks and limitations.

The purpose of this chapter is to reflect on the experiences of the United Nations with counter-terrorist activities—its resolutions, its assistance programs, and its creation of new institutions—and to consider their implications for the monitoring and enforcement efforts outlined in UNSCR 1540. Four issues will be addressed:

—innovative features of the UN's counter-terrorism efforts after September 2001;

—the effectiveness to date of its counter-terrorism measures;

—lessons learned about the implementation of counter-terrorism measures since September 2001 that may be useful in considering how best to implement UNSCR 1540; and

—some of the current challenges and new policy directions in this general area.

Innovative Aspects of the UN's Counter-Terrorism Efforts

One of the most creative and institutionally innovative features of the UN's counter-terrorism efforts has been the reporting and monitoring processes established after the passage of UN Security Council Resolution 1373. Before its passage, most member states' reporting on the implementation of UN Security Council resolutions (typically associated with reports requested on the implementation of multilateral sanctions) consisted of minimal statements, rarely indicating more than that a country was complying with the terms of the resolution "to the best of our ability." Little information or detail was provided beyond the simple declaration of compliance. UNSCR 1373 departed from this pattern by establishing the Counter-Terrorism Committee (CTC), which introduced an innovative and extensive reporting and monitoring system requiring states to report on specific actions taken to implement the Resolution. The CTC also created an interactive, dynamic monitoring process in which member states have to ensure accountability and to improve their ability to restrict the finances, mobility, and general support for groups committing acts of terrorism.

As the resolution was invoked under Chapter VII of the United Nations Charter, the CTC introduced mandatory reporting requirements on all member states. Successive reports were due initially at intervals of six months. Once the reports were submitted, they were translated and placed on the UN website, in an accessible format. Member states were given explicit guidelines by the Committee as to what aspects of implementation they were expected to report upon; and if they failed to address an element in one report, they could be asked to elaborate on it in a successive report. The CTC reduced the frequency of reporting over time, less than the initial requirement of a report every six months, and forty-two member states had submitted their fifth report by August of 2006.[1]

Besides requiring regular reporting, the CTC periodically invited ambassadors or representatives of member states to meet with members of the Committee or its designated experts to elaborate upon or answer specific questions about the implementation of policy measures described in their reports. Thus it established an innovative, interactive process of reporting and monitoring, with responses to specific questions asked by the Committee reflected in subsequent reporting to it. From reading successive reports posted on the UN website, it is possible to gain a glimpse into the dynamics of this iterative process. And for the UN, there was an unprecedented amount of transparency in the reporting process.

At the outset, the CTC focused on building a legal basis in all member states so as to criminalize the provision of financing to groups committing acts of terrorism. It also emphasized the importance of establishing administrative mechanisms in member states in order to freeze funds expeditiously. Attention was given as well to extending the measures beyond the formal financial sector, to include the operations of charitable organizations and the activities of informal money transfer systems, commonly known as *hawalas*. Besides attending to the financing of terrorism, UNSCR 1373 called upon member states to suppress recruitment, eliminate the supply of weapons, and prevent the movement of terrorists or terrorist groups across national boundaries. Finally, it urged countries to sign and ratify the 1999 UN Convention on Terrorist Financing.

It was soon apparent that many states lacked the capacity to implement important aspects of the ambitious new counter-terrorism agenda. The UN Security Council passed Resolution 1377 in November 2001, calling upon member states with technical capacity to assist those that were unable to implement the terms of the preceding counter-terrorism resolutions. Shortly after the passage of this resolution, the CTC began a technical assistance program that concentrated on coordinating bilateral offers of assistance—in addition to offers of technical assistance from international, regional, and subregional organizations—with the needs of member states requesting assistance for their counter-terrorism efforts.

Much of the credit for the creation of this innovative reporting and monitoring scheme goes to Sir Jeremy Greenstock, Britain's then ambassador to the UN, in his capacity as the first chair of the Counter-Terrorism Committee. The British mission to the UN had both the institutional capacity and the political will to provide dynamic leadership in this area, and the reporting and monitoring framework established under British direction illustrates well the role of innovative individual policy entrepreneurship in the UN. One of the lessons of the Stockholm Process on Implementing Targeted Sanctions was the importance of the role of chairs of sanctions committees for the effectiveness of their operations (technically, the CTC is not a sanctions committee). The manual produced by the Stockholm Process concluded that the CTC's reporting and monitoring procedures established precedents that should serve as a model for future sanctions resolutions.[2]

After the second and third rounds of reports were submitted to the Counter-Terrorism Committee, the momentum of the process began to slow down. Seeking to "revitalize" the CTC and the UN's ongoing engagement with the global counter-terrorism effort, the UN Security Council passed Resolution 1535 on March 26, 2004. The chairmanship of the Committee had by this time passed from the United Kingdom to Spain, and the revitalization effort both retained the CTC as the primary mechanism to assist states in combating terrorism and entailed the creation of the Counter-Terrorism Executive Directorate (CTED). The CTED was established as a special political mission alongside the CTC for monitoring the implementation of UNSCR 1373. It is not necessarily a permanent institution, but its initial term extends to the end of 2007, after a comprehensive review at the end of 2005.

The UN's counter-terrorism efforts are not restricted to activities undertaken under the auspices of the Counter-Terrorism Committee alone. One of the Security Council's sanctions committees, the Al-Qaeda and Taliban Sanctions Committee, established by UNSCR 1267 (October 15, 1999), has been at the forefront of the operational aspects of enforcement activities. The 1267 Committee, as it is widely known, maintains a global list of individuals, corporate entities, and groups designated as supporting or engaging in acts of terrorism. Over time this committee has expanded the list of terrorist entities against which all member states are required to restrict financing. It has steadily improved the quality of the information that it provides to member states on designated individuals, groups, and their financial supporters. The Committee has also responded, at least in part, to concerns of human rights groups about the bases for the listing of individuals and has developed innovative procedures for the de-listing of incorrectly named individuals.

In 2003 and 2004 the 1267 Committee increased its oversight and monitoring of member states' implementation and enforcement efforts with regard to actions against specific individuals and groups; and it too introduced reporting and evaluation procedures (modeled, at least in part, on the innovative procedures developed by the CTC). The Committee monitors the actions by member states to block specific transactions and their efforts to bring prosecutions against individuals and groups on the list it maintains. Thus in contrast to the CTC, which concentrates on the medium- to long-term, strategic aspects of countering terrorism through changes in legislation and the strengthening of administrative institutions and enforcement mechanisms, the 1267 Committee focuses on the short- to medium-term, tactical aspects of the issue, maintaining a list of specifically designated individuals and groups.

Soon after the terrorist attacks in Beslan, Russia, in September 2004, the UN Security Council passed Resolution 1566 (October 8, 2004). This resolution contains elements of a definition of terrorism, something the international community has been unable to agree upon, in spite of attempts in twelve international conventions on the issue. The resolution describes acts of terrorism as

> criminal acts against civilians committed with the intent to cause death or serious bodily injury, or taking of hostages, with the purpose to provoke a state of terror in the general public or in a group of persons or particular persons, intimidates a population or compel a government or an international organization to do or to abstain from doing any act . . . constitute offences within the scope of and as defined in the international conventions and protocols relating to terrorism (paragraph 3, UNSCR 1566).[3]

The resolution also contains a provision that can be (and has been) interpreted as a call for an expanded, global list of individuals and groups, beyond the former members of the Taliban regime in Afghanistan and members of Al-Qaeda. More concretely, it established a working group with a mandate to work on both the definition of terrorism and an expanded list as well as to consider the feasibility of establishing a fund for victims of terrorism. Thus as acts of terrorism have continued, the UN has continued to respond and adapt its activities in order to address the issue.

The Effectiveness of UN Counter-Terrorism Measures

It is too early to conclude definitively how effective the CTC's and other efforts against terrorism have been, but there are indications of progress and changes in countries' legal and administrative procedures to restrict terrorist financing. Based on a preliminary assessment of the data available, primarily from an examination of reports from countries in Europe, North America, the Middle East, and East Asia, there is good evidence to suggest that the UN process has made significant progress in criminalizing terrorist financing and improving the financial administrative capacity of member states to act against it. For analytical purposes, it is useful to distinguish between evidence of effectiveness at the global level and evidence of changes at the national level in assessing the UN's various counter-terrorism efforts.

Evidence at the Global Level

At the global level, it is possible to assess the UN's performance in reporting, in managing requests for technical assistance, and in gaining continued acceptance of the twelve international conventions on terrorism.

About reporting, it is significant to note that every one of the member states of the United Nations has reported to the Counter-Terrorism Committee on its compliance with counter-terrorist resolutions. This in itself is an extraordinary achievement. Most states have filed more than one report, and the majority of the reports submitted follow the detailed structure laid out in the guidelines distributed by the Counter-Terrorism Committee. The majority of member states (107) have filed at least four reports, and, as indicated above, more than one fifth of the organization's members have submitted five reports. The 1267 Committee has been somewhat less successful with its more recent introduction of reporting requirements after the passage of UNSCR 1455 in January 2003. By August 2006 a total of 142 member states had submitted reports to the 1267 Committee, but only a handful of members had submitted more than one report. Also, members of the 1267 Monitoring Group have expressed concern about the quality of some of the reporting by member states. With the passage of UNSCR 1617 (July 29, 2005), the 1267 Committee introduced additional innovations for reporting, including forms for providing detailed identifier information for those listed, standardized criteria for the basis for listing, and a checklist to report on actions taken with regard to specific individuals and entities listed.

There is evidence from a close reading of the contents of many of the reports that both the quality of reporting and progress on criminalizing terrorist financing have improved. In the first round of reports submitted to the CTC in late 2001 and early 2002, many states argued that they already had sufficient legal instruments to criminalize the funding of terrorist activity: they were using legislation against money laundering to meet this legal obligation. Reviews of second- and third-round reports to the CTC (completed in 2002 and in 2003) suggest that as the dialogue between member states and the CTC proceeded, states began to move beyond reliance on anti-laundering legislation and promulgate new laws specific to terrorist financing. The Monitoring Group established to assist the 1267 Committee noted in its August 2004 report that a legal basis for freezing assets related to Al-Qaeda existed in 188 of the then 191 UN member states.

UNSCR 1377 invited member states to seek assistance with the implementation of mandatory provisions to criminalize the financing of terrorism, and it called on them to assist each other in implementing the UN resolutions fully. Ambassador Curtis Ward, a former adviser on technical assistance to the CTC, reported that "over fifty States indicated in their first reports that they needed assistance to implement resolution."[4] By the end of 2003 more than 160 states had requested or received capacity-building assistance through the CTC. This number grew as more states apparently came to a clearer understanding of what was expected of them. According to Ward, the greatest needs for assistance appear to have been in drafting anti-terrorism laws and developing banking and financial laws and regulations.[5]

Since the passage of UNSCR 1377 in November 2001, the CTC has facilitated anti-terrorist financing assistance in legislative drafting, support to banking supervisory bodies, and the establishment of financial intelligence units in almost sixty countries. A total of 89 countries have participated in CTC-sponsored workshops, and training in countering terrorist financing has been provided to seventy-one countries. In response to a parallel effort to provide technical assistance, the World Bank has reported receiving more than 100 requests from countries for help in building the capacity to deal with money laundering and terrorist financing. There is also evidence that bilateral cooperation on this issue independent of the CTC initiatives has increased.

As for the signing and ratification of international conventions relating to terrorism, by September 2001 only four countries were parties to the 1999 International Convention for the Suppression of the Financing of Terrorism. But by the end of June 2006 that number had increased to 154 states. Thus with regard to reporting, requests for technical assistance, and the signing and ratification of international conventions, there is good evidence that the UN's counter-terrorism efforts have had some positive effects. The particular reasons why different countries do not comply tend to be contextually specific:

for example, a country may be reluctant to sign one of the conventions because it believes it lacks the technical capacity to ensure that goods or cargoes passing across its borders contain nuclear, chemical, or biological materials. The real test of the effectiveness of the UN measures is in changes at the national level.

Evidence at the National Level

In building on previous work on the implementation of targeted financial sanctions, it is useful to differentiate between four aspects of policy implementation when searching for evidence of change at the national level: the establishment of a legal framework; the creation or strengthening of an administrative infrastructure; the introduction and use of a variety of different regulatory compliance measures; and evidence of enforcement.[6]

In dealing with legal changes, most countries have, as already indicated above, shown progress on criminalizing the willful collection of funds for terrorism and on providing a legal basis for the expeditious freezing of the funds of terrorist groups and individuals. New legislation has either been adopted or is formally under review in most countries. As Curtis Ward has reported, every state has had to adopt new legislation in order to meet fully all the requirements of Resolution 1373.[7] Although regulations against money laundering have been tightened, most countries have recognized, in part owing to CTC policy dialogues, that those regulations alone were not sufficient to suppress terrorist financing. States also need to be able to identify and freeze terrorist funds quickly, without lengthy formal judicial proceedings. Because this typically requires the decision of competent financial authorities, even if the freeze is a temporary measure, many states need new legal provisions.

Most states report changes in their administrative infrastructure, to deal with terrorist financing, and many have formed financial intelligence units or other intra-governmental mechanisms in order to address these issues for the first time. In an effort to support the establishment of an administrative infrastructure to implement counter-terrorism measures, the CTC has appointed an assistance team to dispatch information about common standards and best practices. In addition, the CTC has created a directory of assistance. It is not clear how many states have used this Internet-accessible resource, but CTC assistance teams, in bilateral consultations with different states, evaluate gaps in administrative capacity and facilitate assistance from willing donors. Most countries have identified an agency or intra-governmental mechanism for administering controls on terrorist financing, and nearly all have identified central contact points for the CTC.

With regard to regulatory measures, there is evidence that in most countries banks and financial institutions have been notified about new regulations on the financing of terrorism. Many countries have introduced new reporting requirements for banks and financial institutions, especially "know your client" provisions and reports on suspicious transactions. Formal audits have been used less frequently. Few states have pursued measures to regulate charities other than their registration with government officials. Saudi Arabia, however, has announced an ambitious program for monitoring the activities of all charities operating in the kingdom. Members of the European Union tend to be the most likely to conduct audits of financial institutions and investigations into charitable organizations and to introduce special measures for high-risk (offshore) centers under their jurisdiction.

Until 2002 no state except the United Arab Emirates had created measures for the regulation of *hawalas*, informal money transfer systems. The Saudis claimed in some of their first reports to the CTC that *hawalas* simply did not operate in their country and that every financial institution was under the administrative mandate of the Saudi Monetary Authority. The U.S. government has registered well over 16,000 money service businesses under the provisions of the U.S. PATRIOT Act. Australian officials have taken similar measures, and Hong Kong has been described by Australian regulators as "setting the standard" in this area.[8] Pakistan and the United Arab Emirates have also introduced new legislation about the operations of *hawalas*.

As an example of enforcement at the national level, officials from the U.S. Department of the Treasury have claimed that $112.2 million in terrorist assets was frozen worldwide in the first few months after September 11, 2001. There is some concern that these initial figures may be inflated, because they may include funds frozen under UNSCR 1267 going back to November 1999. In November 2003 the Department of the Treasury reported that more than $136 million in assets had been frozen globally and that the United States had worked with other governments to seize well over $60 million.[9] Juan Zarate, the assistant secretary of the treasury, stated that "[o]ver 170 countries have taken relevant freezing measures and other steps to ensure that terrorists are deprived of the means and channels of funding."[10] He raised the total figure of assets frozen to $147 million at a briefing for the 1267 Committee in January 2005.[11] Of this figure, some $36 million has been frozen by the United States and $111 million has been blocked by other countries (approximately $24 million by Switzerland, $11.9 million by the United Kingdom, $5.5 million by Saudi Arabia, and an undisclosed amount by the United Arab Emirates).

The 1267 Committee estimates that a somewhat lower amount of terrorist assets has been frozen, in part because its lists are not as extensive as those maintained by the U.S. Treasury. Only thirty-four of the countries reporting to it in early 2006 indicated that they had frozen any assets. The total amount affected came to approximately $93.4 million.[12] Pakistan, Saudi Arabia, Switzerland, Turkey, and the United States alone accounted for about $70 million of this amount. A significant part of the assets involved funds attributed to the Taliban, and they have subsequently been returned to the new government of Afghanistan.

No countries have indicated that they have frozen tangible assets such as businesses or property. None of the eleven states reporting to the 1267 Committee that they had detected the presence of Al-Qaeda–related cells in their country said any assets had been frozen. Some mentioned investigations being pursued or under way, but few offered new evidence of concrete success. Many countries still assert that their financial system is not susceptible to misuse by terrorists.

Prosecutions have been pursued, especially in the United States, Germany, Indonesia, and the United Kingdom, but thus far few have resulted in the freezing of additional funds. There has been some extraterritorial applications of the U.S. PATRIOT Act (actions against correspondent accounts in Israel, Oman, Taiwan, India, and Belize), which have allegedly resulted in the seizure of an additional $2 million, but federal judges have sealed the records on most of them. There is virtually no evidence of the suspension of any banking licenses, but there have been convictions in the United States for the provision of "material support." Only the United States and the European Union have developed their own lists of groups and individuals legally identified as terrorists. Most other countries rely instead on the lists provided by the 1267 Committee.[13]

There have been important changes in policy introduced at the national level throughout the world, from Europe and Russia to traditional offshore locations such as Bahrain and Hong Kong. These changes have accompanied significant expressions of a global willingness to do something about terrorist finances, even if material progress to date has been relatively modest. But it is uncertain how effective these changes will be in the long run. Acts of terrorism such as those committed in Indonesia, Turkey, Morocco, Saudi Arabia, Spain, the United Kingdom, Russia, Iraq, Israel, and Egypt serve to underscore the threat that terrorism represents to all states, not just the United States; and continuing acts of terrorism tend to propel the global regulatory effort forward. In the final analysis, however, as the 9/11 Commission's *Monograph on*

Terrorist Financing stated, completely choking off the money to Al-Qaida and affiliated groups is "essentially impossible."[14]

The UN's Counter-Terrorism Experience: Lessons for UNSCR 1540

There are four broad lessons from the UN's experience with reporting, monitoring, and effecting change that are relevant to the implementation of UNSCR 1540 and the monitoring effort associated with the resolution. First and foremost, political will is necessary for the effective implementation of UN Security Council resolutions. An extraordinary amount of political will was present after September 11, 2001, and at the time of the passage of UNSCR 1373, little more than two weeks after the attacks. The outpouring of sympathy and support for the United States immediately following September 11 has largely dissipated, particularly since the U.S.-led intervention in Iraq in March 2003. Nevertheless, the momentum created in 2001, combined with constant reminders of the genuine threat to state interests posed by continuing acts of terrorism, has succeeded in maintaining much of the political will that was evident just after September 11. For an illustration of the consequences of the absence of political will, one need only recall the relative ineffectiveness of the comprehensive sanctions regime directed against Iraq, which eroded over the course of the 1990s. There was less political will behind the passage of UNSCR 1540 than the initial counter-terrorism resolutions, and some states questioned their relevance to its enforcement and resisted reporting. Although its adoption by the Security Council was unanimous, the fact that its committee was given an initial mandate of only two years raised questions about the political commitment to the counter-proliferation, counter-terrorism process. It is worth noting, however, that despite initial reluctance, as of June 2006, 132 states had filed reports to the 1540 Committee.

The second lesson from the UN's experience with counter-terrorism efforts is that political will alone is not enough. Capacity-building and technical assistance are also necessary for those countries that have the will but lack the institutional means to implement the terms of UN Security Council resolutions. UNSCR 1377 recognized this fact and established both a coordinating function within the Counter-Terrorism Committee and institutional mechanisms in order to ensure that member states needing assistance were able to obtain it. The technical assistance "matrix" produced by the CTC was used to match donor abilities and intent with recipient need, and there is strong evidence that member states requested and received appropriate levels and types of assistance. But over time coordination problems emerged, and the efficiency of the matching effort suffered. This led to proposals for the formation of a counter-terrorism action group (CTAG) at the G-8 meeting in Evian in 2003. The CTC continues to play a central role in the provision of technical assistance, but CTAG (with the United Kingdom in the chair) has tended to be more proactive on the issue. UNSCR 1540 recognizes that some states may require assistance in implementing the provisions of the Resolution, and in operative paragraph 7 it invites states to request or offer assistance, as appropriate. As of March 2005 nearly one year after the passage of the resolution, neither the United States nor the United Kingdom, two likely sources of technical assistance, had reportedly received any requests for assistance.

A third lesson of the UN's experience with counter-terrorism measures for the implementation of UNSCR 1540 is that the reporting and monitoring process itself can lead to institutional learning and better national-level implementation of the terms of UN Security Council resolutions. The improvement in the quality of reporting on counter-terrorism measures has already been discussed. The fact that the process was transparent and that successive reports were made available to the general public created an incentive for reports increasingly to follow the detailed outline of specific questions asked by the CTC. More importantly, the process of calling ambassadors and representatives before the committee made them publicly accountable for the actions of their governments and contributed to a growing realization that legislation against money laundering alone would not be sufficient to criminalize the willful provision of funds for terrorism. It also drew attention to the fact that the expeditious blocking of the movement of funds would require new legislation. Most countries have introduced new legislation criminalizing willful provision and providing a legal basis for freezing funds expeditiously since the reporting process began. In addition, many have, as noted, created a financial intelligence unit for the first time. The reporting processes of UNSCR 1540 remain to be assessed fully. When the 1540 Committee's mandate was renewed by UNSCR 1367 on April 27, 2006, a total of 129 member states, about sixty-five percent of the United Nations' membership, had submitted initial reports. The future work of the Committee will include obtaining the remaining states' reports.

Fourth and finally, periodic reporting to the media has facilitated ongoing attention to the issue of counter-terrorism, reminded states of their role in implementation, and proved to be important for the sustained operation of the Counter-Terrorism Committee and the 1267 Committee. Periodic press releases and press conferences serve the function of keeping attention focused on the core issues. They also sustain momentum and ensure that not only member states but also the Security Council committees themselves are held accountable. There have been times in recent years when changes in committee behavior with regard to public outreach have led to a perception of stagnation and inactivity on the part of the UN. On the other hand, there have been occasions too when public outreach has been used for grandstanding.

Current Challenges and New Policy Directions

The UN's experience with counter-terrorism illustrates well the virtues of an innovative and elaborate reporting scheme. Over time, however, the CTC's reporting process began to run out of steam, and the utility of repeated reporting began to be questioned. UNSCR 1540 replicates this process, which undoubtedly has the value of raising global awareness about the dangers of non-state actors gaining access to weapons of mass destruction and their means of delivery, at least at the beginning stages of reporting. The preparation of a report for the 1540 Committee is itself an important and useful process, one that is likely to increase attention to, and knowledge about, potential vulnerabilities. But beyond reporting, there are important questions about how desired policy changes can be institutionalized better and implemented effectively by member states.

To begin with, there is a strong need for a more effective system of monitoring both compliance and enforcement by member states. This is particularly the case for those critically placed states that have the capacity but lack the will to implement the terms of Security Council resolutions. Two central questions are, who should monitor implementation, and how can the monitoring process itself be thorough and independent without becoming watered down for fear of offending the political sensitivities of individual member states?

The four phases or components of effective implementation at the national level—establishing a legal framework, creating an administrative infrastructure, introducing appropriate regulatory compliance measures, and enforcing the new measures—remain to be determined. Most of the Counter-Terrorism Committee's reporting and monitoring provides evidence for the first and second of these components, but it is based largely on self-reporting, not verification. To date, there has been relatively little or no assessment of the effectiveness of the regulatory compliance measures, in particular how they are perceived by private sector actors, on whom enforcement ultimately depends. There has been even less attention to enforcement efforts. The Counter-Terrorism Executive Directorate, under CTC auspices, has initiated visits to selected member states, but its scope and effectiveness have yet to be determined. The 1267 Committee's reports are intended to provide evidence of enforcement, but compliance with reporting has been partial. Reports may be accurate, but some of them leave important things unsaid and important issues unaddressed. The 1267 Monitoring Group is also beginning to explore regulatory measures, and is beginning to assemble a database on individual member state compliance. Ultimately, the evaluation of compliance and regulation requires field research and independent assessment.[15]

The eagerness to learn from and imitate the various counter-terrorism committees' experience with member state reporting has led to a new challenge within the UN system: the problem of "reporting fatigue." Following the innovations of the 1373 Committee, the 1267 Committee introduced a similar model of reporting on enforcement. This is another example of policy innovation and the crucial role played by UN Security Council committee chairs, this time by the Chilean ambassador Heraldo Muñoz. The quality of the reporting to the 1267 Committee has generally been quite high, even if not as comprehensive as reporting to the Counter-Terrorism Committee. In view of the fact that the CTC, the 1267 Committee, and the 1540 Committee have all introduced extensive reporting requirements, there is a growing problem of "reporting fatigue."

Small member states from the developing world with limited institutional capacity often have great difficulty in keeping up with the demands of successive rounds of reporting. If too many demands are placed on reporting alone, the quality of that reporting may begin to decline. There is evidence that this is already taking place. The 1267 Committee Monitoring Group report of August 2004 contained an analysis of non-reporting states and concluded that "an important reason for non-reporting has been the complexity and volume of reports required from member states which clearly lack the capacity to produce them."[16] Some member states have indicated that they literally cut and paste parts of one report into another. Others complain that they have difficulty in keeping separate the different mandates and concerns of Security Council committees requiring reports. There is also growing evidence of overlap and duplication of effort. The 1267 Monitoring Group members have indicated that some member states have been confused about the different reporting requirements and believe that they have already reported as required, for example to the CTC.

There is also evidence of mission creep: the committee chairs or monitoring groups, correctly perceiving the interrelationship among the issues, use this insight to expand their requests for information into each other's domains. In some instances, this is a product of the composition and content of the resolutions themselves. Perhaps it is time to begin to think of some form of greater coordination within the UN that would lead to integrated assessments of interrelated issues such as counter-terrorism and the proliferation of weapons of mass destruction. Given the growing concern about the danger of those weapons falling into the hands of terrorist groups—a concern that recognizes the potential linkages between counter-terrorism efforts and non-proliferation efforts—the advent of UNSCR 1540 may be an appropriate time to consider the greater coordination of reporting and monitoring efforts with the other committees.

Finally, because it invokes Chapter VII and is therefore mandatory for all member states, Resolution 1540 is considered by some as illustrative of a growing "democratic deficit" within the UN system. As some critics have pointed out, the frequency with which the UN Security Council invokes Chapter VII and passes a mandatory resolution binding on all member states has increased in recent years, from sanctions resolutions to counter-terrorism issues and now to proliferation. Because the Security Council consists of only fifteen member states (five permanent members and ten members elected on rotating two-year terms), it is not a globally representative or democratic body, even if the ten elected members are chosen to represent different regions of the world. The urgency of issues of terrorism and the potential use of weapons of mass destruction by non-state actors has prompted some member states within the UN to urge the organization to act and provide leadership on emerging issues. Pragmatists within the organization argue that to do otherwise would render the UN increasingly irrelevant, particularly in the eyes of the world's major power, the United States. However, critics contend that the Security Council is legislating global change without democratic legitimacy.

In a related vein, UNSCR 1540 has also recently come under criticism from some quarters for unnecessarily duplicating the efforts of existing international organizations and operating conventions with broad membership, particularly the International Atomic Energy Agency (IAEA) and the Chemical Weapons Convention's Organisation for the Prohibition of Chemical Weapons (OPCW). Effective implementation of the operational measures of the resolution will require greater coordination with, and even reliance upon, existing specialized international institutions such as the IAEA. There is little reason to try to recreate the institutional capacity that already exists within these organizations in view of the limited staff resources of the 1540 Committee and its Experts Group. Despite the criticisms of institutional duplication and overlap, however, some advocates of an organization for the verification of the Biological and Toxin Weapons Convention (BTWC) view Resolution 1540 as a way to increase global recognition of the issue and a means to introduce aspects of regulation in the absence of an agreed international convention. There are also important states not parties to the Nuclear Non-Proliferation Treaty and the Chemical Weapons Convention that are now legally required to implement measures related to the handling of nuclear and chemical materials under the provisions of UNSCR 1540 in the light of its legal standing in relation to Chapter VII.

Conclusion

Recent experience with counter-terrorism measures taken under UN auspices has seen policy innovation, adaptation, and institutional learning. The United Nations remains inflexible and slow to adapt in certain respects, but there is also evidence of a growing pragmatism within the organization and recognition that given the nature of current security threats, it cannot always afford to rely upon the procedurally inherited, ponderous, and often inefficient processes of the past. UNSCR 1540 is very much an indication of this emergent tendency. However, it faces important challenges that go beyond simple reporting: it must deal with the duplication of reporting and increase coordination with existing international institutions with specialized capabilities in the management of nuclear, chemical, and biological materials. Its leadership will need constantly to adjust and adapt in order to maintain its legitimacy and effectiveness.

Notes

1. See Counter-Terrorism Committee, at www.un.org/Docs/sc/committees/ 1373/submitted_reports.html.

2. Peter Wallensteen, Carina Staibano, and Mikael Eriksson (eds.), *Making Targeted Sanctions Effective: Guidelines for the Implementation of UN Policy Options*, Final Report, Stockholm Process on Implementing Targeted Sanctions, paragraph 127, p. 57, at www.smartsanctions.se.

3. The text of UNSCR 1566 is available on the UN website via www.un.org/Docs/ sc/unsc_resolutions04.html at http://daccessdds.un.org/doc/UNDOC/GEN/N04/542/ 82/PDF/N0454282.pdf?OpenElement, p. 2.

4. C. A. Ward, "Building Capacity to Combat International Terrorism: The Role of the United Nations Security Council," *Journal of Conflict & Security Law*, Vol. 8, No. 2 (2003), p. 302.

5. Personal communication.

6. *Targeted Financial Sanctions: A Manual for Design and Implementation, Contributions from the Interlaken Process*, Part 2, published by the Swiss Confederation in cooperation with the UN Secretariat and the Watson Institute for International Studies, Brown University, 2001, pp. 79–112.

7. Ward, "Building Capacity to Combat International Terrorism," fn. 4, p. 299.

8. Interview with a senior Australian government official by members of the Watson Institute Targeting Terrorist Finances Project, August 2003.

9. Juan C. Zarate, deputy assistant secretary, Department of the Treasury, "Securing the Financial System against Rogue Capital," Keynote Address before the Investment Company Institute, November 10, 2003, at www.ustreas.gov/press/releases/js984.htm.

10. Ibid.

11. "Security Council Committee Meets Senior U.S. Officials to Discuss Implementation of Sanctions Against Al-Qaeda, Taliban," Press Release SC/8288, January 11, 2005, at www.un.org/news/press/docs/2005/sc8288.doc.htm. For a report on its content, see Judy Aita, "Coordinated Efforts Key to Fighting Terrorism, United States Says," *Washington File*, at http://usinfo.state.gov/ei/archive/2005/jan/12-645777.html.

12. Fourth report of the Analytical Support and Sanctions Monitoring Team appointed pursuant to Security Council resolutions 1526 (2004) and 1617 (2005) concerning Al-Qaeda and the Taliban and associated individuals and entities, March 10, 2006, at www.un.org/docs/sc/committees/1267/1267mg.htm.

13. The lists are operated typically through ministries of finance. The European and U.S. lists differ for purposes of national or regional foreign policy, as they are associated with measures not contained in the UNSCR. For example, the United States maintains lists of Palestinian individuals and groups not listed by the UN or by the European Union while the EU has listed groups such as ETA that are not on the UN lists.

14. National Commission on Terrorist Attacks upon the United States, *Monograph on Terrorist Financing*, Staff Report to the Commission, Prepared by John Roth, Douglas Greenberg, and Serena Wille, 2004, p. 2.

15. For an example of an independent assessment effort, see Appendix C of the 2004 Council on Foreign Relations report by its Independent Task Force on Terrorist Financing. This appendix contains a comparative survey of implementation in the Islamic world, which was prepared by the Targeting Terrorist Finances project at the Watson Institute for International Studies at www.cfr.org/publication.html?id=7111.

16. Available at www.un.org/docs/sc/committees/1267/1267mg.htm.

ELIZABETH M. PRESCOTT

3

UNSCR 1540 and the Scientific Community as a Non-State Actor

Curbing the proliferation of high-consequence materials that could be used in biological, chemical, radiological, and nuclear weapons and related delivery systems has received increasing attention in recent years. Most of these materials and delivery technologies have legitimate uses in society and continue to be researched with the aim of improving the human condition. However, the potential exists for the inappropriate and unauthorized use of these materials and technologies, which could result in great harm. Thus setting oversight standards for non-state actors in science and technology requires a delicate balance between maximizing benefits and reducing adverse consequences.

This chapter examines the status and role of the non-state actor in the general threat posed by high-risk materials and technologies, including know-how. In this context, non-state actors consist of scientists, technicians, auxiliary staff, and engineers in the academic, industrial research, and life science communities. Research into high-consequence or sensitive materials will continue, and the world must develop appropriate mechanisms for controlling them and those with expertise in their use. Although this issue is not particularly new—the advent of nuclear technology for producing nuclear weapons as well as nuclear energy occurred in the 1940s—the globalization of biotechnology advances implies a new, wider availability of materials and know-how for developing a biological weapon capability among non-state actors. In particular, the SARS experience and the potential for an avian flu pandemic has led more and more to calls for all states to improve their public health capacities, and this necessarily involves the transfer of life sciences and biotechnologies globally in order to augment this public health capacity.

To this end, United Nations Security Council Resolution 1540 (UNSCR 1540) instructs member states to promulgate regulations that address non-state actors and the role they might play in the proliferation of high-consequence materials. The Resolution defines the non-state actor in a footnote as an "individual or entity, not acting under the lawful authority of any State in conducting activities which come within the scope of this resolution." Unlike non-state actors traditionally examined in relation to the proliferation of weapons of mass destruction (WMD), such as potential terrorist end-users of nuclear, biological, and chemical weapons and materials, the scientific community has distinct characteristics that present it as a source of information and materials that could contribute to illicit proliferation. The science and technology communities thus pose regulatory challenges for purposes of the Resolution, particularly as operative paragraph 8(d) calls upon all states "to develop appropriate ways to work with and inform industry and the public regarding their obligations under such laws [as required by the Resolution]." Proliferation controls resulting from UNSCR 1540 thus must proactively address the needs of the scientific community if they are to be sustainable and effective without putting in jeopardy the economic development, health, and security of states.

This chapter focuses on the biological and life science communities. The varied technology of this sector is one for which there is no international organization directly recognized by UNSCR 1540. For example, in contributing to the achievement of Resolution 1540's objectives, all states are called upon "to renew and fulfil [sic] their commitment to multilateral cooperation, in particular within the framework of the International Atomic Energy Agency, the Organisation for the Prohibition of Chemical Weapons [OPCW] and the Biological and Toxin Weapons Convention, as important means of pursuing and achieving their common objectives in the area of non-proliferation and of promoting international cooperation for peaceful purposes" (operative paragraph 8(c)). Compared to the International Atomic Energy Agency and the OPCW, the main international organizations related to the treaties that address the non-proliferation of nuclear weapons and chemical (and toxin) weapons, the Biological and Toxin Weapons Convention does not have an equivalent treaty-related organization.[1] UNSCR 1540 encourages states to become parties to these treaties, which, although focused on state-based WMD programs, require ratification, a legislative or related process that leads to domestic laws covering persons and entities in the state, that is, non-state actors. Significantly, however, even if states are not party to these treaties, UNSCR 1540 requires them to enact criminal and civil legislation that criminalizes the proliferative activity of non-state actors—as though they were state parties.

The life science community plays a positive role in numerous industries that have a profound impact on global health and development. Creating non-proliferation incentives broad enough to incorporate all those able to proliferate without unduly dampening technological development requires understanding the stakeholders in the scientific research and development community and their interests.

The Life Science Community: Salient Characteristics

Biological materials are fundamentally different from chemical, radiological, or nuclear materials.[2] Pathogens are easy and inexpensive to replicate. A small sample of material can be substantially increased in volume with limited resources, skill, and time. The operator who is highly trained and has the potential to (re)generate high-risk materials presents challenges to the control of dissemination because efforts simply to lock up potentially dangerous materials are insufficient for preventing proliferation if a trained specialist can readily recreate them.

As large, elaborate, and expensive facilities for pathogen generation or manipulation are no longer necessary (except for high-containment facilities for safety from particularly dangerous items), new suppliers cannot always be immediately recognized in an otherwise global marketplace. Additionally, with the exception of smallpox, which has ostensibly been eradicated, high-consequence agents can be found in nature, and there is an active and economically necessary trade in pathogens for legitimate research purposes.[3] The characteristics of biological materials have led the research community to evolve in such a way that the traditional approach to securing materials solely through pathogen control and facility protection has become inadequate.[4]

Integrating and Expanding

The global biological research community is constantly expanding in size and scope. The demand for new treatments for disease and for more sophisticated crops is growing. It will continue to receive significant support from public and private sources in an effort to achieve faster and more comprehensive solutions to global problems. Even in the case of genetically modified organisms—where consumer concern has greatly reduced global demand for products—research continues on products such as drought-resistant, cold-resistant, or more nutritious foods that may provide great benefit to the world's growing population.[5] Evidence suggests that future technologies resulting from tinkering with biological systems will be integrated more broadly into society, with biological systems being explored for products that until recently might have been confined to the pages of science fiction.[6] The integration of advances in the life sciences into new areas can create impediments to identifying would-be malefactors and enforcing regulations against them.

The societal integration of biotechnology also increases the demand for life scientists, highlighting the perverse relationship between expanding the talent base for science and technology and creating a larger pool of potential sources of proliferation. The boom in funds, primarily in the United States, for research to counter bioterror agents has created more facilities with more scientists who are familiar with and have access to the high-risk agents. The world is relying on these scientists to discover and develop interventions for use in the event of an attack, but they could use their knowledge, knowingly or unwittingly, to ill effect.

The proposed new facilities with the highest level of safety in the United States alone far outnumber the current and near-term global projections of scientists qualified to use them. This requires rapidly increasing the number of individuals trained to operate in this challenging climate, but probably the demand for suitable candidates will exceed the supply. And once these scientists are trained to work on high-risk pathogens, there is a need to ensure that their skills are used productively. The rewards, in the short and long term, from training more scientists to focus on high-risk pathogens create the risk of an expanding pool of potential bioterrorists, or at least those who might contribute to acquisition and trafficking.[7]

Mobility

Personnel in the scientific community can be highly mobile. An accomplished scientist is expected to have apprenticed in different laboratories, gaining exposure to diverse subjects, researchers, and techniques. This develops the scientist's flexibility and fosters the creativity necessary for important discoveries in the life sciences. Laboratories, staffed by nationals from many countries who often return home upon completion of their apprenticeship, facilitate the interaction of scientists with their global counterparts. Essential to the advancement of the global life science enterprise, this also creates challenges for the control of individuals and the insider knowledge they possess: there are few impediments to gaining employment in another high-risk environment for a scientist dismissed for suspicious behavior.

Academic versus Private

Fundamental differences between research in the academic sector and that in the private sector have important regulatory implications. Academic scientists are trained to push beyond the current body of knowledge, and there is an emphasis on questioning or debunking established beliefs. Rewards are given for creative, high-risk research that is unlikely to result in a marketable product but promises to elucidate system functions and could answer questions raised by other investigators. Academic laboratories usually have less institutional oversight than private sector ones, which must demonstrate an effective allocation of resources. By contrast, the private sector is tasked with creating an end product that can be sold in order to recoup funds invested in research and development. This requires a more deliberate path of research based on an expected outcome and time frame. The allocation of funds is based on the probability of success and the potential for financial returns. Although the primary rewards bestowed on private sector life scientists are resource-based, the knowledge of participating in the development of a directly useful product can be a strong motivating factor.

The academic and private sector research communities are far from distinct groupings of practitioners. Almost all traditionally trained scientists come from the academic sector, and may move between the academic and private sector depending on career preferences. Their simultaneous involvement in both sectors is increasingly common, as biotechnology firms look to develop discoveries in academia into marketable products. This fluidity of movement between academic and private facilities presents potential proliferators with an opportunity to select a base with desirable characteristics. Preventing proliferation will require strategies that consider both the academic and the private life science sectors in order to prevent a perpetrator from shifting location when impediments are encountered.

The potential for proliferation goes beyond individuals with primary research functions. Anyone with access to a pathogen, from the laboratory cleaning staff to those working with endemic disease in agricultural environments, should be considered as possible proliferators. Training would probably be necessary in order to manipulate a final agent, but relocating a pathogen would require little expertise. Auxiliary facilities that provide services or supplies also present opportunities for proliferation, as was revealed by the discovery of a potentially devastating strain of influenza inadvertently (but legally) being dispensed as a laboratory control to thousands of laboratories around the world. This should serve as a reminder of the range of non-state actors that have become relevant to non-proliferation strategies.[8]

The above attributes of the scientific community do not always apply to the classified research community, whose experiments are performed at the direction of a few and about which there is no open outside access to information. Restrictions over the flow of information prevent evaluation by the broader scientific community, thus requiring an alternative method of oversight. In this environment there are fewer levers with which the wider community can impose sanctions, and a select group determines what research should be performed and rewarded. Strategies for managing the tension between limited access to potentially high-risk research and the need for transparency are not easily implemented.[9] Generally, however, the control exercised over access to results from classified research mitigates much of the concern about proliferation caused by the absence of rigorous community oversight.

The Worldwide Biotechnology Industry

In order to enter this economically promising industry, countries court fledgling biotechnology sectors with monetary incentives, regulatory incentives, or both. These efforts have borne fruit, as the scope and scale of the biotechnology industry continues to expand in many emerging markets. Currently the majority of biotechnology companies are in developed countries, but there are extensive efforts to foster biotechnology in the developing states. Although the OECD compiles statistics available for member countries, the vague usage of the term *biotechnology* and the absence of standardization make global generalizations challenging.[10] Statistics available in the United States show a vigorous and expanding industry that has increased markedly in size and breadth since its infancy.[11] A study of several countries—Brazil, China, Cuba, Egypt, India, South Africa, and South Korea—highlights the commonalities and individual challenges that countries face as they attempt to establish and develop world-renowned medical biotechnology sectors.[12] However, fragmentation within the biotechnology sector makes it difficult to gauge the volume of business that results globally from the life science enterprise.

Some developing countries, eager to share in the economic benefits of technology, tout positive political environments for biotechnology and large science and technology workforces, which could challenge America's supremacy in biotechnology in the coming decades. However, nascent biotechnology sectors that fail to thrive could create conditions in which new risks of proliferation arise. Developing countries have advantages in performing research into diseases, including infectious ones, that are local health burdens.[13] Scientists in these environments are gaining expertise in many of the pathogens that are feared most for their potential as biological weapons. If nascent biotechnology sectors were to cut back their workforces or to fail to hire local scientific talent, the surplus highly trained individuals would need to seek alternative employment. Although this could present an opportunity for employment in the aforementioned new high-containment facilities, scientific talent might be redirected to research and application with malicious ends.

Those implementing UNSCR 1540 must avoid imposing excessive regulatory burdens on emerging life science industries. Focus must be placed on strengthening the weakest links and improving minimum standards for the highest-risk countries and activities. Realizing that it would be counterproductive to impose standards that countries are unable to implement technically or financially, the drafters of UNSCR 1540 have allowed different degrees of development of biomedical infrastructure to be accommodated. UNSCR 1540 (operative paragraph 6) recognizes the utility of effective control lists for high-risk materials at the national level with a flexible time frame for compliance. Compiling a control list at a national level—as an international list of controlled agents is usually only a guideline—allows accommodation to be made for unique national circumstances, such as libraries of infectious agents derived from naturally occurring diseases. Countries with well-developed life science sectors or unique pathogen collections will require specific regulatory measures in order to avoid dampening growth or the forced destruction of rare pathogen collections.

Organizations that perform life science research are important stakeholders in legislative changes to limit proliferation. Recognizing this, UNSCR 1540 (operative paragraph 8(d)) instructs member states to "work with and inform industry and the public" of forthcoming mechanisms for proliferation control. This gives domestic life science sectors a role in crafting practicable regulatory requirements so that overly restrictive regulations do not hinder legitimate biotechnology research, prevent economic and health gains for the country, or exacerbate the potential for proliferation by non-state actors.

Self-Regulation

The life science research community is deemed to be highly ethical, and recognizes the importance of effective oversight. There is an ever-present tension between a keen awareness of the power and objectivity of biological systems and pushing the limits of what is known in order to further a career or publication record. But ethical standards vary between individual scientists and are heavily affected by community, national, and regional perceptions of what is appropriate. In most areas of research, there are formalized systems of oversight that enable proactive and mandatory consultation with peers about the ethics of proposed experiments.[14] These systems are generally seen as effective mechanisms of oversight when implemented appropriately.[15]

The life science community thus places tremendous value on peer review and the oversight generated by the peer review process. A negative peer review can have serious consequences for a researcher's career and livelihood, creating complex incentives because competitors are often those who determine whether or not a grant will be renewed or a paper accepted. Research suggests that scientists are more amenable to the "informal constraints" imposed by peer review than to official and overt regulation.[16] Scientists readily report misconduct: they recognize the need for self-regulation in order to retain the legitimacy of the research enterprise.[17] Recent events surrounding the South Korean stem cell scientist Hwang Woo-suk provide a vivid example. The scandal heated up after a collaborator and also co-author of a prestigious publication drew global attention to his concern about deception in the research. The accuracy and ethical integrity of the research were considered to be more important than the personal benefit gained from silence.[18] Whether at the academic or the industrial level, feedback from peers is an important ingredient in evolving ideas. The threat of sanction by the community is a strong deterrent to unacceptable behavior; it is a powerful mechanism for constraining proliferation.

The peer review process relies on prompt and comprehensive sharing of information. The dissemination of ideas to the global research community usually occurs through publications or conference presentations. Transparency of research greatly accelerates discovery and eliminates erroneous data. Results open to replication and evaluation by others allow the scientific community to challenge data or conclusions. This creates a constant process of review by experts with minimal structure and enables the evaluation of the research and the researcher. In the private sector of life science research, community oversight of proprietary information is more difficult, but intellectual property protections confer ownership, allowing for wider dissemination. Overall, the free and expeditious mobility of ideas is needed for the self-disciplining mechanism of peer review to function properly.

As with any subjective standard, it is inevitable that individuals will deviate from what the majority believes is appropriate. In cases where research is performed outside what is deemed acceptable, its practitioners are usually isolated from the normal rewards bestowed by the community, including publication in highly regarded journals, further research grants, and invitations to speak at conferences. Rewards are instrumental in career advancement in academic science, but they can also have an impact on the private sector because the opinion of the scientific community is essential to the development of a product at many levels. On occasion, individuals actively decide to violate community norms and pursue research that the community finds inappropriate. In these instances, previous sources of funding and information exchange must often be abandoned and alternatives must be sought. For example, attempts to clone a human being employ technology that is generally accepted for use on animals but is viewed as highly contentious when used on humans. Scientists who do use this technology on humans lose the respect of peers and thus resources. Impediments of this kind can significantly delay research and may ultimately undermine success. The human reproductive cloning example is intuitive, but it can be difficult for the scientific community to agree upon the ethical boundaries for all research. A researcher in pursuit of a countermeasure for a bioterror agent may create a research tool or an early-stage product that is contentious to others but seems justified in view of his or her focus on the end goal. Unlike with human reproductive cloning, in which a scientist openly violates community norms, this researcher believes that he or she is working within the norms of the community. Although cloning draws greater attention, this researcher is the greater challenge to effective proliferation control.

Pandemics

Escalating concern about the proliferation of WMD coincides with rising awareness of vulnerability to epidemics in a globalized world. Microbes do not stop at political borders, so there are renewed calls for strengthening the global public health infrastructure.[19] Society feels defenseless against public health decisions made in far-off countries, heightening the political and diplomatic focus on infectious diseases. International organizations such as the UN Food and Agriculture Organization, the World Health Organization, and the World Organization for Animal Health assist by coordinating disease surveillance and response. These organizations increase the pressure for transparency, but ultimately responsibility for dealing with an animal or human health challenge falls on the country where the disease occurs. The domestic capacity to handle a disease is vital to the prevention of its global transmission. Bolstering the public health infrastructure is a long-term project that requires broad regulatory reforms and cultural awareness in order to achieve its goals. Countries have begun to identify changes needed to strengthen surveillance and response through an expansion of the human and animal health infrastructure and the capacities of public health professionals.

Regulatory requirements for research performed on plants and animals are different from those for human-related research. On occasion, the interrelatedness of ecosystems highlights the need for the human and animal research communities to work together. In 2003 the SARS epidemic drew widespread attention because it was an animal pathogen adapted to human hosts and had global health implications. Avian influenza, another primarily animal pathogen with a similar potential for causing significant social dislocation and human suffering, also demands interdisciplinary collaboration. Close interaction between different scientific disciplines and colleagues around the world is important for effectively dealing with challenges of this nature.

As new public health capacity develops, additional opportunities for the proliferation of high-risk materials and technology will emerge too. A reconstruction of the 1918 influenza pandemic strain highlights the conflict between generating knowledge about a disease and creating additional concern about proliferation.[20] The threat of microbial disease will continue to occupy diplomatic agendas, increasing the pressure on countries to rapidly expand their public health infrastructure and to undertake research into areas where risks are high.

Dealing with complex transnational challenges such as infectious diseases requires not only flexibility and differentiation between regions but also overarching international engagement. Allowing more nuanced policies to address the transnational problem of proliferation, UNSCR 1540's operative paragraph 3 empowers member states to address the problem domestically, in acknowledgment that a single global solution will be insufficient. Additionally, it encourages international action by calling for collaboration and adherence to international treaties, in this way creating a role for international coordination. As political and diplomatic attention to transnational issues grows, UNSCR 1540 presents an appealing road map for approaching global problems for which innovative regulatory mechanisms are needed.

A Web of Deterrence

Several parts of UNSCR 1540 work to limit the proliferation of high-risk materials by the scientific community. Acknowledging the role of technological expertise, the Resolution encourages deterrence strategies aimed at non-state actors, thereby facilitating a more realistic approach to the potential for proliferation. Codified in operative paragraph 1 is a prohibition on support for non-state actors who attempt to proliferate. As national governments are often a significant source of funding for scientific researchers, scientists found acting outside acceptable norms of proliferation could be denied access to a primary source of financial support. The gravity of this penalty may induce them to take personal responsibility for avoiding even the appearance of proliferation. Additionally, the Resolution's operative paragraphs 2 and 3(a) and (b) direct member states to focus on the physical manufacture, transportation, and possession of high-risk materials by non-state actors. In many countries, the life science research infrastructure is at least partly coordinated and funded by the state, which assists regulatory enforcement. The private sector, often with close ties to facilities and researchers in academic institutions, is thus also likely to feel the impact of regulations on state-funded infrastructure.

UNSCR 1540 operative paragraph 8(d) encourages member states to "work with and inform industry and the public" of forthcoming mechanisms for proliferation control. Collaboration with interested stakeholders enables better visualization of the full impact of proliferation controls and will increase the likelihood of success.

Domestic regulations aimed at curbing proliferation should create deterrents tailored to meet the specific needs of the scientific infrastructure. At the same time, the increased globalization of the life science enterprise and the growth in available life science products require that solutions fit into an internationally coordinated framework. Thoughtful deliberation can improve oversight of the necessarily porous global infrastructure for individuals involved in research science and help to achieve a high degree of security without hampering future advances. As the life science community adapts to meet modern health challenges, regulatory efforts to limit proliferation will need to evolve too.

Within the web of global life science are communities with differing aims, requirements, and modes of control. Moving beyond a one-size-fits-all global mechanism for controlling proliferation, UNSCR 1540 allows member states the autonomy to develop better regulatory oversight without having to impose unnecessarily difficult sacrifices on the domestic life science sector. It presents an opportunity to craft regulations that work with the characteristics of the biological research community, conferring effective and early deterrence of the proliferation of high-risk materials. A comprehensive set of domestic deterrents, applied along the spectrum of weapon development, may influence non-state actors far upstream from weapon generation. The sum, domestic and international, of the multiple and overlapping strategies for deterrence of early-stage malicious activities mandated under UNSCR 1540 may create a tighter web than might be indicated by the separate parts. If successfully balanced, this approach could result in safeguards that work with the nuances of the different scientific communities and thus enhance the impact of counter-proliferation efforts without impinging heavily on economic development.

Notes

1. For further discussion of this feature of the Biological and Toxin Weapons Convention, see chapter 7 by Angela Woodward in this volume.

2. Jonathan B. Tucker, *Biosecurity: Limiting Terrorist Access to Deadly Pathogens* (United States Institute for Peace, November 2004), pp. 17–18.

3. Michael Barletta, Amy Sands, and Jonathan Tucker, "Keeping Track of Anthrax: The Case for a Biosecurity Convention," *Bulletin of the Atomic Scientists*, Vol. 58, No. 3 (May–June 2002), pp. 57–62.

4. See chapter 9 by Jeffrey Almond in this book on the handling and transportation of pathogens.

5. "Planting a Seed," *Economist*, March 27, 2003.

6. "Reinventing Yesterday," *Economist,* March 27, 2003.

7. Michael Barletta, "Biosecurity for Preventing Bioterrorism," at http://cns.miis. edu/research/cbw/biosec/pdfs/biosec.pdf.

8. "Labs Scramble to Purge Virus: Samples Sent out Worldwide Traced to 1957 Pandemic," April 14, 2005, at www.cnn.com/2005/HEALTH/04/13/flu.recall/.

9. *Biotechnology Research in an Age of Terrorism*, Committee on Research Standards and Practices to Prevent the Destructive Application of Biotechnology, National Research Council, 2004. See also *National Laboratories and Universities: Building New Ways to Work Together—Report of a Workshop*, Committee on National Laboratories and Universities, National Research Council, 2005.

10. This information can be found on the OECD web page under the "Biotechnology"topic at www.oecd.org/topic/0,2686,en_2649_37437_1_1_1_1_37437,00.html.

11. More specific information can be found on the Biotechnology Industry Organization web page at www.bio.org/speeches/pubs/er/statistics.asp.

12. H. Thorsteinsdóttir et al., "Conclusions: Promoting Biotechnology Innovation in Developing Countries," *Nature Biotechnology*, Vol. 22, 2004, pp. DC48–DC52.

13. Idem.

14. An example of this would be institutional review boards, which are designated by an entity to review experiments performed on human subjects. More information can be found at www.hhs.gov/ohrp/.

15. *Seeking Security: Pathogens, Open Access, and Genome Databases*, Committee on Genomics Databases for Bioterrorism Threat Agents, National Research Council, 2004.

16. J. Kempener, C. S. Perlins, and J. F. Merz, "Forbidden Knowledge," *Science*, Vol. 307, February 11, 2005, p. 854.

17. Rick Weiss, "Deception by Researchers Relatively Rare but the Few Scientists Who Falsify Data Are Difficult to Police, Experts Say," *Washington Post*, January 15, 2006, p. A19.

18. Constance Holden, "Stem Cell Research: Korean Cloner Admits Lying about Oocyte Donations," *Science*, Vol. 310, No. 5753 (December 2, 2005), pp. 1402–03.

19. Kofi Annan, "A Global Strategy for Fighting Terrorism," Keynote Address to the Closing Plenary of the International Summit on Democracy, Terrorism and Security,

March 10, 2005, at http://english.safe-democracy.org/keynotes/a-global-strategy-for-fighting-terrorism.html.

20. Terrence M. Tumpey, Christopher F. Basler, Patricia V. Aguilar, Hui Zeng, Alicia Solórzano, David E. Swayne, Nancy J. Cox, Jacqueline M. Katz, Jeffery K. Taubenberger, Peter Palese, and Adolfo García-Sastre, "Characterization of the Reconstructed 1918 Spanish Influenza Pandemic Virus," *Science*, Vol. 310, No. 5745 (October 7, 2005), pp. 77–80.

SARAH MEEK *and* CHANDRÉ GOULD

4

Motivations and Means: Scientists in Apartheid South Africa's Nuclear, Biological, and Chemical Weapons Programs and Relevance for UNSCR 1540

For more than a decade the South African apartheid government developed its nuclear, biological, and chemical (NBC) weapons programs in secret. Only those who worked directly on the programs or oversaw their strategic direction, including at least the state president and the minister of defense, knew the details of their existence. In 1993 President F. W. de Klerk announced publicly that South Africa had pursued a program to develop nuclear warheads; until then rumors of it had been unsubstantiated. It was even later, in 1996, that details of the country's chemical and biological weapons programs, referred to as Project Coast, its apartheid-era code name, became public.

By 2005, a fairly detailed record of the evolution, history, and dismantlement of South Africa's NBC programs existed.[1] It showed that the factor most influential in motivating the decision to develop them was the perception that the apartheid state was existentially threatened by internal and external forces. Other factors, such as the availability of technical and scientific expertise, access to raw materials and equipment, and the willingness of scientists to cooperate, also played an important role in creating the conditions in which the decision to proliferate could be made. The policy response to this threat analysis identified the importance of a nuclear deterrent capability and the need to be able to respond to a chemical weapons attack and to improve the means for crowd control within South Africa. Although military and political leaders were motivated by the need to counter the threat to the state, the programs were driven more immediately by the motivations of individuals to test the limits of science and resourcefulness in a country increasingly isolated from the rest of the world.

This chapter focuses on the role of scientists in the establishment and development of apartheid South Africa's NBC programs. It attempts to understand the factors that influenced the decisionmaking process in relation to the initiation and development of those programs and the role that scientists played. The conclusions it reaches suggest how international measures such as United Nations Security Council Resolution (UNSCR) 1540 of April 28, 2004, and the existing international treaty framework covering nuclear, chemical, and biological weapons can contribute to preventing the further proliferation of these weapons, and they also point to those measures' limitations. The chapter briefly sets out the history of the South African nuclear weapons program and the chemical and biological weapons programs, which followed significantly different courses during their establishment and dismantlement. The common denominator is the role of scientists and other skilled professionals, who were able to manipulate the programs to suit their interests and who developed the knowledge and skills necessary to establish and run them. The chapter concludes by identifying lessons from the South African experience for other countries engaged in activities that may skirt the limits of acceptability under international non-proliferation and disarmament regimes. These lessons also apply to countries in which proliferation activities are outside the purview of national regimes, which nonetheless now face having to implement UNSCR 1540.

South Africa during Apartheid

During the 1970s threats, whether real or perceived, to the existence of the apartheid state increased dramatically. Before 1974 South Africa had been buffered from the rest of the continent by its neighbors, which were still under colonial rule. But this changed when in that year the Portuguese government fell in a coup. In 1975 Mozambique and Angola gained independence, and the South African armed forces invaded Angola but were forced to withdraw. Their response was to rearm and reorganize the National Union for the Total Independence of Angola and thereby destabilize the government of the Popular Movement for the Liberation of Angola (MPLA).

The change in the external threat to the apartheid state was mirrored by a simultaneous increase in the internal resistance to apartheid, and by the late 1970s the South African government and military viewed these threats as a "total onslaught" against the country. According to the defense minister Magnus Malan in 1977, this onslaught "involves so many different fronts, unknown to the South African experience, that it has gained the telling but horrifying name of total war. This different but all-encompassing war has brought with it new methods and new techniques which in turn have to be met by countermeasures."[2]

In 1976, when students took to the streets of Soweto to protest against the use of Afrikaans as the primary language of education, the police responded with live ammunition, killing and injuring protestors. The incident focused international attention on Pretoria and its consistent violations of human rights. The government and military were aware that incidents of this kind could not be repeated because they would not be tolerated by the international community. This prompted the military to seek new crowd control measures, the Holy Grail being a chemical agent that could be used to calm crowds. Both General Lothar Neethling, a former South African police forensics chief, and General Constand Viljoen, a former chief of the South African Defence Force (SADF), recalled the military's interest in such agents. Neethling explained to the Truth Commission that "when the riots started in 1976, the South African Police were caught unawares. They had nothing apart from guns, shotguns, and sharp point ammunition. Nobody wanted to use that and that's why there was a surge for various techniques to be applied. . . . I went overseas three times to Germany, England, Israel, America to find the best techniques available."[3]

These considerations prompted the SADF to decide to develop a chemical program that concentrated on creating irritants and incapacitants for crowd control and external operational use and also on making equipment and clothing to protect against the use of chemical weapons, particularly in Angola. The biological weapons program, on the other hand, focused on devising covert assassination weapons for the operational units of the SADF. The development and use of these weapons to eliminate key figures in the liberation movement was in line with the counterinsurgency warfare approach of the military.

During the 1980s, at the height of the cold war, the SADF continued to wage a high-intensity conventional war in Angola against Soviet-backed MPLA and Cuban forces. It occupied large parts of southern Angola almost continuously from 1980 to 1988.[4] Internally opposition to apartheid grew in intensity. The African National Congress (ANC) and the Pan-African Congress received international support from, among others, the Soviet Union and China. Compounding these threats to the state was the international ostracism of the government as a result of its apartheid policies. South Africa faced sanctions from the United Nations and what has been termed a "near-excommunication from Western nuclear suppliers, markets and scientific forums" with which it had cooperated and benefited since 1957, when it had signed a 50-year agreement with the United States under the Atoms for Peace program.[5] But successive American (and British) administrations also adopted opportunistic policies toward the apartheid government. Indeed, the failure, particularly by the United States, to apply sanctions strictly, may have contributed to making the South African government confident that it would not be called to account for its chemical and biological warfare program even if the West came to know that it existed.

In 1977, some twenty years after South Africa had begun its nuclear enrichment and explosives research under the international Peaceful Uses of Nuclear Energy (PNE) banner, there was clear evidence of its militarization.[6] And in 1978, when P. W. Botha succeeded John Vorster as prime minister, he established a high-level committee on nuclear weapons policy. This committee included the prime minister, the ministers of defense, foreign affairs, minerals and energy, and finance and also the chiefs of Armscor (the state's weapons procurement company), the Atomic Energy Board (AEB), and the SADF.[7] By 1979 it had recommended building "deliverable nuclear weapons to acquire a 'credible deterrent capability' and shifting overall responsibility for the program to Armscor."[8] As Botha recalled later, a nuclear arsenal was developed as a "diplomatic weapon to defend South Africa."[9] The decision to build a nuclear weapons capability was taken at the highest level: Prime Minister Vorster is credited with taking the final decision.[10]

Recruiting the Scientists

The nuclear weapons program grew out of existing capabilities. South Africa had a cadre of skilled scientists and engineers who had benefited from international exchanges and shared technology since the 1950s and 1960s. Working for the AEB (as of 1985 the Atomic Energy Committee), they formed the backbone of the nuclear weapons program near Pretoria. The scientists were drawn from earlier programs, including the PNE efforts and a program, subsequently canceled, that drew together approximately two dozen scientists to build a nuclear reactor. Those recognized as the drivers of the South African nuclear weapons program included the head of the AEB/AEC, Ampie Roux, sometimes referred to as the "godfather" of South Africa's nuclear weapons. However, the decision to pursue a weapons-focused nuclear program meant that control of it moved from the AEC to Armscor, where a mix of politicians, scientists, and technocrats became responsible for advancing the program.

Relative to those in the United States and the Soviet Union, only a small number of scientists and engineers worked on South Africa's nuclear weapons program. According to Albright, "by the early 1980s the program employed about 100 people, of which only about 40 were directly involved in the weapons program and only 20 actually built the devices. . . . By the time the program was cancelled in 1989, the work force had risen to 300, with about half directly involved in weapons work."[11] All those working on the program required top secret security clearances, available only to home-born South Africans. As the country relied increasingly on self-sufficiency, the weapons were created from a technological can-do mentality that coincided with its increasing international isolation in the 1970s and 1980s.[12]

Under Armscor's guidance the nuclear program's focus was on developing and manufacturing weapons that met the same military standards as other weapons systems. The first fully weaponized and aircraft-deliverable production model was completed in June 1988. By the time the program was terminated, there were six devices: one completed in 1979, one upgraded pre-production model, and four production models. Nuclear material was available for a seventh device that was never assembled. The devices were gun-type, designed to operate without neutron initiators, and had a calculated explosive yield of ten kilotons. "One of the things that surprised United Nations inspectors who visited South African nuclear plants was that much of the equipment was low-tech. For example, 2-axis machine tools normally used for simple manufacturing were reportedly adapted to create complex 3-dimensional shapes for South Africa's gun-type nuclear device."[13] Although these seven devices were low-tech, more sophisticated concepts had been investigated, in part to maintain the interest of the scientists and engineers involved in the project.

During the course of the program, scientists took part in both its strategic and operational areas. André Buys, a scientist on the AEB explosives team in the 1970s and the general manager of Armscor's nuclear weapons plant Circle by 1983, recalled that "he and other scientists worried that 'nobody actually sat down and worked out a proper strategy for what they wanted to do with [the bombs] . . . '"[14] For this reason he established a working group in 1983 that developed a more specific, three-phase strategy emphasizing "deterrence and diplomatic leverage."[15] Thus the scientists' role changed from being simply providers of technical expertise, the initial requirement of them, to involvement at the strategic level, at their own initiative. Their strategy was subsequently endorsed by President Botha.

However, it was a group of technocrats, largely engineers, rather than scientists that drove the design of the nuclear program as it developed toward a realizable weapons program. These engineers, mainly from Armscor, mixed their knowledge of nuclear weapons with a broader understanding of weapons production and delivery. This resulted in the modification of the program to produce deliverable weapons. Horton argues that although the influence of scientists was particularly high during the earliest phases of the program (up to 1977), during the course of weaponization (from 1977) their influence diminished relative to that of the technocrats and politicians, who alone took the decision to dismantle the program.[16]

In pursuing a chemical weapons program, the first place to which the military turned to find a scientist willing to develop the concept was the Council for Scientific and Industrial Research's (CSIR) Applied Chemistry Unit. The head of the unit, Dr. J. P. De Villiers, had given thought in the 1970s to issues of chemical warfare, particularly to how the SADF could protect itself against the use of chemical weapons in Angola. He was aware too of the potential benefits of using chemical weapons in unconventional warfare. Dr. Wouter Basson, a young military doctor who had close ties with the surgeon general, was tasked with approaching the CSIR chemist, Dr. Vernon Joynt (who worked under De Villiers), to take on the job of leading the program. Joynt was not attracted to the idea of doing secret military work and turned the offer down, leaving the ambitious Basson to step into his place. Basson's own interest in the possibilities that chemical and biological weapons could offer the military, his scientific qualifications, and his ability to impress high-ranking officers with his knowledge played a role in their giving him the freedom to determine the nature and direction of the program.

In 1981, the decision was taken to give the program to the SADF's Medical Services (SAMS). According to Purkitt and Burgess, "the SAMS had ties with Special Forces and was also trained to protect the SADF from all types of attacks, including CBW [chemical and biological weapons]. . . . The connection between SAMS and covert Special Forces provided a secret and loosely managed organizational context for the new CBW program," which had consequences for the management and research direction of the program.[17]

The biological weapons program developed from the relationship between Basson and Dr. Daan Goosen, a veterinarian. Basson tasked Goosen with the establishment of a specialized facility called Roodeplaat Research Laboratories (RRL), where research could be done on biological warfare agents and where the chemical agents produced at its sister company, Delta G, could be tested using animal models. Both were front companies distanced from the military by appearing to be commercial entities. Together Goosen and Basson recruited scientists to RRL, predominantly from the conservative University of Pretoria. The combination of attractive financial benefits and the opportunity for scientists to work in well-equipped laboratories where they could spend part of their time doing their own work was sufficient incentive for most of those who came to work at the laboratory. Few were initially motivated by patriotism.

The veterinarian Dr. André Immelman was the scientist recruited to RRL next after Goosen, and the responsibility for carrying out military contracts fell to him. He was one of the few scientists who confessed to having been, at least to some extent, politically motivated to join the company. He stated in an affidavit to the Truth and Reconciliation Commission (TRC) that he thought he could "make a contribution towards the protection of the South African population."[18] Immelman was ordered to see to the military's requirements and to be the single point of contact between the military and the front company. Although he maintained that the work he was doing was for defensive application, he did admit that after a while he began to be concerned about the legitimacy of his work. When he took this worry to Basson, he was brushed off with the assurance that he would not be personally involved, or bear any responsibility, if the poisons he was making available were misused.[19]

Another scientist, the veterinarian and microbiologist Dr. Mike Odendaal, testified at the TRC and during the criminal trial of Wouter Basson in 1999–2002 that as head of the Department of Microbiology at RRL he had been required to develop some of the biological assassination weapons. He spoke of infecting cigarettes and chocolates with anthrax spores, sugar with salmonella, and chocolates with botulinum. There was no doubt in his mind that these were intended for operational use.[20] In interviews Odendaal initially justified his involvement in the development of assassination weapons by saying that he had done "good" work too, and pointed to the example of an antelope vaccine he had developed at RRL.

In addition, Odendaal oversaw what was probably the most sophisticated work done at the facility. This was carried out by Adriaan Botha, a junior scientist, and the result was genetically modified *E. coli*. He explained that this research was motivated by his personal interest in developing a recombinant vaccine against enterotoxemia in sheep. And, he claimed, in order to get his proposal passed by the management of RRL he referred to its potential military application, despite having no intention of developing a usable weapon.[21]

As noted by Purkitt and Burgess, "Basson was a highly charismatic and effective recruiter, who was apt at identifying and enlisting some of the most promising and highly skilled medical researchers from the military and from the larger civilian scientific community."[22] Although most of the senior scientists and managers recruited to RRL were aware they were employed in front companies whose primary purpose was to attend to the chemical and biological warfare needs of the military, this was not made clear to the more junior staff members. Indeed some of them have claimed they were never aware of being part of a CBW program. Purkitt and Burgess have argued that it was the combination of the career opportunities offered by the front companies and the knowledge that their work was furthering a political agenda most of the scientists supported that led to their recruitment and their decision to stick with the work. "Many of these researchers and scientists joined the program because . . . the intellectual challenges and opportunities to participate in path-breaking research in one of several related disciplines, for example chemistry, anatomy and virology, intrigued them. Almost all were Afrikaaner South Africans who shared a sense of patriotic duty, a nationalistic zeal for the importance of the work and a sense that their research was critical for maintaining national security."[23] Interviews with the junior-level scientists revealed that political motivations were less significant factors in their decision to work at RRL and Delta G than the attraction of the research itself. The political context may have provided a useful justification later on. This was less true for those in positions of authority.

Although the military withdrew fully from the CBW program only as late as 1993, the process of closing down the program began much earlier as it became clear that some kind of negotiated settlement with the African National Congress was inevitable. However, documents from the biological warfare program show that biological assassination weapons were made available to the covert units of the security forces until at least 1989 and that up to this time RRL had considered expanding its facilities. By 1990 it was clear that the facilities would be privatized. The closure of the chemical front company was given impetus by the Chemical Weapons Convention, which opened for signature in 1993.

Motivations and Means

The political landscape of South Africa between 1960 and 1990 profoundly influenced the motivations for the creation and development of the country's NBC programs and also the motivations of the individuals who worked for them. Some scientists, especially senior ones in the CBW program, both shared a common political ideology and were influenced by the political situation at the time. The more junior scientists were, as indicated above, not informed about the true nature of the CBW program. Scientists have spoken of the attraction of having sufficient funds and physical resources to pursue cutting-edge research in the chemical, biological, and nuclear areas; and specifically in the nuclear field they worked to keep up with nuclear technology and to maintain scientific prominence.

The above are universal motivations, which would apply to scientists anywhere in the world. But the inevitable secrecy of illicit weapons programs meant that the scientists did not talk about what they were doing with colleagues outside the program or even with their closest family members. They had only each other with whom to share their justifications for involvement. Thus they were shielded from questions or considerations about the morality of their work. A separate moral economy was inevitable in which the offensive weapons–related work could be weighed in their minds against other work, for example developing vaccines for wildlife, or against the value of scientific advancement.

Together with the motivations of the scientists were the means, provided largely by the state, to enable these programs to flourish. From the 1970s to 1988–89 the political will to support South Africa's NBC programs did not falter, and money, in the form of high salaries, new laboratories, and research facilities with modern equipment, flowed freely. The programs also ran under fairly loose management: those with a clear interest in them determined their direction and output. As a case in point, weak management of RRL from the mid-1980s meant that scientists justified research into areas that interested them by adding the words "may have military application" to their research proposals.

A similar observation was made about the nuclear weapons program: "According to participants and Western government experts, the [plant's] success depended principally on the skill and initiative of its scientists and technicians. They went through years of trial and error before producing significant quantities of enriched uranium. Behind this talent was the government's willingness to provide adequate funding to solve complicated problems."[24]

Thus the motivations of the scientists and engineers who worked on South Africa's NBC programs differed little from those of any individual who finds an interesting field of work. The most significant difference is that in some instances they were violating South Africa's treaty obligations under the Biological and Toxin Weapons Convention (BTWC) and were following a clear lead from Pretoria to ignore the Nuclear Non-Proliferation Treaty (NPT).[25]

In the context of the CBW program, treaty obligations were consistently underplayed or not addressed at all by Basson. His reports frequently conflated chemical and biological weapons and placed emphasis on issues relating to chemical agents. By avoiding a discussion of the international implications of biological weapons development, he gave himself the space to pursue an agenda that would have gained him the approval of at least the head of Special Forces, General A. J. (Kat) Liebenberg. A document written by Basson in the 1990s indicates that he believed there was little adherence to the BTWC anyway. "It is also often a problem for the scientists of RRL (who are not trained to think strategically)," he said, "to keep perspective in the light of the renewal of Western attempts to ban chemical and biological weapons. It appears to them that South Africa should abide by these calls. *The fact that no country involved is really weighing up the possibility of moving away from biological weapons is not clear to them*" [26] (emphasis in original).

Although a philosophy was developed with regard to the use of chemical weapons both inside and outside South Africa, there is as yet no document made public that indicates a similar doctrine was developed for the use of biological weapons. Because the focus of the biological program was on the development of weapons for covert assassination, it is extremely unlikely that such a document exists. A document by Basson provides some insight into why this may have been the case. He argues that the SADF's philosophy about using chemical weapons "does not cover any aspects of Biological warfare. Because of the more controlled nature of Biological Warfare [sic] there are many more international control measures. The production of Biological weapons is not allowed anywhere in the world."[27] This suggests that there may have been a policy for the development of biological weapons but that given the nature of the ban on biological warfare, it remained unwritten. This is consistent with the way in which the South African security forces operated under apartheid.

As noted by Purkitt and Burgess, it is not unusual for countries operating under a militaristic regime to place national interests ahead of international obligations. It was only in the early 1990s, as a democratic transition became inevitable in South Africa, that the Department of Foreign Affairs took responsibility for international treaty obligations and was able to provide the required reassurance to the international community and ensure that South Africa was no longer considered a proliferator of NBC weapons technology.[28]

Scientists and the Modern World

One of the challenges of the modern security environment is to try to learn the lessons of history so that measures to prevent proliferation can be put in place. The desire to learn from South Africa's NBC programs is no different. However, as has been noted by others, each state's path in acquiring proliferation technology is unique and often entails the involvement of non-state actors. But as the world is faced with a handful of states remaining outside international non-proliferation and disarmament regimes and as there is an increasing focus on non-state groups that attempt to access weapons of mass destruction material and technology, it seems relevant to attempt to identify examples of past experience that may be relevant to current non-proliferation efforts.

At the level of the state, it is clear that national legislation will not stop states from proliferating if that is their intent. Thus the means that are available to the international community to prevent, combat, and eradicate such tendencies become a delicate interplay of coercion and threat, with the stakes high that either approach could push a country closer to the brink of prolif- eration. Analyses of South Africa's decision-making process in deciding to pursue a nuclear program have not yielded any conclusive arguments that one theoretical argument trumped others during the process of deciding to develop nuclear weapons.[29] In fact, it has been noted that the "political lead- ership took advantage of its scientists' eagerness to demonstrate South Africa's technical prowess at a time when the military had no rational operational requirement" to develop a nuclear deterrent.[30] A lack of apparent rational decisionmaking would further complicate efforts to engage with states on these issues.

At least within the context of international peace and security, there is a framework within which to operate for those states that willingly participate in international control regimes. But the tendency to want to push states out of these regimes for non-compliance (or not to actively try to keep them in a regime when they are intent on leaving) can make it very difficult to find chan- nels for negotiation. In the case of South Africa, Horton observes that "U.S. pol- icy to minimise proliferation by punishing South Africa for not joining the NPT backfired and resulted in a greater, not reduced proliferation risk."[31] Waldo Stumpf, who oversaw the dismantlement of the country's nuclear pro- gram, makes a similar assertion: "although international political isolation may be an instrument to contain individual cases of nuclear proliferation, a point in such an isolation campaign may be reached where it actually becomes counter-productive and really pushes the would-be proliferators towards full proliferation."[32] He argues that this stage was reached in South Africa when the United States cut off its supplies of fuel to the two nuclear reactors in South Africa in the 1970s. "The little leverage the U.S. had over the South African nuclear program was lost."[33] On the other hand, effective means to address suspected or proved violators of agreements are extremely important. States observing the agreements have to ensure that they are effective and that sup- port for them is clearly demonstrated. Otherwise, the argument that "no-one else takes them seriously" becomes an easy justification for non-compliance.

The isolation of South Africa played to its advantage as its programs be- came more advanced. There were rumors that weapons programs were being pursued, but without confirmation from Pretoria, although individual scien- tists are known to have spoken to non–South Africans about the programs.

Visitors to South Africa during the 1970s report the AEC scientists were proud of their efforts and privately revealed their nuclear research. They found the scientists to be well trained and pursuing their work with an attitude of "wanting to show the world what South Africa can do." Many during this early stage had studied abroad but in later years the opportunities for overseas training and contact through international conferences were severely reduced. This likely contributed to a highly parochial worldview on their part but does not appear to have impeded their technical skills. . . . [34]

Such isolation also reinforces perceptions of insecurity and external and internal threat. The resulting national security assessments are often what tips the balance toward proliferation. In contrast a change in such assessments toward a more secure environment (whether real or perceived) can mean the reversal or cancellation of weapons programs. But Stumpf also notes that the "roll-back option" South Africa followed for threshold non-nuclear-weapon states "is not an easy path to follow as the NPT and its associated instruments were not designed to deal with such an eventuality."[35]

At the level of individuals, the motivations discussed above remain relevant to countries other than South Africa. Their calculation may be based on financial inducements, prestige, and career advancement or on a strong belief in a political cause. Whatever the reason, if the individual perceives that the benefit ultimately outweighs the cost, then proliferation of technology and knowledge may be the result.

To elaborate all the possible responses to such a wide range of challenges is beyond the scope of this chapter. Nonetheless, one very clear lesson can be drawn from South Africa's experience. This is the need for strong, mutually reinforcing NBC regimes and approaches that combine oversight and enforcement with international cooperation and technical assistance, which in turn encourage states to pursue a peaceful path of nuclear technology and commercial-only chemical and biotechnology industries. These regimes should be entrenched at national, bilateral, regional, and multilateral levels so that the options for negotiation and acquiescence are greater. UNSCR 1540 has such an approach because its effectiveness depends on national and international enforcement and also on other means of cooperation in trying to stem possible proliferating activities by non-state actors.

Conclusion

The South African experience of WMD development, while small-scale, illustrates that states will pursue policy options that are in their best security interests. In this example, it was not only South Africa that set aside its international commitments in order to develop weapons programs for its security needs but also Western nations that put their security concerns ahead of the need to uphold these obligations.

The international security environment has set unprecedented challenges for controlling the spread of weapons, especially NBC programs. At one level, countries concentrate on the need to prevent the spread of technology and equipment that may assist in the manufacture of WMD while they ignore or find too difficult the need to deal with knowledge and its transfer by individuals. There remain countries, and actors within countries, who are focused on attaining illicit weapons at any cost and by any means. But, as seen in the case of South Africa, it is also important to concentrate on those who conceptualize and implement the programs, that is, the scientists and the engineers. With the universal and mandatory requirements of UNSCR 1540, states not willing to comply with the Resolution are now under increasing pressure to explain actions that might be seen to involve proliferating activities by members or groups on their territory.

South Africa remains unique in its renunciation of all three of its WMD programs in the early 1990s. The programs were halted and dismantled, and the scientists and engineers were left to go into private business or to find new lines of work. They were not retrained and reemployed in order to ensure that their knowledge and expertise were not used for illegal purposes in the future. This was due to a range of factors, including national political sensitivities. The post-1994 ANC government was lampooned by the national press when it was discovered that Wouter Basson had been reemployed by the military. The fact that his reemployment was at the request of the American and British governments, which were concerned about his potential role in assisting proliferation in Libya, was not taken into consideration in the court of public opinion. What South Africans saw was that the post-apartheid government was prepared to employ and pay a man believed to have been responsible for gross human rights violations. The large-scale reemployment of scientists from the NBC programs would have found little support from ANC supporters and would have been very difficult for the ruling party to justify to the electorate.

There is no single factor, be it an international treaty, national legislation, or a code of conduct for scientists, that will be sufficient to deter a country or group intent upon proliferation from pursuing an option that it believes is in its or its country's best security interests. The primary lesson for disarmament from the South African experience is that deterrents on many levels are required in order to increase sufficiently the disincentive for individuals as well as states to seek weapons of mass destruction.

Notes

1. See, for example, Lt. Col. Roy E. Horton III, "Out of (South) Africa: Pretoria's Nuclear Weapons Experience," USAF Institute for National Security Studies, Occasional Paper 27, August 1999; D. Albright, "South Africa's Secret Nuclear Weapons," ISIS Report, May 1994; Waldo Stumpf, "Birth and Death of the South African Nuclear Weapons Programme," paper presented at the conference "50 Years after Hiroshima," September 28–October 2, 1995, Unione Scienzati per il Disarmo, at www.fas.org/nuke/guide/rsa/nuke/stumpf.htm; Peter Liberman, "The Rise and Fall of the South African Bomb," *International Security*, Vol. 26, No. 2 (Fall 2001), pp. 45–86; and Chandré Gould and Peter Folb, *Project Coast: Apartheid's Chemical and Biological Warfare Programme*, UNIDIR, 2002.

2. Quoted in Jacklyn Cock and Laurie Nathan (eds.), *War and Society: The Militarisation of South Africa* (Cape Town: David Philip, 1989), p. xiii.

3. Testimony of General Lothar Neethling in the transcript of the Truth and Reconciliation Commission hearing into chemical and biological warfare, Cape Town, June 11, 1998.

4. Jeremy Grest, "The South African Defence Force in Angola," in Cock and Nathan (eds.), *War and Society*, p. 116.

5. NTI, South Africa profile, at www.nti.org/e_research/profiles/SAfrica/Nuclear/index_2153.html.

6. Liberman, "The Rise and Fall of the South African Bomb," fn. 1, p. 49. In 1977 it was suspected that South Africa was planning an underground cold test. In response to strong protests by the United States, the Soviet Union, and France, the government canceled the test. The resulting sanctions and the cancellation of U.S. cooperation pushed South Africa from a "peaceful nuclear explosives" approach to a more aggressive, weapons-focused research and development program, initially under the Atomic Energy Board and then Armscor, the state weapons agency.

7. As quoted in Liberman, "The Rise and Fall of the South African Bomb," p. 53.

8. Idem.

9. Ibid., p. 59.

10. Ibid., p. 52.

11. David Albright, "South Africa's Secret Nuclear Weapons," ISIS Report, May 1994, p. 9, at www.isis-online.org/publications/southafrica/ir0594.html.

12. Ibid., p. 1.

13. "South Africa's Nuclear Autopsy," *The Risk Report*, Vol. 2, No. 1 (January–February 1996), Wisconsin Project on Nuclear Arms Control, at www.wisconsinproject.org/countries/safrica/autopsy.html.

14. Correspondence with A. Buys, December 10, 1999, as quoted in Liberman, "The Rise and Fall of the South African Bomb," p. 55.

15. Ibid., p. 56.

16. In September 1988 South Africa sent a letter to the then director general of the International Atomic Energy Agency (IAEA), Hans Blix, expressing its willingness to accede to the Nuclear Non-Proliferation Treaty if certain conditions were met, primarily that South Africa be allowed to market its uranium subject to IAEA safeguards. The dismantlement of the program quickly followed, and was completed two years before President de Klerk announced in 1993 that South Africa had had a nuclear weapons program.

17. Helen Purkitt and Stephen Burgess, "Paths to Disarmament: The Rollback of South Africa's Chemical-Biological Warfare and Nuclear Weapons Programs," paper presented at the 2001 annual meeting of the International Studies Association, p. 7, at www.isanet.org/archive/disarm.html.

18. Affidavit of Dr. André Immelman to the Truth and Reconciliation Commission, Pretoria, June 4, 1998.

19. Idem.

20. Chandré Gould and Marlene Burger, *Secrets and Lies: Wouter Basson and South Africa's Chemical and Biological Warfare Programme* (Cape Town: Zebra Press, 2002), pp. 36–37.

21. All RRL research proposals had to be authorized by the departmental head and the head of research (in this case Mike Odendaal and Schalk Van Rensburg).

22. Purkitt and Burgess, "Paths to Disarmament," p. 7.

23. Dr. Ian Phillips, African National Congress defense expert, quoted in ibid., p. 7.

24. Ibid., p. 4.

25. South Africa signed the Nuclear Non-Proliferation Treaty only in 1991, but it had been a party to the treaty negotiations and had held a seat on the International Atomic Energy Agency's board of governors until 1977–78, when it was suspended owing to its nuclear ambitions. It was later barred from participating in the IAEA's general conference. South Africa signed the BTWC in April 1972 and ratified it in November 1975, well before it initiated the biological weapons program.

26. Wouter Basson, *Authorisation for the Sale of Assets: Project Coast,* document written for the purpose of securing the authorization of the minister of defense, Magnus Malan, for the privatization of RRL (HSF/UG/302/6/C123), SADF Top Secret document, August 19, 1991.

27. Wouter Basson, "Presentation to the Reduced Defence Command Council: Proposed Philosophy for Secret Chemical Warfare for the South African Defence Force—Principles and Feedback on Current Status in the SA Defence Force," October 3, 1990, South African History Archives.

28. Purkitt and Burgess, "Paths to Disarmament," p. 16. It has also been noted that the negotiation of the Chemical Weapons Convention, with a strict compliance regime, convinced South Africa that it would not be able to sustain a clandestine chemical weapons production capacity, thus hastening that program's closure.

29. For discussion, see, for example, Liberman, "The Rise and Fall of the South African Bomb," and Purkitt and Burgess, "Paths to Disarmament."

30. Horton, "Out of (South) Africa," p. 15.

31. Ibid., p. 14.

32. Stumpf, "Birth and Death of the South African Nuclear Weapons Programme."

33. Ibid.

34. Horton, "Out of (South) Africa," p. 5.

35. Stumpf, "Birth and Death of the South African Nuclear Weapons Programme."

PART II

UNSCR 1540 and Existing Controls, Organizations, and Treaties

RON G. MANLEY

5

Restricting Non-State Actors' Access to Chemical Weapons and Related Materials: Implications for UNSCR 1540

UN Security Council Resolution 1540 places a number of duties on UN member states, including to "adopt and enforce appropriate effective laws which prohibit any non-state actor to manufacture, acquire, possess, develop, transport, transfer or use nuclear, chemical or biological weapons and their means of delivery, in particular for terrorist purposes" (operative paragraph 1). The primary mechanism for ensuring the non-proliferation and eventual elimination of chemical weapons is the Chemical Weapons Convention (CWC).[1] UNSCR 1540 encourages states not only to adopt this convention but also to meet, in full, their obligations under it.

The Chemical Weapons Convention

The CWC, which opened for signature in 1993 and entered into force on April 29, 1997, prohibits the development, production, stockpiling, and use of chemical weapons by its states parties, numbering 178 as of June 2006. They are also required to declare and undertake the destruction of any stocks of chemical weapons that they possess. Moreover, all facilities used for the production of chemical weapons since 1946 must be declared and destroyed or, subject to the prior approval of the conference of states parties of the CWC, converted for use for peaceful purposes. In addition, states parties are obliged to declare any chemical production facilities, whether commercial or military, that produce either highly toxic chemicals or the precursor chemicals necessary for their synthesis and that are listed on the schedules contained in the CWC's Annex on Chemicals.

The CWC has an intrusive and effective verification regime. Stocks of chemical weapons, chemical weapons–related facilities, and both military and commercial plants producing or, in some circumstances, processing or consuming certain toxic chemicals are subject to inspection. These inspections are undertaken by teams of international inspectors employed by the technical secretariat of the Organisation for the Prohibition of Chemical Weapons (OPCW), the organization mandated by the treaty as responsible for overseeing its implementation. During the nine years since the CWC's entry into force, these inspection teams have carried out almost 2,500 inspections at 945 different sites in seventy-six states parties.[2] Over 1,000 of these inspections were of chemical industry–related sites.

By June 2006, there were 178 states parties that had signed and either ratified or acceded to the CWC. A further eight countries had signed the Convention and thus made a commitment in principle to its objectives, but they have not yet taken the final step of formally ratifying it. Only eight states remain completely outside the Convention. Of the remaining states not party to the CWC, at least five are suspected of either having or having had stocks of chemical weapons or chemical weapons programs, and their continued non-membership is thus of particular concern. The five countries are Egypt, Iraq, Israel, the Democratic People's Republic of Korea (North Korea), and Syria.[3] Indications are that Iraq will accede to the Convention once an elected government is in place.[4] Israel has signed the CWC, but to date it has not ratified it. Even though the other non-states parties may neither possess chemical weapons nor have chemical weapons programs, they could still become, intentionally or otherwise, a safe haven for non-state actors seeking to obtain or produce chemical weapons. In October 2003 the member states of the OPCW, recognizing the need to continue to strive for universal adherence to the Convention, adopted an action plan specifically aimed at encouraging the remaining non-states parties either to ratify or to accede to the Convention.[5] This plan has had some success, and a further twenty-two have joined the CWC in the period following its adoption. Efforts to encourage the remaining non-states parties to join are continuing. As a result, the risk from chemical weapons produced by states is gradually being reduced and the manufacture and use of the key precursor chemicals necessary for their production are being brought under greater international control.

The CWC requires those states parties that possess chemical weapons to destroy them within ten years of its entry into force, by April 29, 2007.[6] However, a provision to extend this deadline by a maximum of five years, to April 2012, is also provided for if the OPCW's conference of states parties to the CWC is satisfied that the request for an extension is justified.[7] It is already evident that the two states with the largest stockpiles of chemical weapons, the Russian Federation and the United States, will be unable to meet the first deadline and thus will need to seek an extension.[8]

Since the entry into force of the Convention, more than 8.6 million chemical weapons have been declared by the six "possessor" states parties.[9] By June 2006 approximately 2.5 million of these weapons had been destroyed, leaving around 6.1 million remaining to be destroyed.[10] Although their destruction is the responsibility of the individual "possessor" states, there is a significant risk that without additional support from other states parties, even the 2012 deadline may not be met. All the chemical weapons are safely stored at sites in the six "possessor" states and are regularly monitored by inspectors from the technical secretariat of the OPCW, but their existence provides a potential source for those non-state actors seeking such weapons. Greater effort by the "possessor" states, in combination with additional support from the other states parties, is required in order to ensure that these weapons are destroyed as soon as practicable.

One of the important obligations placed on all states parties to the CWC is to adopt, in accordance with their constitutional processes, the necessary national measures to implement the Convention.[11] The adoption of appropriate national implementing legislation is viewed by the OPCW as an essential step in enabling states parties to meet fully their obligations under the CWC, an approach that is adopted too by Resolution 1540. In 2003 the executive council of the OPCW, recognizing that many states parties were failing to meet this obligation, drew up and adopted an action plan, to encourage states parties to rectify this situation by enacting the required comprehensive national implementing legislation.[12] Despite the considerable efforts of the OPCW's technical secretariat, assisted by a number of states parties, to implement the executive council's plan, it has met with only limited success. In a report to the ninth session of the conference of states parties, the director general of the technical secretariat stated that as of October 31, 2002, only 96 states parties (56 percent) had reported that they had some form of national implementing legislation in place. Of these, only 53 (32 percent) were judged to have adopted sufficiently comprehensive implementing legislation.[13] Many states parties appear to have taken the view that as they neither possess chemical weapons nor undertake any other related activities, there is no need for them to divert national resources from other important issues to drafting and implementing the necessary legislation. As explained below, the existence of comprehensive national implementing legislation not only is necessary for a state party to meet fully its obligations to the CWC but also is a vital step in preventing non-state actors from gaining access to chemical weapons. This has now become a mandatory requirement because UNSCR 1540 has been adopted under Chapter VII of the United Nations Charter.

Ratifying or acceding to the CWC and fulfilling their obligations under it will enable states, whether big or small, to make a major contribution to the reduction in the global threat posed by chemical weapons and related materials. It should be noted, however, that this action on its own may not be sufficient to meet fully the objectives of UNSCR 1540 with respect to the prevention of the use of chemical weapons by non-state actors. This is because the CWC, as negotiated and adopted, was intended primarily for eliminating the development, production, and use of chemical weapons by states. Its verification regime, including both declaration and inspection requirements, was, and still remains, directed principally at the activities of states rather than at those of non-state actors. For example, only those chemicals listed in the three schedules contained in the Convention's Annex on Chemicals are subject to declaration and routine inspection. In addition, routine verification is restricted to what was judged at the time of the treaty negotiations to be militarily significant quantities of those chemicals on the lists. As illustrated below, non-state actors planning a chemical attack may have very different requirements.

The CWC and the Global Chemical Industry

Many of the toxic chemicals used as chemical weapons are also key intermediates in the production of chemicals for the legitimate, commercial chemical industry. Because of their dual purpose, it was essential that the CWC's verification regime extended not only to military sites but also to commercial chemical industry sites producing or using those chemicals for legitimate, peaceful purposes. However, the concept of allowing international teams of inspectors to undertake inspections at those sites was, and remains, unprecedented. The full involvement and support of the global chemical industry, in the negotiation of the Convention as well as in its implementation, were essential if the CWC were to have any chance of succeeding. Fortunately, most of the major chemical industry associations throughout the world, realizing the importance of the CWC, chose to play a major part in its negotiation; and their support has continued since the Convention entered into force.

The potential impact of the CWC on the commercial chemical industry meant that in drafting the verification regime, it was necessary to establish a careful balance. On the one hand, there was the need to provide sufficient transparency to enable a state party to demonstrate its compliance with the Convention. On the other hand, it was necessary to minimize the impact on the national chemical industry and thereby enable companies to protect their commercial business information. This was not an easy task, and the successful negotiation of the CWC's verification regime inevitably involved a number of compromises.

The dual nature of the majority of toxic chemicals and their precursors meant that their inclusion in the Annex on Chemicals or a lowering of the threshold for their declaration placed a greater burden on the global chemical industry. Phosgene and hydrogen cyanide, for example, which have both been extensively used as chemical weapons, are key intermediates in the production of a large number of commercial chemicals. The global production of these two chemicals alone runs into millions of tons a year. Banning their production would simply not have been a feasible option, and the sheer scale of their manufacture meant that only limited verification of their production was considered to be practicable. Many other toxic chemicals that could be used as chemical weapons or could serve as precursors for their manufacture pose similar problems. For this reason, the Annex on Chemicals was the subject of extensive negotiation. Inevitably, the outcome was a compromise, designed to provide a balance between the perceived chemical weapon risk and the need to protect national chemical industries and the international trade in chemicals. As a result, although the Annex on Chemicals contains the most militarily significant chemical weapons and their precursors, it is by no means exhaustive. Many known toxic chemicals and potential precursors, judged not to pose a significant military risk, are not included or are subject only to limited verification. To counter these potential limitations, additional provisions, such as the general purpose criterion (GPC), incorporated in paragraph 1 of Article 2 of the CWC, and the clarification process and challenge inspection mechanism, contained in Article 9, were incorporated into the text of the Convention.

Article 9 and the General Purpose Criterion

The provisions of Article 9 provide a mechanism for any state party believing it has evidence of non-compliance by another state party either to seek clarification from that state party or to request an immediate challenge inspection of the location where it believes the non-compliant activity is taking place. A challenge inspection may be requested at any location within a state party, whether it has been previously declared or not. However, the requesting state party must provide sufficient information to the executive council of the OPCW to demonstrate that its request for an inspection is justified. The inspection will automatically proceed unless the executive council votes by a three-quarters majority of all forty-one of its members not to go ahead. The challenged state party is required, within a very short time, to permit an OPCW inspection team to visit the location and investigate the allegation. The provisions of Article 9 thus give a means to counter some of the unavoidable limitations of the CWC's routine verification activities.

In recent years many individuals, and even some states, have tended to take the view that the CWC applies only to those chemicals listed in the Annex on Chemicals. Although it is true that declaration and routine verification is limited to these chemicals, the reach of the CWC is much broader than this—it is comprehensive.

The drafters of the CWC were fully aware that the schedules in the Annex on Chemicals could not be exhaustive. They understood as well that the introduction of declaration thresholds, to ease the burden on the global chemical industry, carried with it the potential danger of the Convention's circumvention. To counter this problem a catchall clause, known as the general purpose criterion (GPC), was inserted into the definition of a chemical weapon.[14] This clause stipulates that "Chemical Weapons means the following, together or separately: a) Toxic chemicals and their precursors, *except where intended for purposes not prohibited under this Convention, as long as the types and quantities are consistent with such purposes* [emphasis added]; b) Munitions and devices. . . ." It follows that with the exception of the circumstances emphasized in the above text, all toxic chemicals are defined as chemical weapons and are thus covered by the CWC.[15] This general purpose criterion is viewed by many as the key to ensuring the long-term effectiveness of the CWC. It is also, unfortunately, perhaps one of the most poorly understood parts of the Convention, and this has, albeit inadvertently, led to the adoption by some of a more limited view of its scope.

Non-State Actors: The Main Problem?

It is important to keep in mind that the GPC and those provisions contained in Article 9 are aimed primarily at the activities of states. Taken as a whole the CWC attempts to establish a balance between its primary purpose of eliminating the threat of the use of chemical weapons as a means of warfare and the need to support and foster the global development of chemistry for peaceful purposes. However, this carefully negotiated balance is now in danger of being disturbed by the increasing threat of the use of chemical weapons or related materials by non-state actors. To restore the balance, additional action by the states parties to the CWC, as well as by states that are not members, is necessary.

Although in theory the CWC's challenge inspection mechanism should be equally effective against the activities of states and non-state actors, in practice this may not always be the case. For example, in order to be able to accept a short-notice challenge inspection, states need to have in place the legislation necessary to grant immediate access by a team of international inspectors, and this provision will normally form part of its national implementing legislation for the CWC. But providing this access to non-commercial properties such as private residences poses problems for some states. Because the main purpose of the CWC was seen by many to be directed at the activities of states rather than individuals, some states decided not to include the provision for this type of access in their national implementing legislation. Accepting a challenge inspection in relation to the activities of non-state actors at, for example, a private residence may pose difficulties for those states that have chosen to go down this route.

The quantities of toxic chemicals necessary to mount terrorist attacks against unprotected civilian populations are orders of magnitude less than those that would be regarded as militarily significant. In the former case, gram and kilogram quantities may be significant; in the latter case, hundreds or even thousands of tons would be required to mount an effective military campaign or to serve as a deterrent against their use by a potential aggressor. For instance, the chemical weapons stockpiles of the Russian Federation and the United States before the entry into force of the CWC in April 1997 were around 40,000 tons and 30,000 agent tons, respectively.[16] It is estimated that Iraq's chemical weapons stockpile immediately before the 1991 Gulf war was of the order of 6,000 to 10,000 agent tons.[17] The Tokyo subway attack in March 1995, by contrast, involved the use of a small number of devices, each containing a few grams of the nerve agent sarin.

Recognizing the potential limitations of the CWC with respect to the activities of non-state actors, UNSCR 1540 also decides that all states "shall take and enforce effective measures to establish domestic controls to prevent the proliferation of nuclear, chemical, or biological weapons and their means of delivery, including by establishing appropriate controls over related materials and to this end shall: (a)Develop and maintain appropriate effective measures to account for and secure such items in production, use, storage or transport." The definition of related materials, which is contained in a footnote to the Resolution, is "Materials, equipment and technology covered by relevant multilateral treaties and arrangements or included on national control lists, which could be used for the design, development, production or use of nuclear, chemical and biological weapons and their means of delivery." This definition, which also includes chemicals and equipment covered by multilateral arrangements and national control lists—such as the Australia Group (see below), the Proliferation Security Initiative, the G-8's Global Partnership against the spread of weapons and materials of mass destruction, and the EU's strategy against the proliferation of weapons of mass destruction—as well as those chemicals covered by the CWC, is much broader than the three schedules of chemicals in the Annex on Chemicals.

States developing and putting in place legislation and regulations to meet their commitments to both the CWC and UNSCR 1540 thus need to take note of the potential limitations of the CWC with respect to the activities of non-state actors. Even those states that already have national implementing legislation in place to meet their obligations under the CWC may still need to take action to counteract the potential threat of the preparation or use of chemical weapons by non-state actors on their territory. Some of the areas where particular attention may be required are examined below.

The Trade in Chemicals

As explained above, the CWC and its Annex on Chemicals try to strike a careful balance between preventing the proliferation of chemical weapons and fostering the free trade in chemicals among its states parties. Highly toxic chemicals, such as nerve agents, which have little or no use other than as chemical weapons, are listed in Schedule 1 of the Annex on Chemicals, and their production, storage, and transfer by states parties is strictly controlled. For example, transfers to non-state parties of chemicals listed in Schedule 1 are prohibited, and there is no minimum declaration threshold for transfers of these chemicals between states parties.

Although the export to non-state parties of chemicals listed in Schedule 2 is also prohibited, controls on the trade in chemicals appearing in schedules 2 and 3, the vast majority of which are dual-use, are much less stringent. Moreover, a number of chemicals that were not considered to pose a significant military threat or the impact of whose restrictions on the legitimate commercial chemical industry was judged to outweigh the potential military threat were excluded from the Annex on Chemicals. Examples of the former are sodium and potassium cyanide; cases of the latter are chlorine and ammonia. Chlorine, a moderately toxic industrial chemical and the first chemical weapon to be used in the First World War, is produced and traded globally in quantities of millions of tons per year. Additional consideration therefore needs to be given to monitoring the trade and movement of toxic chemicals of types and quantities that might be useful to non-state actors planning to engage in terrorist activities; and, where practicable, further action must be taken to restrict their access to these materials.

A number of states have already put in place additional arrangements to monitor and control the export of certain chemicals and equipment that could be used in the production of chemical weapons. The thirty-eight countries belonging to the export control regime called the Australia Group have, for example, agreed on lists of both chemicals and dual-use chemical manufacturing equipment that they will subject to additional controls.[18] The Australia Group's chemicals list currently contains fifty-four dual-use chemicals that are routinely traded internationally, twenty of which are not included in the Annex on Chemicals. As the CWC also has no mechanism to monitor or to control the export of dual-use equipment, the equipment list is specific to the Australia Group.

It is important to note that the declared purpose of these additional controls is to prevent the potential misuse of the listed chemicals and equipment, not to obstruct the legitimate trade in them. All current members of the Australia Group are also states parties to the CWC, and thus have undertaken an obligation to foster the legitimate trade in chemicals between states parties to it.

Declaration Thresholds

To minimize the impact on the legitimate chemical industry, a number of thresholds were established for the declaration of chemicals listed in the Annex on Chemicals. For example, the production of chemicals listed in Schedule 1 of the annex is strictly controlled and may be undertaken only for research, medical, pharmaceutical, or protective purposes.[19] With one exception, facilities undertaking such work must be declared; and they must provide on an annual basis full details, including the quantities, of all Schedule 1 chemicals produced. These facilities are also subject to regular inspection by the OPCW. The exception is for facilities producing less than 100 grams of these chemicals a year for research, medical, and pharmaceutical purposes.[20] These facilities need not be declared, and thus are not subject to routine monitoring under the CWC. Although quantities of less than 100 grams of these extremely toxic chemicals are deemed to pose no military threat, the potential impact of their use by non-state actors could still be significant. The declaration thresholds for the dual-use chemicals listed in schedules 2 and 3 are much higher, ranging from one kilogram to one ton a year for chemicals on Schedule 2 and over 30 tonnes per year for chemicals on Schedule 3.[21] Facilities producing less than the declaration threshold will be transparent to the OPCW and not subject to routine monitoring by it.

In order to be able to make the required annual declarations, states need to put in place appropriate mechanisms to collect the necessary data. In most cases, these mechanisms are part of their national implementing legislation for the CWC. But to reduce the impact on their national chemical industries, many states parties require only those companies the capacity of whose facilities exceeds the relevant declaration threshold to make the required returns. It follows that in these circumstances they may not even be aware of either the existence or the location of facilities that fall below the declaration threshold. Assessing the degree to which these facilities might serve as a potential source of toxic chemicals for use by non-state actors will be difficult. Where appropriate, states will need to address this problem and to devise their own means of dealing with it.

Riot Control Agents and Toxic Industrial Chemicals

States parties to the Chemical Weapons Convention undertake not to use riot control agents as a means of warfare.[22] However, they may continue to produce, stockpile, and use these chemicals for law enforcement, including domestic riot control purposes.[23] States parties are required to declare the chemical name and structural formula of any chemicals they hold for this purpose, but riot control agents are not listed in the Annex on Chemicals, nor are they subject to routine verification under the CWC. Control of the production, stockpiling, and trade in these chemicals is left to individual states parties.

Even though riot control agents are by definition relatively non-toxic, they can under certain circumstances still be used as an effective terrorist weapon. Recognizing this, some countries, such as the United Kingdom, already have in place legislation to control the production, possession, and sale of these chemicals on their territory.[24] The market is much less strictly controlled in a number of countries; and in some others, personal protection devices containing these chemicals remain readily available to members of the general public. For this reason, legislators will need to give further consideration to how best to control access to these materials.

Many moderately toxic industrial chemicals that were not considered to pose a significant military threat could, in some circumstances, be used as effective terrorist weapons. Some of these chemicals are listed in either Schedule 2 or Schedule 3 and thus are subject to declaration—and in some cases, the facilities producing them are subject to inspection by the OPCW—but many are not. Even where these chemicals are subject to verification under the CWC, this activity is aimed primarily at deterring their diversion for military purposes. Their potential for use by non-state actors for terrorist purposes is not specifically addressed in the treaty. The bulk storage of toxic industrial chemicals and their bulk transport pose a particularly challenging problem in the light of their potential for use by non-state actors in a terrorist attack.

To counter this particular risk, further measures may be necessary regarding the production, bulk storage, and bulk transport of these chemicals. One approach to this problem might be to build, where practicable, on existing relevant national health and safety legislation. Within the United Kingdom, for example, the Major Accident Hazards Regulations already require companies that are producing and storing toxic chemicals in bulk to assess the potential hazards posed by their activities, to take action to reduce these hazards, and to put in place emergency plans to deal with accidents that might arise from them.[25] An amendment to these regulations requiring companies to include in their hazard assessment and action plans the potential for these materials to be used in a terrorist attack would by no means eliminate the problem, but it would lead to an increase in the resilience of facilities to this form of attack.

The possible impact of any additional regulation or other control measures on both the national and global chemical industries will need to be given careful consideration, and the potential gain must be balanced against the likely harmful impact of additional controls.

Conclusion: The Need for National Implementation

Although non-state actors may resort to the use of traditional chemical warfare agents, there are, as illustrated above, other readily available toxic chemicals that might also serve their purposes. When drafting their national legislation, states should thus bear in mind that the CWC's general purpose criterion has an important role in dealing with the potential use of toxic chemicals by non-state actors. Fully enacting the GPC in national implementing legislation by, for example, criminalizing the preparation, possession, use, or intent to use toxic chemicals for terrorist or criminal purposes will not only strengthen the CWC but also provide individual states with a valuable tool in their fight to prevent the diversion and misuse of these chemicals by non-state actors.

It is in the interest of all states wishing to prevent the proliferation of chemical weapons either to ratify or to accede to the CWC and to take action to enact the national implementing legislation necessary to meet fully the obligations arising out of their membership of the Convention. States not parties to the CWC will, in meeting fully the requirements of Resolution 1540, also need to address a wide range of issues; and, where appropriate, they will need either to adjust existing legislation or to draft new laws and regulations. In doing so, they will need as well to give careful consideration to minimizing the impact on their national chemical industries and research institutions. The eventual success or failure of both Resolution 1540 and the CWC in restricting access by non-state actors to toxic chemicals will, in the end, depend on the effectiveness of the national implementing legislation put in place by individual states.

Notes

1. See the Convention on the Prohibition of the Development, Production, Stockpiling and Use of Chemical Weapons and on Their Destruction, 32 I.L.M. 800, January 13, 1993, at www.OPCW.org.

2. S. Spence, "Developments in the OPCW - *Quarterly Review*, No. 38," in M. Meselson and J. Perry Robinson (eds.), *The CBW Conventions Bulletin*, Issue No. 66 (Brighton, U.K.: Science and Technology Policy Research Unit, University of Sussex, December 2004), pp. 6–21.

3. Arms Control Association, "Fact Sheet: Chemical and Biological Weapons Proliferation at a Glance," September 2002, at www.armscontrol.org/factsheets/cbwprolif.asp.

4. OPCW Press Release Number 34, July 20, 2004, at www.OPCW.org.

5. Report of the Eighth Session of the Conference of States Parties, C-8/7, October 24, 2003, at www.OPCW.org.

6. CWC, Article 4, paragraph 6.

7. Paragraph 26, Part 4 of the verification annex to the CWC.

8. "Extension of the intermediate and final deadlines for the destruction by the Russian Federation of its category 1 chemical weapons," C-8/DEC.13, Eighth Session of the Conference of States Parties, October 24, 2003, at www.OPCW.org, and "Extension of the intermediate and final deadlines for the destruction by the United States of America of its category 1 chemical weapons," C-8/DEC.15, Eighth Session of the Conference of States Parties, October 24, 2003, at www.OPCW.org.

9. The declared "possessor" states are Albania, India, Libya, the Russian Federation, the United States of America, and a state party that has elected to have its name withheld.

10. Spence, "Developments in the OPCW - *Quarterly Review*, No. 38," pp. 6–21.

11. CWC, Article 7, paragraph 1.

12. Plan of action regarding the implementation of Article 7 obligations, C-8/DEC.16, Eighth Session of the Conference of States Parties, October 24, 2003, at www.OPCW.org.

13. Spence, "Developments in the OPCW - *Quarterly Review*, No. 38," pp. 6–21.

14. CWC, Article 2, paragraph 1.

15. The meaning of *toxic chemical* is defined in paragraph 2 of Article 2 of the CWC as "any chemical which through its chemical action on life processes can cause death, temporary incapacitation or permanent harm to humans or animals."

16. G. S. Pearson and R. S. Magee, "Critical Evaluation of Proven Chemical Weapon Destruction Technologies," *Pure and Applied Chemistry*, Vol. 74, No. 2 (2002), pp. 187–316.

17. *Iraq's Weapons of Mass Destruction: A Net Assessment* (London: International Institute for Strategic Studies, 2002), pp. 45–46.

18. See www.australiagroup.net.

19. CWC, Part 6 of the verification annex.

20. CWC, Part 6, paragraph 12 of the verification annex.

21. CWC, Part 7, paragraph 3 and Part 8, paragraph 3 of the verification annex.

22. CWC, Article 1, paragraph 5.

23. CWC, Article 2, paragraph 9(d).

24. Section 5(1)(b) of the Firearms Act (1968) (London: HMSO).

25. Statutory Instrument 1999 No. 743: *The Control of Major Accident Hazards Regulations 1999* (London: TSO Customer Services).

TARIQ RAUF *and* JAN LODDING

6

UNSCR 1540 and the Role of the IAEA

Several of the programs and activities of the International Atomic Energy Agency (IAEA, the Agency) are relevant to the objectives of UN Security Council Resolution (UNSCR) 1540. The Agency assists states in, among other activities, preventing nuclear material and related technologies from falling into the hands of non-state actors, and thus its activities contribute to the implementation of Resolution 1540 by member states of the United Nations.[1] The relationship between the IAEA and UNSCR 1540 is specified in the Resolution as complementary: "none of the obligations set forth in this resolution shall be interpreted so as to conflict with . . . or alter the responsibilities of the International Atomic Energy Agency or the Organisation for the Prohibition of Chemical Weapons" (operative paragraph 5). Additionally, the Resolution is for states, not for the 1540 Committee set up by the Resolution, to implement, and it does not override that which is already in place and it serves to reinforce. States are called upon "to renew and fulfil their commitment to multilateral cooperation in particular within the framework of the International Atomic Energy Agency . . . as important means in pursuing and achieving their common objectives in the area of non-proliferation and of promoting international cooperation for peaceful purposes" (operative paragraph 8).

The relevant Agency programs and activities include:

—Legislative assistance, to enable states to adopt the necessary laws for implementing instruments under the Agency's purview, such as safeguards

The views expressed here are purely personal and do not necessarily reflect those of the IAEA.

agreements and their additional protocols and the Convention on the Physical Protection of Nuclear Materials (CPPNM);

—Training state officials in order to strengthen states' systems for controlling nuclear material and related technology and to enable states to implement legal instruments to which they subscribe and to tighten national controls;

—Support to states in their development and implementation of high standards of physical protection of nuclear material and nuclear facilities through the elaboration of standards and through training and assessment services; and

—Support for states' efforts to upgrade border controls so as to improve the detection of illicit trafficking of nuclear material and related technology.

The objectives of both UNSCR 1540 and the IAEA could be served best through mutually agreed coordination and support, as appropriate. Resolution 1540 obliges "all States, in accordance with their national procedures, to adopt and enforce appropriate effective laws which prohibit any non-State actor to manufacture, acquire, possess, develop, transport, transfer or use nuclear . . . weapons . . . , in particular for terrorist purposes . . . [and to] establish domestic controls to prevent the proliferation of nuclear . . . weapons . . . , including by establishing appropriate controls over related materials" (operative paragraphs 1 and 3). To this end, states shall implement a variety of accounting, security, and physical protection measures, as well as border controls and law enforcement efforts, and establish appropriate effective national export and trans-shipment controls (operative paragraph 3(a) to (d)).

Although the Resolution reinforces the Agency's non-proliferation goals, the relevant IAEA programs and activities could help states to implement Resolution 1540, thereby serving the objectives of both. The Resolution recognizes that "some States may require assistance in implementing the provisions of this resolution . . . and invites States . . . to offer assistance as appropriate" (operative paragraph 7). The 1540 Committee, after reviewing the reports by states on their implementation of the Resolution, could inform them as appropriate about requesting legislative and technical assistance and advisory services from the IAEA. This would help them to adopt and implement relevant international control instruments in the nuclear field, as well as domestic controls to prevent the dissemination of nuclear material and related radioactive materials to non-state actors.[2] The 1540 Committee itself does not provide this assistance, but in a clearinghouse capacity it can assist with matching requests and offers as needed.

UNSCR 1540 recognizes the relevant international control instruments in the nuclear field and their objectives at the time of its adoption by acknowledging "that most States . . . have taken effective measures to account for, secure and physically protect sensitive materials, such as those required by the Convention on the Physical Protection of Nuclear Materials and those recommended by the IAEA Code of Conduct on the Safety and Security of Radioactive Sources" (preambular paragraph 11).

Security Council Resolution 1673 (2006) reaffirmed inter alia that none of the obligations in Resolution 1540 (2004) shall be interpreted so as to conflict with or alter the rights and obligations of state parties to the Nuclear Non-Proliferation Treaty (NPT), or alter the responsibilities of the IAEA. UNSCR 1673 extended the mandate of the 1540 Committee for a period of two years, until April 2008, invited the 1540 Committee to explore with states and international, regional, and subregional organizations experience sharing and lessons learned in the areas covered by Resolution 1540, and the availability of programs that might facilitate the implementation of Resolution 1540.

The IAEA's Legislative Activities

The IAEA has a number of legislative instruments in place to verify and facilitate states' compliance with nuclear security undertakings, notably those of the Nuclear Non-Proliferation Treaty and of UNSCR 1540 in respect of non-state actors. These requirements include the safeguards agreements and their updates in the form of additional protocols, as well as the aforementioned CPPNM and the Code of Conduct on Safety and Security of Radioactive Sources.

Safeguards Agreements and Their Additional Protocols

The IAEA safeguards system is designed to verify states' fulfillment of their commitments not to use nuclear material to develop nuclear weapons or other nuclear explosive devices. The system contains a number of elements that include commitments relevant to states' strengthening their control over nuclear material and nuclear-related material and activities. These comprise the following procedures:

—The state system of accounting for and control of nuclear material (SSAC). Comprehensive safeguards agreements, which all non-nuclear-weapons states must enter into under the Nuclear Non-Proliferation Treaty, and comparable non-proliferation treaties and agreements, require states to maintain effective SSACs in order to ensure that nuclear material is accounted for at all times and that any changes in national inventories are recorded and reported to the Agency. States for which additional protocols (APs) incorporating enhancements to IAEA safeguards are in force are also required to provide information to the Agency on their nuclear material activities and holdings, including on nuclear fuel cycle–related research and development activities not involving nuclear material; and

—Export and import controls. IAEA comprehensive safeguards agreements require states to report exports and imports of nuclear material to the Agency. APs expand these reporting requirements to certain specified equipment and non-nuclear material.[3] These obligations assume states maintain import and export controls that enable them to report such international transfers to the Agency. The adoption of UNSCR 1540 now means that maintaining such controls is mandatory.

The Convention on the Physical Protection of Nuclear Material

The Convention on the Physical Protection of Nuclear Material is included in the list of twelve legal instruments of relevance to combating terrorism adopted by the UN.[4] This list increased to thirteen with the completion of the 2005 Convention against Nuclear Terrorism. The CPPNM is the only international legally binding undertaking related to the physical protection of nuclear material aimed at averting potential danger from the unlawful acquisition and use of nuclear material.[5] In particular, certain CPPNM commitments are relevant to the control and protection of nuclear material:

—The protection of nuclear material. The CPPNM obliges contracting states to ensure the protection—on their territories and on their ships or aircraft during international transport—of nuclear material used for peaceful purposes at the levels specified in the CPPNM;

—Export and import requirements. States party to the CPPNM commit themselves not to undertake or to authorize the undertaking of the international transport of nuclear material (such as exports and imports) without providing assurances that nuclear material will be protected at the required levels. Parties must also apply the agreed levels of protection to nuclear material during its transit from one part of their territory to another and while it passes through international waters or airspace; and

—Measures to prevent, detect, and punish offenses relating to nuclear material. States parties are required to make offenses under Article 7 punishable by appropriate penalties under their national laws. These offenses shall be included as extraditable offenses in any extradition treaty existing between parties. Parties that make extradition conditional on the existence of a treaty have the option of considering the CPPNM as the legal basis for extradition in respect of the offenses.

The process of amending the CPPNM to strengthen it finished on July 8, 2005. The amendment, entering into force thirty days after approval from two-thirds states parties, would extend the scope of the Convention to cover, inter alia, the physical protection of nuclear material used for peaceful purposes, in domestic use, storage, and transport, and the physical protection of nuclear material and nuclear facilities used for peaceful purposes against sabotage. This wording reflects that in Resolution 1540's operative paragraph 3. A conference to consider the proposed amendments was held in 2005. Additionally, the Convention against Nuclear Terrorism completed negotiation in spring 2005 and opened for signature at the UN world summit in September 2005.

The Code of Conduct on Safety and Security of Radioactive Sources

The Code of Conduct on Safety and Security of Radioactive Sources deals with radioactive materials, not nuclear sources. [6] In undertaking to implement the Code, states are committed

—to reinforce the responsibilities of manufacturers, suppliers, users, and those managing disused sources for the safety and security of radioactive sources;

—to establish an effective national system of control over the management of radioactive sources;

—to establish legislation and regulations that prescribe and assign governmental responsibilities for the safety and security of radioactive sources; and

—to provide for the effective control of radioactive sources.

In such legislation and regulations, states are particularly obliged to include security measures to prevent, protect against, and ensure the timely detection of the theft, loss, or unauthorized use or removal of radioactive sources during all stages of management.

The International Atomic Energy Agency has an outreach program to encourage and facilitate states' conclusion of comprehensive safeguard agreements and additional protocols.[7] In addition, it organizes teams of legal and technical experts for the purpose of advising states on adherence to and implementation of international instruments relevant to enhancing protection against nuclear terrorism.[8]

IAEA Technical Capabilities in Support of UNSCR 1540

In order to help states to upgrade their ability to control and account for nuclear material and related technologies, the Agency provides advisory services and technical assistance upon request.[9] Much of this type of assistance is provided through the Nuclear Security Plan of Activities, approved by its board of governors in March 2002, which contains a number of programs and activities relevant to protection against nuclear terrorism.

The Agency's technical assistance of relevance to Resolution 1540 consists of four measures. The first measure is capacity building for the maintenance of effective state systems of accounting for and control of nuclear material. An effective State System of Accountancy and Control (SSAC) is fundamental to a state's ability, first, to account for and control nuclear material on its territory and to detect possible losses or unauthorized use or removal of nuclear material; and, second, to fulfill its international nuclear non-proliferation obligations. The IAEA offers an international SSAC advisory service (ISSAS) whereby, among other things, a team of experts, at the request of a state, reviews the legal framework and the regulatory, administrative, and technical systems of SSACs and evaluates the performance of those systems in meeting safeguards obligations. Recommendations are made and an action plan is formulated in cooperation with the state so as to improve its SSAC. The follow-up to such missions may involve, for example, assistance with the procurement of equipment or the training of staff from the SSAC authority and from facility operators.

Next, the Agency provides assistance with the physical protection of nuclear material and nuclear facilities. Its programs in this area aim to strengthen states' capacity to protect nuclear facilities and nuclear material in use, storage, or transport against malicious, criminal, or terrorist acts. The programs include: a) developing internationally accepted recommendations and guidelines for the physical protection of nuclear material in use, storage, and transport and of nuclear installations; b) providing services to states at their request to enable them to evaluate the national physical protection system and its implementation at nuclear installations; and c) providing technical advice, expertise, training, and equipment for specific security arrangements.

The Agency's International Physical Protection Advisory Service helps states to improve physical protection systems at nuclear facilities and convenes a wide range of related training courses, among them ones on the design basis of threat methodology. This service offers international, regional, and national courses for officials from national nuclear operators, regulators, and law enforcement and security authorities.

Third, the IAEA helps with the detection of malicious activities involving nuclear material. It seeks to ensure that effective measures are in place to detect and deal with incidents of theft, illicit possession, and illicit nuclear trafficking. The prevention of theft and illicit possession of and trafficking in nuclear material is by far the most desirable outcome; but if preventive measures fail, states need to have in place the means of detecting such incidents. The Agency helps to achieve this by providing, upon request, assessment services, training, and technical support and by coordinating states' development of up-to-date detection instrumentation. Technical documents providing advice on the detection of and response to illicit nuclear trafficking have been issued, and a program of training courses on combating illicit nuclear trafficking is being conducted at the regional, subregional, and national levels. The Agency is implementing as well a coordinated research project involving eighteen member states designed to improve the technical measures available for detecting and responding to illicit trafficking.

The IAEA also has an illicit trafficking database (ITDB), established in 1993, to provide an authoritative source of information on illicit trafficking incidents and to help facilitate the exchange of this information among states. Its unique strength is that it is built upon information provided by the states in whose jurisdictions the incidents occurred. The Agency disseminates reports on individual incidents and analytical assessments of the information in the database. More than eighty states currently participate in the ITDB program.

Finally, the IAEA gives assistance with national legislation. Compliance with international obligations usually requires states to pass national legislation as part of the ratification process. The Agency helps states, upon request, to adopt national rules and regulations pursuant to the obligations contained in the relevant bilateral or multilateral instruments. In this way, it supports states in their development of a comprehensive nuclear law governing radiation protection, nuclear and radiation safety, nuclear liability, safeguards, and physical protection. Through the years, the Agency has assisted a large number of states to develop their nuclear law in conformity with the international instruments to which they subscribe, including the setting up of independent regulatory authorities, which are most often responsible for the control and licensing of nuclear material and related technology.[10] Most of the Agency's work in this area consists of advising states on how to draft specific legal provisions that meet their international commitments and obligations in the nuclear field.

Effective National Export Controls

As mentioned above, safeguards agreements, additional protocols, and other legal instruments require subscribing states to monitor exports and imports of nuclear material and related technology. If national authorities request the IAEA's assistance in setting up or strengthening their national control systems, it endeavors to identify ways to help. Moreover, it has gained experience over the years in reviewing nuclear-related imports and exports and has developed much expertise in analyzing covert activities and transactions related to nuclear trade.

Conclusion

Resolution 1540 is designed to prevent the proliferation of nuclear, chemical, and biological weapons and their related components and materials to non-state actors. It requires UN member states to enforce effective measures to establish domestic controls, particularly effective physical protection, border controls, and law enforcement efforts. Security Council Resolution 1673 (2006) reaffirmed inter alia that none of the obligations in Resolution 1540 (2004) shall alter the responsibilities of the Agency. As discussed above, the International Atomic Energy Agency already has in place a number of programs that would assist states to fulfill their obligations pursuant to Resolution 1540. States have been called upon to report to the 1540 Committee on their implementation of the steps called for by the Resolution, and the first and second rounds of reports have been analyzed. In those cases in which states lack appropriate national rules and regulations, physical protection measures, border controls, and law enforcement measures relating to nuclear materials, the 1540 Committee could recommend that such States contact the Agency for relevant assistance and also inform it accordingly. Such an arrangement not only is straightforward and practical but also is in line with the Resolution, which calls on states to fulfill their commitments within the framework of the Agency's Statute and the decisions of its Board of Governors regarding IAEA activities to protect against nuclear terrorism. The Agency already is assisting states in their implementation of UNSCR 1540. Subsequent reports and future activities of the 1540 Committee would provide an appropriate mechanism by which the results of the Agency's assistance could be measured.

Notes

1. The stated objectives of Resolution 1540 could contribute to strengthening international peace and security in that they aim to close gaps between international treaties and national legislation on curbing the proliferation of WMD to non-state actors. Nonetheless it is important to recognize the view expressed by a large number of UN member states that international legally binding instruments need to be negotiated directly by the states concerned and that the Conference on Disarmament is the

sole UN body charged with negotiating multilateral non-proliferation and disarmament treaties and agreements.

2. Radioactive material is nuclear material and other radioactive substances that contain nuclides that undergo spontaneous disintegration (a process accompanied by emission of one or more types of ionizing radiation, such as alpha, beta, and neutron particles and gamma rays) and which may, owing to their radiological and fissile properties, cause death, serious bodily injury, or substantial damage to property or to the environment.

3. States are to report imports at the Agency's request.

4. The text of the CPPNM and related information is found at "Conference to Consider and Adopt Proposed Amendments to the Convention on the Physical Protection of Nuclear Material" at www-pub.iaea.org/MTCD/Meetings/cppnm.html#thecon. For the twelve instruments, see "Conventions on Nuclear Terrorism," at http://untreaty.un.org/English/Terrorism.asp.

5. Nuclear material is plutonium, except that with isotopic concentration exceeding 80 percent in plutonium-238; uranium-233; uranium enriched in the isotope 235 or 233; uranium containing the mixture of isotopes as occurring in nature other than in the form of ore or ore residue; or any material containing one or more of the foregoing. Convention on the Physical Protection of Nuclear Material, Article 1, at www. iaea.org/Publications/Documents/Infcircs/Others/inf274r1.shtml.

6. Radioactive material has been defined above (see fn. 2). The Code does not apply to nuclear material, except sources incorporating plutonium-239.

7. Representatives of more than 130 states have attended Agency regional and interregional seminars on safeguards agreements, additional protocols, and the strengthened safeguards system in the past three years.

8. The IAEA's international team of experts (ITE) has visited more than a dozen countries so far, in West Asia, Central America, Southeast Asia, and Eastern Europe. IAEA international instruments relevant to enhancing the protection of nuclear material against nuclear terrorism include the Convention on the Physical Protection of Nuclear Material at www-pub.iaea.org/MTCD/Meetings/cppnm.html#thecon; safeguards agreements concluded between the Agency and a state (INFCIRC/153 (Corr.)) and an additional protocol thereto (INFCIRC/540 (Corr.)) at http://www.iaea.org/OurWork/SV/ Safeguards/legal.html; the Convention on the Early Notification of a Nuclear Accident (INFCIRC/335) at www.iaea.org/Publications/Documents/Conventions/cenna. html; the Convention on Assistance in the Case of a Nuclear Accident or Radiological Emergency (INFCIRC/336) at http://www.iaea.org/Publications/Documents/ Conventions/cacnare.html; the Convention on Nuclear Safety (INFCIRC/449) at www-ns.iaea.org/conventions/nuclear-safety.htm; the Joint Convention on the Safety of Spent Fuel Management and on the Safety of Radioactive Waste Management (INFCIRC/546) at www-ns.iaea.org/conventions/waste-join convention.htm; the Code of Conduct on Safety and Security of Radioactive Sources (GOV/2003/49-GC (47)/9, July 29, 2003) at www-pub.iaea.org/MTCD/public ations/PDF/Code-2004_web.pdf; and the International Basic Safety Standards

for Protection against Ionising Radiation and for the Safety of Radiation Sources (IAEA Safety Series No.115).

9. Advisory services, carried out by teams of international experts led by the Agency, typically result in recommendations for training and technical upgrades, some of which may be requested through various Agency assistance programs.

10. Since 2000, the IAEA has provided legislative assistance to more than fifty member states by means of written comments, and it has given advice in drafting national nuclear legislation to more than seventy member states. In addition, training on issues related to nuclear legislation has been provided to some fifty-five individuals at the request of member states.

ANGELA WOODWARD

7

The Biological Weapons Convention and UNSCR 1540

The threat posed by biological weapons (BW) has undoubtedly grown in recent years, as non-state actors have now joined states in demonstrating an interest in developing and using these weapons of mass panic, if not destruction. Terrorist groups and individuals have sought to develop and use BW for various purposes, such as to influence political processes, to inflict economic and psychological panic as well as to kill people. The 1984 salmonella poisoning perpetrated by the Rajneesh sect in Oregon in the United States and the 2001 anthrax attacks there illustrate the means and motivations of those seeking to use BW.

The underlying factors that foster the prospective spread of biological weapons and related materials—the dual-use nature of biological agents, equipment, and techniques and the rapid advances in biotechnological science—persist, requiring innovative approaches and layering and reinforcing measures to prevent BW proliferation.[1]

The 1925 Geneva Protocol and the 1972 Biological Weapons Convention (BWC) are central to the legal regime requiring the disarmament and non-proliferation of BW.[2] These legal instruments were augmented by the United Nations Security Council's adoption of Resolution 1540 (UNSCR 1540) on April 28, 2004. This requires states to enact and enforce effective laws and supporting measures to prevent the proliferation of nuclear, biological, and chemical (NBC) weapons, their related materials, and their means of delivery to and by non-state actors, especially terrorists.

This chapter examines the Biological Weapons Convention and the biological weapons–related provisions of UNSCR 1540, including the major concepts governing their scope and operation, and describes their interrelationship. It details states' obligations under each instrument, among them national implementation obligations, and discusses their respective monitoring and verification arrangements. The chapter concludes by highlighting particular challenges in ensuring compliance with these agreements and assessing what UNSCR 1540 adds to the BW disarmament and non-proliferation regime.

The Biological Weapons Disarmament and Non-Proliferation Regime

The legal regime concerning BW comprises a range of international legal instruments, primarily treaties dealing with international humanitarian law, disarmament, and non-proliferation. But multilateral agreements on other, related issues are increasingly being considered in a BW non-proliferation context, for example those dealing with human, animal, and plant disease and environmental protection. This section focuses on the primary BW disarmament and non-proliferation treaty, the Biological Weapons Convention, and on the provisions in UNSCR 1540 related to biological weapons.

The Biological Weapons Convention, which was the first agreement to ban an entire category of weapon, was opened for signature on April 10, 1972, and entered into force on March 26, 1975. As of March 2006 the Convention has 155 states parties[3] and sixteen signatory states.[4] However, twenty-three states have neither signed nor ratified the treaty.[5] In common with certain other multilateral disarmament and non-proliferation treaties adopted during the Cold War, the governments of Russia (formerly the Soviet Union), the United Kingdom, and the United States serve as the treaty's depositaries, by virtue of which they have functional responsibilities concerning the treaty's operation. But states parties have assigned some logistical tasks—principally, convening treaty meetings and handling the confidence building measures data exchange process (described below)—to the United Nations Secretary General, with functional operations being carried out by the United Nations Department for Disarmament Affairs.

UN Security Council Resolution 1540 was adopted unanimously, after consultations with member states, in April 2004. Its provisions, requiring states to prohibit and prevent the proliferation of nuclear, chemical, and biological weapons, are binding on all states.[6] The Resolution specifically refers to states parties' obligations under the BWC.[7]

The following sections detail states' obligations under each instrument, particularly those relating to national implementation, and describe the evolution of their respective arrangements for monitoring and verifying states' compliance with those obligations.

General Obligations

The Biological Weapons Convention explicitly prohibits all activities except research that contribute to the acquisition of a biological weapon, which is defined using a general purpose criterion (GPC), contained in Article 1: "Each State Party to this Convention undertakes never in any circumstances to develop, produce, stockpile or otherwise acquire or retain: 1) Microbial or other biological agents, or toxins whatever their origin or method of production, of types and in quantities that have no justification for prophylactic, protective or other peaceful purposes; 2) Weapons, equipment or means of delivery designed to use such agents or toxins for hostile purposes or in armed conflict."

The treaty negotiators recognized that the inclusion of an exhaustive list of prohibited agents and toxins would quickly become outdated due to new scientific developments that could contribute to the development and proliferation of BW. Hence the prohibition on microbial and other biological agents and toxins[8] was based on criteria assessing their general purpose, which was intended to "future-proof" the treaty against these developments.[9] As the GPC is located specifically, and solely, in Article 1(1), the ban on delivery systems in Article 1(2) is total. States parties are not permitted to develop BW delivery systems, even for defensive purposes. Critically, the GPC enables dual-use materials to be used for peaceful purposes and—combined with the absence of an explicit ban on BW research (although research for offensive purposes is widely understood to be prohibited by the treaty)—allows states parties to pursue a biological defense program intended to develop prophylaxis (vaccines) or protective measures (such as protective clothing and biological agent detectors). To evaluate adherence to the GPC, it is necessary to assess objectively the intent of those using items that are capable of contributing to the development and use of BW. The Convention requires those using dual-use agents and materials to justify that they are doing so for a legitimate purpose in accordance with Article 1.[10]

While the treaty does not explicitly ban the use of BW, any state party doing so would have violated the provisions banning BW development, acquisition, or retention. States parties explicitly declared their understanding that BW use is effectively prohibited under the BWC at the Fourth Review Conference of the BWC in 1996.[11]

The Convention further prohibits states from transferring BW "to any recipient whatsoever" or assisting, encouraging, or inducing any state, groups of states, or international organization to acquire BW (Article 3).[12] The states parties pointedly affirmed at the Fourth Review Conference that this article covered "any recipient whatsoever at the international, national or sub-national levels."[13] The BWC therefore specifically prohibits states parties from transferring BW to non-state actors or assisting them to develop BW.

It also explicitly requires states parties to complete the destruction of items prohibited by the treaty within nine months of its entry into force.[14] States that join the Convention after it has entered into force need to have completed this process before they join it in order to comply with Article 1.

In addition to these responsibilities to ensure BW disarmament and non-proliferation, states parties are afforded certain rights relating to technical cooperation and development under the Convention, although states parties only "undertake" to realize them. Article 7 provides for cooperation in cases of violations so as to assist affected states parties. Rights to economic co-operation and scientific and technological exchanges in support of peaceful purposes are detailed in Article 10.

Under UN Security Council Resolution 1540, all states are required to pro-hibit and prevent a range of activities relating to BW under operative para-graphs 1 to 3. Additional obligations arise under operative paragraph (OP) 8, but these are not strictly mandatory.

OP 1 stipulates that states are obliged not to support efforts by non-state actors to acquire BW and their delivery systems, including related activities (development, manufacture, transportation, and transfer), or to use BW. The Resolution does not provide an exhaustive definition of "support," which widens its potential scope. An interpretation of its ordinary meaning, however, would encompass at least financial and logistical assistance as well as techni-cal knowledge and expertise. States are also obliged, under OP 2, to prohibit non-state actors from attempting to participate or participating in these activ-ities and from providing support. Notably, UNSCR 1540 (unlike the BWC) does not explicitly prohibit states from providing support to other states, although this would be achieved through effective implementation of the national measures that are required under OP 3. Unlike the BWC, the Reso-lution does not balance states' obligations with rights to economic develop-ment by using biological sciences for peaceful purposes or assistance in response to violations.

Requirements for National Implementation

The method by which a state gives legal effect to its international obligations depends on its constitutional arrangements and the nature of its legal system. States with a civil law system often have constitutional arrangements whereby international law is directly enforceable in their national legal jurisdiction and certain treaties may be considered to be "self-executing."[15] Nonetheless, specific national implementing measures are likely to be necessary to fulfill certain treaty obligations. States that follow a common law tradition need to adopt specific national implementing measures so as to translate their obligations under international law into measures that are enforceable in their national legal jurisdiction. Examples of national measures include legislation, regulations (a form of secondary, or subordinate, legislation), executive orders, and administrative decrees.

The Biological Weapons Convention

The BWC contains an explicit requirement in Article 4 for states parties to ensure national implementation of the Convention: "Each State Party to this Convention shall, in accordance with its constitutional processes, take any necessary measures to prohibit and prevent the development, production, stockpiling, acquisition, or retention of the agents, toxins, weapons, equipment and means of delivery specified in Article 1 of the Convention, within the territory of such State, under its jurisdiction or under its control anywhere."

This requirement is mandatory, and its fulfillment is essential for facilitating states parties' compliance. Although the BWC does not specify what national measures are necessary to give effect to the obligations in it, as more recent disarmament treaties tend to do,[16] the broad "any necessary measures" formulation in the Convention provides for a wide range of measures (laws, regulations, and so on) to be adopted on many different issues affected by it in accordance with each state party's constitutional arrangements.[17] The complexity of states' obligations under the BWC means that it cannot realistically be considered to be self-executing by states with a civil law system.

The BWC requires that states parties' national implementing measures prohibit and prevent the activities banned under Article 1 from occurring in their territory or in any other area that is under their jurisdiction or control, such as diplomatic posts and military bases abroad. This applies to any natural person (citizens, including military personnel) and legal person (companies and other entities recognized as having legal personalities in the domestic legal jurisdiction).

The prohibition of activities relating to the acquisition (through development, production, transfer, or other method), stockpiling, or proliferation of agents, toxins, equipment, and other items specified in Article 1 requires a range of issues be addressed through national implementation, such as the criminalization of activity prohibited by treaty, law enforcement, and export controls.

Issues relating to biosafety (the application of knowledge, techniques, and equipment to prevent personal, laboratory, and environmental exposure to potentially infectious agents or biohazards) and biosecurity (measures to control access to pathogens and toxins and to prevent unauthorized access) are also increasingly being recognized by states parties as essential to effective national implementation of the BWC.[18] For example, during the 2003 BWC meeting of experts, held under the intercessional meeting process agreed at the treaty's Fifth Review Conference in 2002, states parties held a structured discussion on constituent elements of a biosecurity strategy. It addressed the following issues:

—Legal, regulatory, and administrative measures (including national and international models and standards, risk assessment, program design, and consequence management);

—Facilities (including facility planning and management and the storage, containment, custody, and disposal of dangerous pathogens);

—Personnel (including personnel issues for pathogen management and training and continued education in pathogen security);

—Transport and transfer (including issues of the transport and transfer of dangerous pathogens and the type of recipient facility); and

—Oversight and enforcement (including issues of licensing, accreditation, and authorization).[19]

UNSCR 1540

Operative paragraph 2 of Resolution 1540 requires all states to adopt and enforce appropriate effective laws that prohibit non-state actors from carrying out a range of activities—to manufacture, acquire, possess, develop, transport, transfer, or use—relating to BW (as well as chemical weapons and nuclear weapons) and their delivery systems. Broadly defined, laws are the range of national measures that establish legally binding norms in a state. OP 2 does not prescribe the *type* of national law required to give effect to this provision (as it does in OP 3), simply requiring that such laws should be adopted and enforced "in accordance with their national procedures." States will likely require criminal legislation in order to give effect to this paragraph of UNSCR 1540. Significantly, OP 2 establishes a binding obligation on non-states parties to the BWC to take and enforce national legislation relating to BW non-proliferation and explicitly requires all states to *enforce* such national laws.

Operative paragraph 3 provides detailed requirements for the scope and, for certain obligations, the type of national measure necessary for states to give effect to their obligations under this paragraph. The general requirement for states to take and enforce national measures to prevent the proliferation of biological (and other) weapons and their means of delivery is contained in the chapeau paragraph of OP 3. This requirement is operationalized through specific types of control measures for "related materials," which are detailed in four subparagraphs (OP 3(a)–(d)).

OP 3(a) requires states to "[d]evelop and maintain appropriate effective measures to account for and secure" BW and their means of delivery during their "production, use, storage and transport." This is akin to the materials accounting systems already applied to nuclear and chemical materials under their respective treaty regimes. Yet materials accounting systems cannot be readily applied to bacteriological (biological) agents and toxins, as the baseline holdings of biological agents increase at varying rates and these agents are capable of self-replication and synthetic production.[20] This increases the difficulty in designing and implementing a monitoring system capable of detecting illicit diversions. UNSCR 1540 does not provide guidance on what system states might use to "account for" such materials and delivery systems. A layered approach that includes monitoring and biosecurity measures and activities will be necessary.

UNSCR 1540 addresses the issue of what should be accounted for by noting, in OP 6, the usefulness of "national control lists" in implementing the Resolution. States' development of effective national control lists for BW-related materials will be difficult, especially for non-states parties to the BWC that may be less familiar with BW control issues. The range of related materials and their dual-use characteristics will also complicate the design and implementation of the required security measures. In practice, states will probably need to prioritize certain materials for increased security.[21] For guidance on the scope of BW export control measures necessary to comply with this provision in UNSCR 1540, states may have recourse to BWC states parties' discussions at treaty review conferences on requirements under Article 3 of the Convention and to the control lists of the Australia Group's export control arrangement.[22] The latter specify agents and equipment that the states participating in this group consider to be at risk of diversion for BW.

OP 3(b) contains obligations relating to biosecurity, by requiring states to "develop and maintain . . . effective physical protection measures" over materials related to BW and their means of delivery.[23] The inclusion of this biosecurity requirement is a positive step because it should lead to continued discussion and consideration and, ideally, to guidelines on what measures are regarded to be appropriate.

Under OP 3(c) states are obliged to establish systems to "detect, deter, prevent and combat" illicit trafficking and brokering through border controls and law enforcement. These combined activities by border control and law enforcement officials will serve to establish a national monitoring system, at least with respect to trafficking and brokering, and they point to a need for international cooperation. The requirement in OP 2 that states *enforce* their laws prohibiting non-state actor activity involving NBC weapons also inherently requires a monitoring system, but it is by no means certain that all states have the capability or expertise to establish one. In practice, those countries will need to work together at the national level and with colleagues worldwide in order to fulfill these requirements. This problem is compounded for many non-state parties to the BWC, for which BW non-proliferation obligations are entirely new and which will probably need assistance so as to identify, implement, and monitor national biosecurity measures.

OP 3(d) requires states to "establish, develop, review and maintain" controls for the export, transit, trans-shipment, reexport, and end-user verification of materials related to BW and their delivery systems through national laws and regulations. This may be achieved under any legal measure; but most states will have primary legislation establishing export controls, with goods and materials subject to export control identified in subsidiary regulations. The Resolution also obliges states to sanction violations of export control laws through criminal or civil penalties, which will probably require specific implementing legislation. This effort to stem the non-proliferation of NBC weapons through a licensing system for organized trade (compared with the Resolution's provisions that identify non-state actors which are subject to prohibitions) gives the Resolution direct relevance to other entities with a distinct legal status (that is, "legal persons"), such as companies. Notably, it specifically calls upon states to work to inform industry, as a named group, of its obligations under national laws in order to prevent NBC proliferation.

Monitoring and Verification

Verification is the process of gathering and analyzing information in order to make a judgment about a state's compliance or non-compliance with its obligations. Monitoring is a means of obtaining information for verification purposes.[24]

A significant flaw of the Biological Weapons Convention is that it lacks effective monitoring, compliance, and verification mechanisms. There is a modest compliance mechanism, comprising a consultative procedure, in Article 5 which may be invoked in a bilateral and multilateral mode.[25] However, since the signing of the Convention, states parties have fleshed out a procedure for using a multilateral mode whereby a formal consultative meeting (FCM) can be held to consider an allegation of non-compliance. The procedure supports partial information collection and assessment, based solely on information provided by interested states parties and consultations by the FCM's chair. There is no provision for independent information collection or evaluation using other sources under these procedures.

Ultimately, the Security Council has a role in verifying and enforcing compliance with the BWC, either under its UN Charter mandate to maintain international peace and security or after a referral by a BWC state party under Article 6 of the BWC. That provision enables a state party to bring a case of non-compliance to the attention of the Security Council by lodging a complaint that includes "all possible evidence" relating to its finding of a breach by another state party. But even assertions of non-compliance supported by overwhelming and credible evidence have not been referred to the Security Council under this procedure; and the Security Council has not initiated action, as this would probably have drawn a veto from one of its permanent five members.

The UN Secretary General also has an inherent authority under the UN Charter to inform himself, through fact-finding missions, of cases that may threaten or breach international peace and security in order to brief the Security Council. The General Assembly and the Security Council have both endorsed this authority with respect to alleged uses of biological and chemical weapons.[26] This mechanism may be used to investigate cases involving any UN member state because its authority derives from the UN Charter and resolutions of the General Assembly and the Security Council, not the BWC.[27] As a state's approval is needed for fact-finding mission activities on its territory, this mechanism is therefore less effective in cases involving intransigent, opaque, or defiant states.

Recognizing that further measures were necessary to improve transparency and strengthen compliance with the treaty, the BWC states parties agreed to a modest transparency mechanism at the treaty's Second Review Conference in 1986 by requiring an annual confidence building measure (CBM) data exchange. The CBMs, which were enhanced and extended at the treaty's Third Review Conference in 1991, comprise eight forms on prescribed topics.[28] States parties' participation in this process is patchy, and there is no procedure to translate and analyze the reports or to assess their correctness and completeness. States parties only share these reports with each other, in an effort to limit the dissemination of potentially sensitive information, although much of the information reported can be obtained through open sources. However, a few states have published their reports on government websites or provide them to researchers on request.[29]

States parties considered means to strengthen the Convention under the Verification Experts (VEREX) consultations of 1992–93, the 1994 Special Conference, the Ad Hoc Group (AHG) discussions of 1995–96, and negotiations from 1997 to 2001 on a draft verification protocol. The draft protocol proposed the establishment of an international organization for the prohibition of biological weapons that would oversee implementation of the BWC, including technical assistance, and conduct monitoring and verification.[30] The negotiations on the protocol broke down in 2001, resulting in the inability of the Fifth Review Conference later that year to conclude a final document. The chair, Ambassador Toth, suspended the meeting for one year, and the reconvened session in 2002 was able to agree to a modest work program of intercessional meetings in 2003–05 in advance of the Sixth Review Conference, held from November 20 to December 8, 2006, in Geneva.

The five topics listed for consideration in the intercessional process signify a trend away from collective consideration by the states parties of multilateral verification arrangements for the Convention toward a reliance on national compliance, which may be facilitated and assisted by individual states, regional organizations, or other international organizations working on BWC-related topics.[31] The involvement of these organizations in the program of work, including briefings and background papers, is an important and effective innovation of the intercessional meeting process over the BWC review conferences, the VEREX consultations, and the AHG negotiations.

The meetings held under the intercessional process were obliged "to discuss, and promote common understanding and effective action on" five topics, including national implementation measures at the meetings held in 2003. There was no attempt to determine which states have enacted effective measures to implement the BWC or even to formalize legal technical cooperation for states that have identified that need. States likely to benefit most from this information exchange do not participate regularly in these meetings.

It has been difficult to assess the status and effectiveness of states parties' national measures to implement, and comply with, the BWC. Since the treaty's entry into force in 1975, states parties have failed to share information regularly on their adherence to Article 4, either through the CBM exchanges or Convention meetings, and to conduct regular assessments of the effectiveness of their national measures. Poor levels of participation in the CBM exchanges mean many states parties have not used that opportunity to review the effectiveness of their biological weapons legislation. States ought to consider routinely the effectiveness of their national measures to cover, among other issues, new scientific developments that affect BW development in order to fulfill the Article 4 mandate.

In addition to the efforts of the United Nations Department for Disarmament Affairs to collect states parties' reports on their measures to implement the BWC prohibitions, a parallel collation of states parties' implementing legislation, including texts where available, was conducted from June 2002 to November 2003 by the non-governmental organization VERTIC.[32] Its assessment determined that states had taken different approaches to implementing their treaty obligations through national measures and that some states had not used treaty definitions for prohibited items and activities, creating potential loopholes in treaty compliance.[33] National measures to give effect to the treaty could not be identified in many states parties, particularly those in Africa, Asia, and Latin America.

For its part, UNSCR 1540 establishes a rudimentary monitoring system that is based on states' declarations on implementation. Operative paragraph 4 establishes a Security Council committee (the 1540 Committee), comprising all members of the Security Council, for a two-year period to receive and review reports that states are obliged to provide on the steps they have taken, or intend to take, to implement the Resolution. The committee's mandate was renewed for a further two years in April 2006, and was extended to provide for a work program, to include dialogue, assistance, and cooperation activities.[34]

The 1540 Committee's assessment of states' reports is necessarily restricted to considering the status of their implementation of the Resolution's requirements relating to national measures, not their compliance with its provisions per se. For example, it cannot assess the effectiveness of a state's laws, such as by analyzing enforcement. Although the Resolution does not provide for the Committee or its experts to have recourse to other sources of information in assessing states' reports, even when these are available publicly, the experts have been authorized to collect and analyze this information from open sources, including the information states have unilaterally made available publicly or to related treaty organizations.[35]

UNSCR 1540 does not provide a compliance procedure or mechanism for dealing with suspected violations. Cooperative efforts to rectify deficiencies are more appropriate in ensuring national implementation, especially when non-compliance may realistically be due to lack of awareness or capacity. States that persist in failing to rectify deficiencies in their national laws, despite the availability of appropriate technical assistance, will come to the attention of the UN Security Council through the 1540 Committee reports to the UNSC.

Although a more detailed, if largely ineffective, compliance mechanism is available under Article 5 of the BWC, Resolution 1540 prescribes a more effective system for requiring and reviewing state declarations than is currently available through the BWC's confidence-building measure data exchange process. Regional workshops on UNSCR 1540 issues will be held under the new work program. However, the functions of the 1540 Committee of raising awareness, facilitating legislative technical cooperation, and assessing implementation could be further enhanced by enabling it to conduct in-country visits.[36] This is even more necessary with respect to the BW obligations in UNSCR 1540 given the absence of a multilateral verification organization that would otherwise conduct in-country activities relating to implementation assistance, monitoring, and verification—activities themselves serving to deter non-compliant activity.

The reporting requirement under UNSCR 1540 has led states to assess critically their existing measures, to identify shortcomings, and to share a wealth of information on their NBC weapons legislation. This has significantly increased transparency over the status of national implementation measures for the major nuclear weapons, chemical weapons, and biological weapons treaties as well as Resolution 1540. The assessments of states' implementation reports by the 1540 Committee and its expert group are provided only to the Security Council. Nonetheless, the public availability of states' reports facilitates compliance assessments by other governments and civil society.

UNSCR 1540's Impact on the BW Regime

The provisions related to biological weapons in UNSCR 1540 are important as they extend to those states that continue to remain outside the BWC obligations to prohibit and prevent the proliferation of BW. The adoption and enforcement of national measures required under the Resolution by those states—as well as those BWC states parties that have failed to implement their treaty obligations effectively to date—serves to strengthen the norm against BW. In addition, as non-state parties to the BWC adopt the BW measures required under Resolution 1540, it is to be hoped that the benefits of treaty membership may serve as an incentive to their subsequent accession to the Convention.

UNSCR 1540 is also fulfilling a functional compliance role: it requires BWC states parties to review their compliance with the Convention's BW non-proliferation obligations, using criteria for national implementation provided in the Resolution that are more detailed than those specified in the BWC, and to improve the deficiencies identified. The information provided in states' reports to the 1540 Committee, especially if further reports and additional, clarifying information are requested, is a significant advance in the provision of information for monitoring national implementation of BWC obligations, as reflected in more precise detail in Resolution 1540. The publication of states' reports on implementation has significantly increased transparency concerning their legislation on nuclear, chemical, and biological weapons disarmament and non-proliferation. In May 2006 the 1540 Committee made available an online "Legislative Database" of states' national measures to comply with UNSCR 1540—the first publicly available, online repository of nuclear, biological, and chemical weapons–related legislation—which further enhances transparency concerning states' compliance with the BW-related provisions of UNSCR 1540 as well as BWC state parties' compliance with Article 4. Compared with the present process for handling information provided under the BWC mechanisms, states' reports to the 1540 Committee are subjected to stringent review. However, assessment of states' reports is only one layer of a verification system. In order to be able to determine states' compliance with either UNSCR 1540 or the BWC, more sophisticated information collection and evaluation procedures will be necessary.

An ongoing process of awareness raising and capacity building activities will be necessary in order to overcome a lack of understanding of BW issues and to ensure that states are kept informed of scientific developments that may affect requirements for implementation. In this respect, the promotion of obligations under UNSCR 1540 will have an important role in raising awareness about these issues. The Resolution's specific reference to the international verification organizations for nuclear and chemical weapons, which carry out substantial technical assistance and training programs, is another painful reminder of this lacuna in the BW field. It is clear that activities under the 1540 Committee's new work plan, provided for under UNSCR 1673, cannot redress this gap in the BW field.

Conclusion

The international legal framework relating to the prohibition and prevention of BW is rooted in the international treaties and customary international law that comprehensively prohibit the development, proliferation, and use of biological weapons. UNSCR 1540 serves to strengthen this normative framework by requiring states to adopt specific national measures to prohibit non-state actors' acquisition of a BW capability and prohibiting states' support for that acquisition. Although UNSCR 1540 tackles the problem of BW proliferation through strengthened national implementation and compliance, adherence to the norm against BW remains unverified. UNSCR 1540 does not seek to address this lacuna in the BW regime, but it does add another supportive layer to the normative framework for the non-proliferation of biological weapons.

Notes

1. For a discussion of the persistent factors contributing to the biological weapons problem and the dynamic biological weapons threats, see Jez Littlewood, "Managing the Biological Weapons Problem: From the Individual to the International," Weapons of Mass Destruction Commission, Paper No. 14, Stockholm, Sweden, August 2004.

2. See the Protocol for the Prohibition of the Use in War of Asphyxiating, Poisonous or Other Gases, and of Bacteriological Methods of Warfare, signed June 17, 1925, and the Convention on the Prohibition of the Development, Production and Stockpiling of Bacteriological (Biological) and Toxin Weapons and on Their Destruction, signed April 10, 1972.

3. States parties are those that have both signed and ratified, or acceded to, the treaty.

4. The BWC signatory states comprise Burundi, the Central African Republic, Côte d'Ivoire, Egypt, Gabon, Guyana, Haiti, Liberia, Madagascar, Malawi, Myanmar, Nepal, Somalia, Syria, Tanzania, and the United Arab Emirates. In accordance with Article 18 of the Vienna Convention on the Law of Treaties, signatory states are obliged "not to defeat the object and purpose" of the treaty.

5. These states are Andorra, Angola, Cameroon, Chad, the Comoros, the Cook Islands, Djibouti, Eritrea, Guinea, Israel, Kazakhstan, Kiribati, the Marshall Islands, Mauritania, Micronesia (Federated States of), Mozambique, Namibia, Nauru, Niue, Samoa, Trinidad and Tobago, Tuvalu, and Zambia.

6. See other chapters in this volume on the binding nature of UNSCR 1540.

7. See operative paragraph 8(c). The Resolution also encourages (in preambular paragraph 13) states parties to disarmament treaties and agreements to implement fully their obligations under these arrangements.

8. References to agents in this chapter include all "microbial or other biological agents, or toxins whatever their origin or method of production."

9. The 1993 Chemical Weapons Convention's Annex of Chemicals serves primarily to facilitate verification; it is its general purpose criterion that bans all chemicals as weapons except where permitted by treaty. See chapter 5 by Ron Manley in this book.

10. States parties may require a proactive demonstration of peaceful intent through, for example, national licensing systems for facilities working with pathogenic material.

11. "The use by States Parties, in any way and under any circumstances, of microbial or other biological agents or toxins, that is not consistent with prophylactic, protective or other peaceful purposes, is effectively a violation of Article I of the

Convention." *Final Declaration*, Fourth Review Conference of the Parties to the Convention on the Prohibition of the Development, Production and Stockpiling of Bacteriological (Biological) and Toxin Weapons and on Their Destruction, November 25–December 6, 1996, BWC/CONF.IV/9/Part 2, Article 2, paragraph 3.

12. These are termed "inchoate" or incomplete, attempted offenses in domestic law.

13. *Final Declaration*, BWC/CONF.IV/9/Part 2, Article 3, paragraph 1.

14. States parties must destroy or convert to peaceful purposes all agents, toxins, weapons, equipment, and means of delivery described in Article 1 within nine months of the treaty's entry into force. BWC, Article 3.

15. This is effected through a national law, such as a state's ratification law for the treaty.

16. For example, the 1993 Chemical Weapons Convention requires states to adopt national legislation to criminalize chemical weapons activities and to establish a national authority to oversee treaty implementation (Article 7), and the 1997 Ottawa Landmine Convention obliges states to adopt national legislation establishing criminal offenses and penalties (Article 9).

17. For a detailed discussion on national implementation measures for the BWC see Treasa Dunworth, Robert J. Mathews, and Timothy L. H. McCormack, "National Implementation of the Biological Weapons Convention," *Journal of Conflict and Security Law* 2006 11(1), 93–118.

18. These concepts are elaborated in chapter 9 by Jeffrey Almond in this volume.

19. Report of the Meeting of Experts (Part 1), Meeting of the States Parties to the Convention on the Prohibition of the Development, Production and Stockpiling of Bacteriological (Biological) and Toxin Weapons and on Their Destruction, August 18–29, 2003, BWC/MX/4 (Part 1), September 18, 2003.

20. Toxins, which are a by-product of certain biological agents and a derivative of certain chemical agents, are also subject to chemical weapons control regimes such as the CWC.

21. For example, the United States prioritizes certain agents for increased physical and biosecurity by using a "select agent" list.

22. These are "Control list of dual-use biological equipment and related technology," "List of biological agents for export control," "List of animal pathogens for export control," and "List of plant pathogens for export control." See www.australia group.net.

23. *Biosecurity* refers to the implementation of measures to control access to pathogens and toxins and to prevent unauthorized access.

24. For more information on monitoring and verification techniques and processes, see UNIDIR and VERTIC, *Coming to Terms with Security: A Handbook on Monitoring and Verification* (Geneva: United Nations, 2003).

25. See Nicholas Sims, *The Evolution of Biological Disarmament*, SIPRI Chemical & Biological Warfare Studies, No. 19, Stockholm International Peace Research Institute, Stockholm, Sweden, 2001, pp. 31–52. The United States used the bilateral procedure to discuss the suspicious anthrax outbreak in Sverdlovsk in the Soviet Union in April

1979 immediately before the First Review Conference. As later confirmed through on-site investigation, including epidemiological analysis and a Soviet admission, the discussions concluded that the outbreak emanated from a biological weapons facility. Cuba invoked the multilateral procedure in June 1997 by requesting the Russian Federation to convene a consultative meeting to consider its claim that a U.S. overflight had released crop agent *thrips palmi* and that there was a causal connection between this overflight and the subsequent, and economically devastating, outbreak of this insect pest throughout the island. The Formal Consultative Meeting chair's final report noted that owing to the technical complexity of the subject and the length of time since the alleged incident, it had not been possible to reach a definitive conclusion over Cuba's concerns. Despite this, there was general agreement that Article 5 and the enhanced procedures had been fulfilled "in an impartial and transparent manner." Letter addressed to all states parties to the Biological and Toxin Weapons Convention from Ambassador Soutar (United Kingdom), Chair of the Formal Consultative Meeting, dated December 15, 1997.

26. The authority relates to the suspected use of both biological and chemical weapons due to its inception as a provisional measure to strengthen the 1925 Geneva Protocol and its incorporation before the adoption of the 1993 Chemical Weapons Convention.

27. The UN Secretary General has carried out missions to investigate the alleged use of chemical weapons in Afghanistan and Indochina ("yellow rain," 1981 and 1982), Iran and Iraq (1984–88), Azerbaijan (1992), and Mozambique (1992).

28. States parties are to provide information on, inter alia, research centers and laboratories, national biological defense research and development programs, outbreaks of infectious diseases, and declarations of past activities in offensive or defensive biological research and development programs.

29. For example, Australia, the United Kingdom, and the United States.

30. For detailed information on the verification protocol negotiations, see Jez Littlewood, *The Biological Weapons Convention: A Failed Revolution* (Aldershot: Ashgate, 2005).

31. The organizations participating in or observing these meetings include the Food and Agriculture Organization, the International Atomic Energy Agency, the International Committee of the Red Cross, the International Criminal Police Organization (Interpol), the Organisation for the Prohibition of Chemical Weapons, the UN 1373 Committee, the UN 1540 Committee, the United Nations Monitoring, Verification, and Inspection Commission, the World Customs Organization, the World Health Organization, and the World Organization for Animal Health.

32. See *The Information Repository of the Follow-Up Process of the Biological Weapons Convention*, CD-ROM compiled by the UN Department for Disarmament Affairs, 2003, and VERTIC, Dataset: Biological Weapons Convention: Collection of National Implementation Legislation, at www.vertic.org/datasets/bwlegislation.html.

33. VERTIC, *Time to Lay Down the Law: National Legislation to Enforce the BWC* (London: VERTIC, 2003).

34. UN Security Council Resolution 1673, April 27, 2006.

35. Examples of public sources are government websites with the state's laws, which are necessarily public information, and case law, which is increasingly available online from subscription databases.

36. The committee established pursuant to UNSCR 1373 (2001) commenced on-site visits for consultations with government officials, although this procedure was added by a subsequent resolution.

TED WHITESIDE

8

UNSCR 1540 and "Means of Delivery"

UNSC Resolution 1540, adopted on April 28, 2004, is a very important step in the international community's response to one of the challenges of the proliferation of weapons of mass destruction (WMD). The Resolution calls upon all states to "refrain from providing any form of support to non-State actors that attempt to develop, acquire, manufacture, possess, transport, transfer or use nuclear, chemical or biological weapons *and their means of delivery*" (operative paragraph (OP) 1, emphasis added). The last element, "means of delivery," is the focus of this chapter. The analysis explores in particular the broader framework of the potential relationship of Resolution 1540 to existing international non-proliferation instruments in the area of means of delivery in view of the development since the 1980s of a number of tools to attempt to stem the proliferation of missiles and related systems.

Background: UN Security Council Statement S/23500

It is useful to consider Resolution 1540 in the historical context of earlier UN Security Council (UNSC) work on WMD proliferation. UNSC Statement 23500 (S/23500) of January 31, 1992, is the first statement in which the Security Council affirmed that the proliferation of WMD constitutes a threat to international peace and security.[1] In the paragraphs dedicated to "Disarmament, Arms Control and Weapons of Mass Destruction," it expresses the commitment of the members of the Security Council to take concrete steps to

This chapter is written in the author's personal capacity. The views expressed here do not necessarily represent those of NATO, its member governments, or any other organization.

enhance the effectiveness of the UN in the areas of disarmament, arms control, and non-proliferation. It underlines the need for UN member states to fulfill their obligations in relation to arms control and disarmament in order to prevent the proliferation of all WMD, and it emphasizes the importance of the early ratification and implementation of international and regional arms control arrangements, such as the Strategic Arms Reduction Treaty (START), which concerned the launchers and means of delivery of American and Soviet strategic nuclear systems.

UNSC S/23500 also affirms the commitment of the members of the Security Council to preventing the spread of technology related to the research for or the production of such weapons and to taking appropriate actions to that end. In the area of nuclear proliferation, it emphasizes the importance of states' effective implementation of International Atomic Energy Agency (IAEA) safeguards, as well as the importance of effective export controls. In addition, it states specifically that members of the UNSC will take appropriate measures in case of any violations reported to them by the IAEA.

The political significance of the Statement is found in the importance it places on ratification of the main international arrangements or treaties on WMD proliferation. This has helped to underpin and strengthen the normative basis of these treaties and has put pressure on all UN member states to join them in the future. Its issuance was also at a time when negotiation of the Chemical Weapons Convention (CWC) was coming to fruition—it opened for signature in 1993.

It is important to highlight that UNSC S/23500 did not address expressly the problems of delivery systems or the potential risks from proliferation related to non-state actors. But over the past decade, intelligence assessments have increasingly focused on the critical area of means of delivery. Furthermore, concern has gone beyond only missiles; it now also includes simpler, less sophisticated means of delivering nuclear, biological, and chemical (NBC) weapons. By way of example, the United States National Intelligence Estimate 2002 weighed the probability of a cruise missile attack from a freighter offshore of the United States in relation to a ballistic missile attack.[2]

Of equal concern is the fact that many radio-controlled aircraft and other types of unmanned air platforms have a large operational range and could be used by non-state actors. This indicates that the potential means of delivery available to non-state actors are by their very nature more diverse and basic than those in the inventory of state actors. Non-state actors usually have fewer resources for acquiring sophisticated missile systems and less capability to do so. Moreover, as their aim is more to cause massive disruption than to inflict destruction, the means of delivery as well as the actual nuclear, radiological, chemical, or biological device used can be very rudimentary.

For this reason, the issue of means of delivery is addressed more specifically and alongside concerns about NBC weapons in UNSCR 1540. The Resolution is the first one that imposes an obligation on states to implement and enforce effective legislation and controls on NBC weapons, related materials, *and* their means of delivery. It requires states to establish domestic controls, so as to prevent non-state actors from proliferating NBC weapons *and* their means of delivery, by establishing appropriate controls over related materials. These controls constitute "appropriate effective measures to account for and to secure such items in production, use, storage or transport; . . . appropriate effective physical protection measures; . . . appropriate effective border controls and law enforcement efforts to detect, deter, prevent and combat . . . the illicit trafficking and brokering in such items; . . . appropriate effective national export and trans-shipment controls over such items" (OP 3).

Means of Delivery: The UNSCR 1540's Definition

Resolution 1540 defines (only in a footnote) means of delivery as "missiles, rockets and other unmanned systems capable of delivering nuclear, chemical, or biological weapons that are specially designed for such use." It is relevant to note that NBC weapons did not require an explicit definition in the Resolution. This is because the international community implicitly shares a common understanding of the nature of these materials through work on the 1968 Nuclear Non-Proliferation Treaty (NPT), the 1972 Biological and Toxin Weapons Convention (BTWC), and the 1993 Chemical Weapons Convention (CWC).

It is useful to analyze the definition by noting, first, that means of delivery are missiles, rockets, and other unmanned systems. The Resolution does not include manned systems such as crop-dusters or other small commercial or private aircraft—devices that some experts consider to be potential means of delivery by non-state actors, especially in attempts to spread chemical or biological agents—nor does it include much more rudimentary devices such as postal envelopes or delivery boxes.

In this regard, the definition provided by Resolution 1540 seems at first reading to be limited to militarily significant means of delivery, in particular those specially designed for delivering NBC weapons. But a closer reading provides a broader understanding of means of delivery: OP 3 stipulates that "all States shall take and enforce effective measures to establish domestic controls to prevent the proliferation of nuclear, chemical, or biological weapons *and their means of delivery*, including by establishing appropriate controls on related materials" in the ways outlined above (emphasis added). "Related materials" are defined in a further footnote as "materials, equipment and technology covered by relevant multilateral treaties and arrangements, or included on national control lists, which could be used for the design, development, production or use of nuclear, chemical and biological weapons and their means of delivery."

It should be noted that this definition relates to international regimes or arrangements or national control lists covering means of delivery, although there may be states that are not signatories of such regimes or that currently do not use national control lists along these lines. The definition does not cover specifically the problem of intangible exchange, such as technological know-how, other than through arrangements or national control lists that address that technology.

On the other hand, and this is one of the important merits of UNSCR 1540, the Resolution highlights the key role played by non-proliferation instruments related to means of delivery such as the Missile Technology Control Regime (MTCR). Thus it promotes a greater understanding and application of these instruments throughout the international community, thereby encouraging all states to adopt such practices. Although up to April 2004 the NPT, the CWC, and the BTWC had promoted greater understanding of export control principles such as those contained in the Australia Group and the Nuclear Suppliers Group, export control measures related to means of delivery had not been discussed widely within the international community as a whole. Resolution 1540 therefore carries with it the Security Council's implicit support for all non-proliferation instruments related to means of delivery.

The second part of UNSCR 1540's definition of means of delivery specifies that they must be capable of delivering NBC weapons. In the light of terrorist events such as the September 11, 2001, attacks on the World Trade Center and the Pentagon, non-state actors could try to spread unconventional substances and materials, non-weapons-grade chemical or biological agents, or radiological materials (so-called dirty bombs) in order to cause significant casualties as well as economic disruption and social strains.

The third part of the definition of means of delivery indicates that the systems must be "specially designed" for use in delivering NBC weapons. This is potentially a challenging area for implementation of the Resolution, and may require further clarification among experts regarding criteria related to dual-use devices. Unmanned aerial vehicles (UAVs) are an interesting example. UAVs, air-breathing vehicles that perform their entire mission within the earth's atmosphere, may fly computer-guided routes or routes controlled by a human operator. Many unmanned air vehicles are used for reconnaissance missions and thus are not clearly "specially designed" for delivering NBC agents or weapons. However, because of their relatively long range, ease of acquisition, and relatively low cost, UAVs are regarded to be potential means of delivery or vehicles for NBC agents, even if the initial design of the platform may not have been that of a weapon delivery vehicle.[3]

As outlined in this preliminary reading of the definition of means of delivery in Resolution 1540, there remains the potential challenge of subtle differences in its overall implementation. For this reason, it will be important that states take into consideration the relationship of the Resolution to other international instruments related to missiles and similar technologies.

Export Control Regimes

In the field of export controls on means of delivery, UNSCR 1540 requires all states to take and enforce effective measures for establishing domestic controls so as to prevent the proliferation of NBC weapons, their means of delivery, and related materials. In particular, OP 3(d) draws attention to states' obligations to establish, develop, review, and maintain appropriate effective national export and trans-shipment controls over such items. The Resolution's inclusion of export controls over means of delivery and related materials therefore draws attention to export control expectations that have been addressed previously by two well-known international regimes: the Wassenaar Arrangement (WA) and the Missile Technology Control Regime.[4]

The WA, adopted in 1996 upon the demise of CoCom (the Coordinating Committee for Multilateral Export Controls), is an international regime for export controls on conventional and dual-use goods. Its aim is to promote transparency, data exchange, and policy coordination in exports of conventional arms and dual-use goods and, after the adoption of counter-terrorism clauses, to strengthen its members' capabilities to combat the threat of terrorism. Its members exchange specific information on transfers of arms covered by the categories of the UN Register of Conventional Arms and also on transfers (or denials of transfer) of certain controlled dual-use items. In the field of means of delivery (category 7, Missiles or Missile Systems), members of WA exchange information on guided or unguided rockets, on ballistic or crude missiles capable of delivering a warhead or weapon of destruction over a range of at least twenty-five kilometers, and on technical material designed or modified specifically for launching such missiles or rockets. It also includes remotely piloted vehicles with the characteristics of missiles as defined above, called Man-Portable Air Defense Systems or MANPADS, but it does not include ground-to-air missiles.

The Missile Technology Control Regime, established in 1987, is an informal and voluntary association of thirty-four countries. Its aim is to control the proliferation of rockets (ballistic missiles, space launch vehicles, and sounding rockets) and unmanned air vehicle systems (cruise missiles, drones, UAVs, and remotely piloted vehicles) capable of delivering WMD and also the proliferation of their associated equipment and technology. Following the adoption in 2002 of counter-terrorism clauses in the MTCR work program, the Regime also works to strengthen the capabilities of its members to combat the threat of international terrorism. It seeks to coordinate national export licensing efforts aimed at preventing the proliferation of rockets and unmanned air vehicle systems. Its export controls focus on complete rocket and unmanned air vehicle systems capable of delivering a payload of at least 500 kilograms over a range of at least 300 kilometers and their major subsystems and related technology (category 1) and on propulsion and propellant components, launch and ground support equipment, various other missile-related components and related technology, as well as certain other missile systems (category 2). In contrast to the export of category 1 items, which is subject to a strong presumption of denial, the export of category 2 items is subject to a case-by-case review against specified non-proliferation factors.

UNSCR 1540 requires that, among other measures, states maintain effective national export and trans-shipment controls on such items. The Resolution also calls upon states to present national reports to the 1540 Committee of the Security Council. However, it does not establish and clarify the minimum acceptable standards for legislation and subsequent legislative implementation. In a similar manner, although the WA and the MTCR constitute the main multinational arrangements about export controls and the transfer of missile equipment, material, and related technologies, they do *not* establish mandatory criteria for export control provisions. They provide guidelines only. The information is exchanged on a voluntary basis: states freely choose to introduce export controls on conventional weapons as well as to introduce export licensing measures on rocket and other unmanned air vehicle delivery systems or related equipment, material, and technology. Indeed, each country implements these arrangements according to its national legislation, but Resolution 1540 means that this legislation is now mandatory.

Implementation of UNSCR 1540 will be carried out in the broader framework of evolving practices in both the WA and the MTCR. For example, the MTCR's Equipment and Technology Annex is modified from time to time in order to improve its clarity and especially to reflect changing technologies that could be used for rockets and unmanned aerial vehicles. Owing to increasingly sophisticated attempts at procurement by non-state actors, the MTCR's members also address the issues of the intangible transfer of technology; transit, trans-shipment, and brokering controls; and the need to curtail the activities of intermediaries and front companies. All these important issues relate to the general effective implementation of the Resolution.

The Development of Civilian and Space Launch Technology

The principal focus of UNSCR 1540 is the non-state actor, defined in yet another footnote as an "individual or entity, not acting under the lawful authority of any State in conducting activities which come within the scope of this resolution." Given this focus, it would appear logical that means of delivery are principally expected to be platforms of a relatively rudimentary nature rather than sophisticated ballistic or cruise missile technologies. Nonetheless, the risk of non-state actors obtaining more sophisticated technology continues to exist, and the implementation of the Resolution will therefore have to take into consideration a balanced approach to dual-use technologies in this context. As an illustration, some states may express concern that technologies such as space launch vehicle technology and legitimate drone technologies must not be hindered by too restrictive an implementation of the legislation to be set in place for compliance with Resolution 1540.

The risk of tension between rigid rules to deter the proliferation of means of delivery for NBC weapons and the development of civilian technology (space launch technology in particular) is already being considered, not only by the MTCR but also by the more recent International Code of Conduct against Ballistic Missile Proliferation (ICOC). The MTCR, although it limits the export of technology for space launch vehicles and major subsystems, including rocket stages, reentry vehicles, and rocket engines and also guidance systems (category 1), specifically points out in its Guidelines for Sensitive Missile-Relevant Transfers that it is not designed to impede national space programs or international cooperation in them. The MTCR focuses its attention only on delivery systems (means of delivery and related technology) that could be used for delivering WMD or conventional warheads. For this reason, the MTCR considers in its guidelines two criteria: (1) the capabilities and objectives of the missile and space programs of the recipient state and (2) the significance of the transfer in terms of the potential development of means of delivery for WMD.

The ICOC, better known as the Hague Code of Conduct against Ballistic Missile Proliferation (HCOC), was adopted by an international conference in

The Hague in November 2002. It is the result of an initiative taken by the MTCR plenary meeting in Helsinki in October 2000.[5] This code is meant to supplement the MTCR, but its membership is not restricted to MTCR countries. Some 120 states from all regions of the world have already subscribed to the Code, which can best be considered as a politically binding instrument of verification and confidence building.[6] The HCOC is not intended to hinder states from benefiting from the peaceful use of outer space. It aims simply to curb the proliferation of WMD-capable ballistic missiles and particularly to introduce transparency measures such as annual declarations and pre-launch notifications regarding ballistic missiles and space launch programs. For this reason, and given the similarities between the technology used in ballistic missiles and civilian rockets, the HCOC calls upon states to exercise restraint in the development, testing, use, and spread of ballistic missiles. And in the area of space launch vehicle programs, it requires states to provide an annual declaration on national space launch vehicle policies and land launch sites, to give annual information on the number and generic class of space launch vehicles launched during the preceding year, and to consider (on a voluntary basis) inviting international observers to their land launch sites. In addition, the HCOC requires states to exchange pre-launch notifications on their ballistic missile and space launch vehicle launches and test flights. (These should include the generic class of the space launch vehicle, the planned launch notification window, and also the launch area and the planned direction of the test flight.)

Much as Resolution 1540 must address the threat posed by the use of dual-use technologies for NBC weapons without affecting legitimate peaceful commercial uses and industrial research, so implementing 1540's provisions on means of delivery must take into consideration the legitimate development of delivery technologies that can be used for surveillance purposes or other kinds of commercial activity.

Final Observations

The unanimous adoption of UNSCR 1540 in April 2004 has been a key development in the international community's ongoing efforts to address the challenge of WMD proliferation, specifically as this problem relates to non-state actors. The Resolution underlined the need for all member states to resolve peacefully any problems threatening or disrupting the maintenance of regional and global security and affirmed support for multilateral non-proliferation treaties. In view of this, it is an important step in responding to the grave concern that non-state actors might acquire, develop, traffic in, or use nuclear, chemical, and biological weapons and their means of delivery.

The definition of means of delivery as stipulated in UNSCR 1540 can be understood best in the broad context of existing non-proliferation arrangements. Because international non-proliferation arrangements dealing with means of delivery are not yet universal and because export control arrangements are not universal either, it will be important to proceed on the basis of a clear and common understanding within the international community as to how the provisions on means of delivery are to be implemented in this Resolution, which is universal. The 1540 Committee, with its considerable expertise, has been examining country reports and identifying any gaps in understanding or actual implementation. It is expected that the 1540 Committee will be in a position to address the means of delivery challenge and promote the robust role that the Resolution will play in stopping the potential proliferation of delivery technologies and capabilities.

Notes

1. Statement of President, UN Security Council meeting at the level of Heads of State and Government, (S/23000), January 31, 1992, at http://disarmament.un.org:8080/advisoryboard/42nddocs.html.

2. United States National Intelligence Estimate: Iraq's Continuing Programs for Weapons of Mass Destruction (Washington, D.C.: The White House, October 2002).

3. "Nonproliferation: Assessing Cruise Missile/UAV Technology Export Controls," Hearing, Subcommittee on National Security, Emerging Threats and International Relations, Committee on Government Reform, U.S. House of Representatives, March 9, 2004.

4. For further information on the Wassenaar Arrangement, see www.wassenaar.org; and for more information on the MTCR, see www.mtcr.info.

5. Press Release, Plenary Meeting of the Missile Technology Control Regime, Helsinki, Finland, October 10–13, 2000, at www.mtcr.info/english/press/helinski.html.

6. Its text is found at Ministry of Foreign Affairs, The Netherlands, at www.minbuza.nl/default.asp?CMS_ITEM=MBZ460871. See also "Fact Sheet," Bureau of Nonproliferation, January 6, 2004, at www.state.gov/t/np/rls/fs/27799.htm.

PART III

New Controls, Legislation, and Enforcement

9

JEFFREY ALMOND

Industry Codes of Conduct

New legislation to comply with United Nations Security Council Resolution 1540 will affect the pharmaceutical and the biotechnology industries, most notably in relation to their work on developing drugs and vaccines against infectious diseases. Access to dangerous microorganisms and to expertise in genetic manipulation is an obvious area of concern for security authorities intent on limiting the spread of potentially dual-use technology. However, safety practices are already in place throughout much of these industries (referred to below as the industry) and academia. Developed in response to biosafety concerns, to the need for quality standards for drug and vaccine products, and to general security concerns, they already constitute good governance, and this can be built upon. However, it is important that new legislation does not overly restrict research or stifle innovation in this commercially important area. Consultation with scientists in the industry is vital to ensuring the continued health of the biotechnology and the pharmaceuticals sectors, and, apart from other measures, can contribute to the process of combating the biological weapons threat.

This chapter seeks to provide insights into how industry and academia can assist states with their obligations under UNSCR 1540. It highlights the challenges arising from advances in the biotechnology and the pharmaceutical industries and academia, the biosafety and biosecurity issues arising from the handling and transportation of potentially dangerous biotechnologies,

The views expressed here are those of the author in his personal capacity; they do not necessarily represent the consensus views of the pharmaceutical and the biotechnology industries or of particular companies.

and the codes of conduct and culture of responsibility that already exist among scientists aimed at maximizing the benefits of their research while minimizing its adverse effects, misuse, or criminal use. States need to understand these issues so that they can develop, implement, and enforce appropriate legislation and controls in compliance with UNSCR 1540 without unnecessarily restricting vital research and development. The formulation of new legislation for stemming the proliferation of biological technology and materials to commercial actors neither bona fide nor authorized could also raise awareness of the ways in which current biosafety and biosecurity procedures might contribute to averting or defending against a bioterrorist attack, however unlikely. The terms *biosafety* and *biosecurity* overlap significantly and may in some forums be used interchangeably. For the purposes of this discussion, *biosafety* refers to the safe handling of biological materials (especially microorganisms) through the use of processes and practices that protect individuals and the environment from accidental infection, release from the laboratory, or both. *Biosecurity* refers to the procedures for authorizing and restricting access to biological materials, their secure containment, and the monitoring of any work carried out on them.

The Spread of Technology and Knowledge: Its Challenges

Three examples illustrate the significance of recent scientific and technological advances and their double-edged implications. The first is a scientific publication in 2001 that caused a great deal of concern among security authorities.[1] The experiments reported indicate that the insertion of an immune system regulator, interleukin-4, into the mousepox virus can dramatically increase its virulence in certain breeds of mice. Even more disturbing was the observation that interleukin-4 suppressed immune memory responses, thereby allowing the virus to overcome preexisting immunity. These results implied that similar manipulations of the closely related human smallpox virus could result in a highly virulent strain that might overcome the immunity provided by vaccination. Moreover, if the method were applicable to a range of pathogens (which today, fortunately, it is not), the stockpiling of antivirus vaccines would be rendered useless. Although the conduct and publishing of these experiments may be criticized, research in this general area is justified for many by the need to improve knowledge of the pathogenesis of viruses generally and of the pox viruses in particular. Several strains of the pox virus group are used or are being developed as vectors of foreign antigens in vaccine design, and it is vital that we fully understand what makes these viruses pathogenic. For example, several genetically engineered fowlpox and canarypox viruses are licensed for use as veterinary vaccines, and trials using engineered canary pox and cowpox as human vaccines against AIDS and malaria are well advanced. Nevertheless, the publishing of these experiments has led to calls for greater government oversight of the scientific community in terms of what experiments should be conducted and what findings should responsibly be published.

The second example is the readily available know-how in the field of influenza virology. The potential severity of influenza outbreaks is well recognized: the Spanish influenza of 1918–19 is estimated to have killed over forty million people worldwide. Fears of a pandemic of similar or even greater severity have been heightened recently by the (so far small) outbreaks of H5 avian influenza in humans in East Asia. Although the H5 influenza strains isolated to date seem to be unable to spread efficiently from human to human, there are fears that further evolutionary change could lead to human-adapted viruses that could be transmitted rapidly and be as pathogenic for humans as some of these strains are for bird populations. H5 and H7 influenza outbreaks in the poultry industry in the past have had a devastating impact, with mortality rates of more than 90 percent and very rapid and easy transmission among birds. But not all avian influenza viruses are pathogenic, and we are beginning to understand the molecular determinants that distinguish those of high virulence and those of low virulence. Studies with this purpose are important in order for the scientific community to better assess the threat of pandemic influenza and to influence vaccine design. At the same time, science also provides information that could be misused. For example, it would be technically possible today, using a technique called reverse genetics, to build into a human influenza strain some of the molecular structures found in those avian strains that have a mortality rate greater than ninety percent. This information is published in high-profile internationally available journals, and the techniques are relatively standard for those skilled in molecular biology and virology. It is difficult to predict precisely the effect of such manipulations on a human strain of influenza, but it is clear that the results could be extremely threatening.

The third example of a powerful new technology that could have double-edged applications is gene shuffling, also known as molecular breeding. This technology can condense thousands and even millions of years of evolution into a test tube experiment that may take just a few hours, resulting in the creation of myriad variants of the original genes, some of which will have novel properties. Related but divergent genes are mixed together with an appropriate DNA polymerizing enzyme and billions of copies are made under conditions that favor recombination or shuffling between the parent genes. The process is not limited to exchanges between two starting genes; multiple parents (of the same or different sex) can be used, resulting in a veritable sexual orgy in the test tube. Examples of the beneficial use of this technology are appearing in the literature, and the novel genes created and their gene products offer significant advances in various aspects of agriculture and medicine. As discussed above, however, this technology in the wrong hands could be used to create novel toxins or viruses that might be resistant to antitoxins and vaccine-induced immunity.

In spite of the worries raised by developments such as the above examples, continued progress across the whole of molecular biology and specifically in the field of microbial pathogenesis is essential if science is to deliver solutions to the more difficult infectious diseases. Today our inability to effectively combat HIV, malaria, and tuberculosis means that approximately six million people die annually according to World Health Organization estimates, and many more are debilitated who could otherwise have healthy and productive lives. Yet we must recognize that increasing knowledge of microbial pathogenesis, together with the development of techniques that allow easy genetic manipulation of organisms, will inform and enable those of malevolent intent.

Pathogens and Risk

Microbes that cause diseases in humans or animals have been handled since the time of Pasteur, and the risks they pose to scientific staff and the environment are well known. Various treaties, laws, regulations, and other legal and political instruments currently govern activities involving dangerous microbes. These have been put in place mainly to ensure localized containment of virulent pathogens, the safety of research personnel, the treatment of research animals, and the preparation of distributed products such as drugs and vaccines. Containment regulations may naturally differ between countries according to the risks the organisms pose in different geographical environments. Although international alignment is perhaps incomplete, consensus views are promulgated and governments are advised via learned societies such as the American Society for Microbiology, the Society for General Microbiology, the European Federation of Microbiological Societies, and the International Committee of Scientific Unions.

In the early 2000s, a discussion paper on possible mechanisms of government oversight of biotechnology research attempted to define dangerous microbial pathogens on the basis of a pyramid scheme that represents three criteria: pathogenicity, transmissibility, and infectivity.[2] At the tip of the pyramid are organisms that are most dangerous to human health, for example the viruses causing smallpox, Lassa fever, Ebola, and Marburg, and the bacteria causing tularaemia (*Francisella tularensis*), Q fever (*Coxiella burnetii*), and bubonic and pneumonic plague (*Yersinia pestis*). Lesser pathogens, such as those causing measles, mumps, and polio, are placed lower in the pyramid scheme, with common commensals and nonpathogens such as soil bacteria at the bottom. Current practices and methods of operation in North America, the continent of Europe, and the United Kingdom do not yet use the pyramid scheme; but in these places risk assessments are part of standard operating procedures, and they take into account factors such as disease-causing potential, transmissibility, potential for survival in the environment, and potential to transmit genetic material to other life forms.

In addition to the classification of natural organisms, it is necessary to consider genetically engineered strains. Genetic manipulation is controlled in most countries by national legislation, guidelines, and codes of conduct. The European Union has enacted a variety of legislative proposals on the handling and use of genetically modified organisms (GMOs). For example, Council Directive 90/219/EEC, on the contained use of GMOs, requires prior notification and approval of research activities in which a facility is using pathogenic microorganisms for the first time. Council Directive 90/220/EEC contains similar notification and approval requirements for the deliberate release of GMOs into the environment for research and development purposes. EU directives cover research not only on human pathogens but also on plant and animal pathogens. Member states reinforce the EU directives. In France, for example, it is mandatory to submit proposals for GMO research to the Commission de Génie Génétique. The review process is by a group of independent experts that assesses the objectives of the genetic manipulation and decides whether permission should be granted. It also advises on the appropriate level of containment for the work. In the United Kingdom the Heath and Safety Executive's Genetic Manipulation Advisory Committee performs a similar function.

Various guidelines and regulations also exist in the United States, to ensure that activities involving pathogens do not pose environmental or public health problems. The most important is the National Institutes of Health's (NIH) Guidelines for Research Involving Recombinant DNA Molecules, which was issued by the NIH's Recombinant DNA Advisory Committee in 1976 in order to provide guidance to researchers on constructing and handling recombinant DNA molecules and the organisms and viruses containing those molecules. Two categories of laboratory research involving recombinant DNA technology continue to be closely scrutinized, and cannot be initiated without the submission of relevant information to the NIH's Office of Biotechnology

Activities. These are the "deliberate transfer of a drug resistance trait to micro-organisms that are not known to acquire the trait naturally if such acquisition could compromise the use of the drug to control disease agents in humans, veterinary medicine, or agriculture" and "the cloning of toxin molecules with LD50 of less than 100 nanograms per kilogram body weight." These guidelines apply to research conducted at institutes in America and those abroad that receive NIH funding. It is likely that many private companies and foreign researchers follow the guidelines voluntarily.

Biosafety and Biosecurity Issues

This governance relating to GMOs has been developed with the strong con-tribution and, importantly, the agreement of scientists in the countries where it has been implemented, notably in the USA, the UK, and other European countries. Between the famous Asilomar conference in 1973 and the issuance of the NIH's Guidelines three years later, the scientific community displayed its collective responsibility and caution by imposing a moratorium on exper-iments in biotechnology until the time when the risks could be reasonably assessed and facilities could be put in place to allow step-by-step progression.

There is also a pharmaceuticals and biotechnology knowledge base about the scale-up of microbial cultures; this is essential for the industry to conduct its business. The safety and security requirements for handling infectious microorganisms at the 10,000-liter scale and beyond rely on a set of practices and operating procedures different from those relevant to the research labo-ratory environment. In addition, there is the sound management of the stocks, banks of cells, and master and working seeds that are required for the biotech-nology business to succeed. These measures are an obvious necessity for the industry's commercial interests and, more importantly, for the health and safety of all employees who handle microorganisms.

It should be recognized too that government legislation is not the only driver of biosafety and biosecurity. From an industrial perspective, there is a need for governance and security measures that restrict access to microbial strains that may have been painstakingly and expensively developed for com-mercial exploitation. As with many other branches of industry, it is in biotech-nology companies' interests that know-how and materials developed within a company do not become widely disseminated and undermine competitive advantage.

Nevertheless, it is necessary in most developed countries to disclose to the relevant government authorities the purpose, the justification, and the detailed protocols for research on biological agents. Details include the origins of the DNA sequences of the agents; the predicted properties of any altered strain; their disposal, retention, or transfer; the purpose for which the recipients require them; and the packaging and tracking that may be required if the organisms are transported. Physical facilities for biological containment and storage, as well as cleanliness, production capacity, and emergency standard operating procedures are among the issues of concern to regulatory authorities. Others include the training of personnel, their level of expertise, and their immune status. Ongoing research is followed up and any changes in protocol are reported on, as are the creation of any novel organisms and their properties, new safety concerns, changes in personnel, safety violations, and transfers. As academia and the industry usually seek to publish their work, departures from accepted protocols will become evident. Also, when a biotechnology company wishes to license a product, it is subject to inspections by, for example, the European Medicine Agency or the U.S. Food and Drug Administration; and biotechnology companies have to comply with their requirements for biosecurity and biosafety. This constitutes an independent review of processes and practices in the biosafety arena.

Strengths and Weaknesses of Current Practice

Today generic security procedures include electronically controlled access to the site and to the building where the work is carried out and strict control over storage facilities. Modern security control even in small companies and academic laboratories is increasingly computer-based, and may incorporate specific personalized data about staff competency, training, level of authority, and, where relevant, immunological status and vaccination history. Typically, authority to work on a project is given only for a defined period of time. Security schemes require formal identification checks and the use of escorts at all times for non-employees visiting sites. Yet more layers of security are now being used: for example, in storage areas access to the relevant refrigerators may be allowed only to those with properly authorized and computer-controlled keys. There are also semi-independent quality-assurance practices that ensure all procedures are correctly followed and recorded. Every procedure is evaluated, and all relevant details of working conditions and activities involving the handling of microorganisms are appropriately presented to local biosecurity and biosafety committees.

However, all safety and security procedures have limitations. For example, it would currently be difficult to prevent motivated laboratory staff from stealing aliquots of microbes from individual vials to which they have professional access. Moreover, it is even possible in some cases (limited so far to certain families of viruses) to create a virus de novo using chemical synthesis, as has been described recently for polio.[3] A further possible point of unease is that as of now there is no vetting process in routine practice in the industry that assesses an individual's suitability to learn biotechnological techniques. Likewise, there is no process for monitoring individuals when they leave the biotechnology field. Experience, expertise, and specializations cannot simply be unlearned, and there is nothing to prevent an experienced individual from leaving the industry or academia and moving to a country or situation where work of malevolent intent can be undertaken. Nevertheless, concern for biosafety and the security of materials is widespread in the industry. Security lapses would tarnish its image, and for this reason there are built-in biosecurity and biomanagement measures.

Even without the legislation that is proposed under UNSCR 1540, for example, that all states take and enforce effective controls such as to account for, secure, and physically protect related materials and their export (operative paragraphs 3(a)–(d)), it is clear from what has been presented above that there are extensive security and safety procedures in place in most laboratories and production facilities in the pharmaceutical and the biotechnology sectors in the developed world. Implementation of UNSCR 1540 should start by recognizing the good governance that already exists and strengthening this where necessary in full consultation with current players. New legislation should avoid excessive bureaucracy and must not stifle innovation and activity in this important sector. Valid judgments about the balance between benefit and danger in this type of research can be made only in the specific context by people capable of understanding both the scientific issues in question and the social consequences.

The Movement of Pathogens and Expertise

The international nature of scientific investigation and the multinational basis of the pharmaceuticals and the biotechnology industries mean that dangerous pathogens need to be transported across international boundaries. Diagnosis, epidemiology, and sharing GMO seeds and vaccine seeds are examples of when rapid transportation is often a public health requirement, an industrial necessity, or both. In many countries, regulations in place demand import and export permits for certain microbes and GMOs together with clear identification, labeling, and appropriate physical containment of biological materials so as to avoid spillage or leaking during transportation. The World Health Organization provides international guidelines, as does the International Air Transport Association, and bodies such as the U.S. Department of Agriculture provide national rules. Although it may be possible in some cases to transport pathogens by separating them into two harmless pieces of genetic material and then reassembling them at the point of destination, this is the exception rather than the rule. Any future legislation in this area that imposes tighter restrictions must recognize the need to enable rapid international reaction to health situations, the sensitive and fragile nature of most biological samples, and the legitimate requirements of international trade in the biotechnology sector.

Legislating for UNSCR 1540

Scientists fully recognize the anxieties of government security agencies and acknowledge the need to review and, where necessary, to strengthen legislation on both biosecurity and biosafety, including the incorporation of powers of oversight of experimentation in certain areas. There is clearly a need to prevent those of malevolent intent from obtaining potentially dangerous biological technology and materials. But although legislative compliance with Resolution 1540 will reduce the ability of non-state actors to act unlawfully, it will not remove it entirely.

In seeking to find the right balance of legislation to meet the objectives of the Resolution while maintaining an environment that preserves academic freedom and enables biotechnology and pharmaceutical research, governments must consult with and build around the needs of industry. It is important that legislation does not become over-prescriptive in seeking to tightly control the movement and activity of individuals operating in the field. Although governments have an expected responsibility to maintain a healthy research base and to safeguard competencies in this area, nature and evolution can be more dangerous than bioterrorism in throwing up threats of infectious disease. New rules should be in keeping with the assumption that most players are legitimate scientists who want to comply with the objectives and who believe that their research does not pose unnecessary risks. Maintaining these balances is one of the challenges for states to implement the resolution's operative paragraph 8(d), "to develop appropriate ways to work with and inform industry and the public regarding their obligations under such laws."

Scientists will be more forthcoming with information about their activities if they are not worried about confusing regulations, unattainable standards, false accusations, or criminal penalties for unintentional errors. Researchers recognize the need to root out malevolent and irresponsible players, but it is important that the recent high-profile prosecutions of academic scientists are not interpreted as government heavy-handedness and punishment for mistakes. The winning of hearts and minds approach can be used to gain cooperation if properly handled.

Scientists in both academia and biotechnology will be supportive if communication is clear and the objectives are logical and recognized as necessary. To date, the biotechnology industry has considered as reasonable calls for international and national legislation that introduces internal controls upon it. Indeed, in their obligations under Resolution 1540's operative paragraph 8(d), states are called upon to "develop appropriate ways to work with and inform industry and the public regarding their obligations under such laws" (as are to be made in conformance with UNSCR 1540).

Conclusion

Although the days of the great amateur are probably gone, scientists such as Louis Pasteur and Edward Jenner could not have made their contributions to bacteriology and vaccinology if they had operated in an environment of government legislation that sought to restrict experimentation and deny access to materials. Innovation in a rapidly changing industry depends upon the continuation of freedom in the pursuit of knowledge. Successful implementation of Resolution 1540 will therefore require the goodwill and cooperation of the scientific community, and its interests must be considered carefully.

It is also important to recognize that biotechnology for beneficial ends must be undertaken in the developing world as well as the developed world because many applications have particular relevance in the former. For example (as mentioned above), one of the more possible routes to the development of an AIDS vaccine relies on the engineering of viruses closely related to that causing smallpox. To systematically deny access to this technology to countries that are severely afflicted by the AIDS epidemic would hardly be ethical. Similar arguments can be made in relation to the potential benefits of biotechnology in agriculture. This could pose risks, but the universal application of Resolution 1540 could provide the impetus for the worldwide spread of the biosafety and biosecurity culture and norms of behavior that exist in developed countries. Increased interaction among scientists, weapons experts, policy analysts, and decisionmakers can facilitate creating more effective legislation at the national level for all states so that they can implement and enforce UNSCR 1540 more effectively.

Notes

1. R. J. Jackson, A. J. Ramsay, C. D. Christensen, S. Beaton, D. F. Hall, and I. A. Ramshaw, "Expression of Mouse Interleukin-4 by a Recombinant Ectromelia Virus

Suppresses Cytolytic Lymphocyte Responses and Overcomes Genetic Resistance to Mousepox," *Journal of Virology*, Vol. 75, 2001, pp. 1205–210.

2. John Steinbruner, Elisa D. Harris, Nancy Gallagher, and Stacy Okutani, *Controlling Dangerous Pathogens: A Prototype Protective Oversight System*, Center for International and Security Studies at Maryland (CISSM), University of Maryland, December 2005, at www.isn.ethz.ch/pubs/ph/details.cfm?id=15118.

3. Jeronimo Cello and others, "Chemical Synthesis of Poliovirus cDNA: Generation of Infectious Virus in the Absence of Natural Template," *Sciencexpress*, July 11, 2002, available at www.sciencemag.org/cgi/content/abstract/1072266v1.

WILL ROBINSON

10

New Border and Customs Controls for Implementing UNSCR 1540

United Nations Security Council Resolution (UNSCR) 1540 provides customs authorities with an important mandate and opportunity to contribute to the non-proliferation of weapons of mass destruction (WMD). Building upon UNSCR 1373 (2001), which requires all UN member states to take action against the harboring of terrorists, their movement using false travel documents, and the financing of terrorism, Resolution 1540 recognizes the need for customs expertise in detecting and preventing particularly the illegal trafficking of WMD, related materials, and delivery systems. It has drawn attention to and codified illicit trafficking as a new form of proliferation.

A New Security Relationship with Customs Controls

Resolution 1540 has the effect of placing customs at the center of the international debate on how best to deal with non-proliferation of nuclear, chemical, and biological weapons and materials. This chapter examines how governments can empower and support their customs administrations in order to comply with the Resolution and develop progressive regimes for detecting potential incidents of WMD trafficking at the border. As this will be a long process, a phased implementation program is required. Customs as an institution is evolving to meet today's diverse challenges, but the 169 member countries of the World Customs Organization (WCO) are at different stages of development. Customs services in developed economies have largely moved away from revenue collection as their main activity to dealing with issues related to the protection of society; in the developing world, the key role remains to collect revenue at the border. How well customs administrations and their governments respond to the challenges of Resolution 1540 by focusing more on security remains to be seen.

As a consequence, capacity building on a broad scale is required in order to improve the organization, laws, procedures, and techniques of customs administrations and international cooperative efforts between national customs authorities. Because an export from one country leads to an import to another, it is important to build an international cooperation system with universal standards against proliferation. This is necessary to disrupt the opportunities for traffickers and terrorists as they attempt to move nuclear, chemical, and biological weapons, precursor elements, and delivery systems across borders.

As part of this process, a radical new approach is required to bolster the more traditional customs role and methods. Governments must recognize the potential for customs administrations to play an important role in detecting and preventing the movement of WMD and related materials at the border; and their contribution should be integrated into a general government non-proliferation effort so that customs administrations fulfill an essential role in that policy as a whole.

Of equal importance is a new approach to risk assessment: this requires the identification of WMD or associated materials at the earliest possible point in the supply chain. It implies having access, where practicable, to better information about consignments before shipment and using modern risk management and intelligence techniques. This approach should be coupled with strategies against corruption so that the efforts of customs officials can retain a high level of consistency and reliability. Weaknesses in integrity are ruthlessly exploited by transnational organized traffickers.

Assistance in improving effectiveness and efficiency can be provided by the World Customs Organization, founded as the Customs Cooperation Council in 1952, an intergovernmental body that is a center of customs expertise and now has 169 member countries in six regions. By developing international trade instruments and control and enforcement methodologies, the WCO aims to make tools available to its member customs administrations to improve their effectiveness and efficiency in dealing with the new challenges for controls that achieve a balance between security and the facilitation of trade.

Customs Control Requirements

Resolution 1540, acting under Chapter VII of the UN Charter, requires all member states to take a range of steps aimed at preventing the proliferation, especially by non-state actors, of nuclear, chemical, and biological weapons, their delivery systems, and related materials. It is binding on all member states. The Resolution imposes three major obligations:

—To refrain from providing any support to non-state actors who are attempting to manufacture, come to possess, transport, or use WMD and their means of delivery;

—To prohibit in their domestic law any such activities by non-state actors, particularly for terrorist purposes, and to prohibit any assistance or financing of such activities; and

—To adopt domestic measures to prevent the proliferation of WMD, their means of delivery, and related materials, including by accounting for and physically protecting such items, establishing and maintaining effective border controls and law enforcement measures, and reviewing and maintaining national export and trans-shipment controls (with appropriate criminal or civil penalties).

The third obligation prescribes special tasks with regard to border security measures and therefore is addressed to customs administrations. These bodies have important powers that exist nowhere else in government: they have the authority to inspect cargo and goods shipped into, out of, and through a country, the authority to refuse entry or exit, and the authority to expedite entry. Customs administrations require information about goods being imported, and will in future increasingly require information to be provided in advance of shipment and by electronic means. Given their unique authorities and expertise, customs can and should play a central role in securing global trade.

In this context Resolution 1540 requires that all states shall "develop and maintain appropriate effective border controls and law enforcement efforts to detect, deter, prevent and combat, including through international cooperation when necessary, the illicit trafficking and brokering in such items in accordance with their national legal authorities and legislation and consistent with international law" (operative paragraph 3(c)) and

> establish, develop, review and maintain appropriate effective national export and trans-shipment controls over such items, including appropriate laws and regulations to control export, transit, trans-shipment and re-export and controls on providing funds and services related to such export and trans-shipment such as financing, and transporting that would contribute to proliferation, as well as establishing end-user controls; and establishing and enforcing appropriate criminal or civil penalties for violations of such export control laws and regulations (operative paragraph 3(d)).

Tasks for customs not only embrace control of the export of sensitive goods but also require a broader approach to the problem. As a result, customs administrations, assisted by the WCO, are becoming involved in security issues to a greater extent. Operative paragraph 7 of Resolution 1540 stipulates that "some States may require assistance in implementing the provisions of this resolution within their territories and invites States in a position to do so to offer assistance as appropriate in response to specific requests to the States lacking the legal and regulatory infrastructure, implementation experience and/or resources for fulfilling the above provisions."

In the future, customs administrations will need to address these specific objectives. As a consequence, they will also be required to respond to national security concerns by instituting controls aimed at combating international terrorism and WMD proliferation. Some customs have already responded to this security challenge, but others are still developing their response. To play an effective role, customs must develop an understanding of how international trade is currently operating, so that controls can be exerted at different stages of the trade supply chain. Logically, controls can commence during the manufacturing and export processes. Exports from a country must take into account the new ways in which the modern global economy is developing and being organized. For example, traditional controls are being enhanced by tracking the movement of sensitive and high-tech strategic goods at each stage of the supply chain and, where possible, by identifying high-risk goods before they reach the point of export.

The traditional controls at the stage of import need to be strengthened as well, to limit opportunities for WMD, precursors, materials, people, and funds to reach their intended destination. This can be achieved by employing new methods of risk management that provide better indications concerning the risk associated with potential suspect consignments. As a direct consequence, these methods would also expedite customs procedures, helping them to balance between the need to facilitate legitimate trade and the need to deal with new security issues.

Other concerns of customs control are goods in transit and trans-shipment movements. Risks in supply chain security are complicated by arrangements for transit, whereby goods are allowed to pass from one country to another under a form of customs control, and trans-shipment, whereby goods pass from one means of transport to another, usually involving repacking, in an intermediary country.

Governments and their customs administrations should be concerned too about the potential for the misuse of free trade zones when trying to establish an unbroken system of control. Free trade zones are used by many governments to promote trade in which a minimum level of regulation is demanded of companies approved to operate within these zones. As a result, companies enjoy a wide range of benefits, including exemptions from duty and taxes, simplified administrative procedures, and duty-free imports of raw materials, machinery parts, and equipment. However, the operation of free trade zones can imply a reduction in customs controls, compounded by a lack of clarity regarding the regulations covering the control of these zones.[1]

Assessing Risk before Shipment: A Fundamental Shift in Thinking

A fundamental shift in thinking is needed in order to fulfill the new tasks set for customs administrations and to achieve effective control of the international trade supply chain. Customs operating in the twenty-first century must develop effective methods of strategic planning and should deploy resources against the relative levels of risk expected to be known and dealt with in their work. The international customs community will need to combine existing skills that facilitate legitimate trade with a radical new role and approach in ensuring the security of international trade.

For the first time, customs will need to look beyond the border, to the farthest point of origin in the international trade supply chain, in order to secure all parts of that chain. Thus customs must shift from exercising exclusive control of the movement of goods as they cross the border to also supplementing this with audit-based controls within its risk management regimes. "Conducting compliance-measurement exercises on traders through post clearance audit is an appropriate method to verify trade transactions reflected in the books and records of international traders."[2]

Customs administrations need to gain the support of all the key players and stakeholders involved in international trade and the key international bodies in order for them to execute this comprehensive level of advanced controls.[3] For this reason, a process of gradual change has to be introduced and managed in customs administrations. Historically, the various types of border control have been performed by different agencies, each responsible for different control regimes, including goods, people, health, security, and safety, for every border crossing movement. This disjointed approach is now giving way to organizations based upon integrated border management so as to prevent duplication of effort and to optimize the effectiveness that can flow from having a single, integrated border control agency.[4]

Another requirement of customs administrations is to keep track of developments in modern trade and to adjust their regimes in order to control and enforce regulations effectively and efficiently and to facilitate economic growth. The current trend for just-in-time business transactions places increased pressure on all players in the supply chain. Customs are required to facilitate these modern trading methods, but this must be balanced against the need for security. Over time, export controls have tended to become more simplified and relaxed while new developments in organized crime and potential links with terrorism suggest the necessity for a review and adjustment of these relaxed controls and the development of new strategies to meet national economic and security requirements within the same integrated border control regimes.

Managing Implementation: New Technical Approaches

Customs administrations need to develop a new technical approach to their controls if they are to meet the new range of challenges. This will require working in advance of shipment and applying controls based on advance electronic information and prescreening before vessels and containers arrive at their destination. The facilitation of both trade and security can be improved as customs administrations combine their efforts, use an agreed set of data elements, and focus on the mutual exchange of information. Such standardization is necessary for trade purposes, but it will also assist security because advance information allows customs administrations to develop a new risk management approach and to identify high-risk consignments at an early stage. At the same time it provides tangible benefits for economic operators, as information can be provided in a single transmission and delays at the border can be reduced.

Security seals are an integral part of the chain of custody and represent a major technical security measure that is constantly being updated. The proper grade and application of a security seal, as well as a detailed sequential analysis of a seal integrity program based on the use of high-security seals conforming to ISO/PAS 177712, is contained in the guidelines to chapter 6 of the general annex of the revised Kyoto Convention (see below) and as appendix III to annex 2 of the Framework of Standards to Secure and Facilitate Global Trade (see below). By using advance electronic information and intelligence methodologies linked with better physical security provided by a seal integrity program, customs has the opportunity to exert better controls and to improve detection of illegal trafficking in arms, hazardous materials, and the materials needed to manufacture WMD. In terms of legal trade the measures have the effect of contributing to the predictable and effective clearance of goods.

WCO Instruments

The World Customs Organization has created a wide range of international instruments and tools that provide a pathway for governments and their customs administrations to follow in instituting modern and effective border controls.

The revised Kyoto Convention is a key international instrument. It describes how a customs administration should establish its organization, management, and procedures in order to create effective border controls.[5] The convention contains detailed annexes, which, when implemented and combined with the provisions contained in the WCO's Arusha Declaration on integrity (an anticorruption instrument),[6] provide a solid foundation for the supporting role that customs play in the area of antiterrorism.

In the area of mutual administrative assistance, the WCO has adopted the Johannesburg Convention (2003), which is available for accession.[7] This new instrument provides for a level of cooperation beyond security: it allows members to work together on a multilateral basis to exchange essential data for identifying high-risk consignments of goods before shipment.[8] Alternative arrangements are available to states through the WCO Model Bilateral Agreement.[9] Both instruments have the potential to improve effectiveness in detecting traffic in arms, explosives, and sensitive materials.

The WCO administers and manages the Customs Enforcement Network, a multilateral database, alert system, and communication tool based on a secure Internet application and available to members on a 24-hour basis. This system, although currently underused for combating terrorism, has the potential to be employed more effectively by states wishing to share essential strategic and tactical information via alerts on the trafficking of arms, ammunition, weapons of mass destruction, and their precursor materials.

The most important recent development has been the adoption in June 2005 of a new international instrument to manage implementation of the tools and guidelines concerning the security of the supply chain: the Framework of Standards to Secure and Facilitate Global Trade (referred to below as the Framework of Standards or the Framework).[10] The Framework provides detailed arrangements for customs-to-customs and customs-to-business cooperation. Further explanation and concrete implementation procedures are contained in its annexes and appendixes, and are supposed to assist those members joining it to improve security standards. Phased implementation will be supported, where appropriate, by technical assistance from the WCO and a capacity building program.

In implementing the Framework of Standards, member countries can employ a wide range of guidelines on security, integrated supply chain management, risk assessment and risk management, and the use and deployment of scanning equipment, seals, and container security; and they can also develop national legislation and business partnerships. These improvements can be fully realized only with the unstinting support and commitment of governments, which in turn contribute to states' capacity "to take cooperative action to prevent illicit trafficking in nuclear, chemical or biological weapons, their means of delivery, and related materials" in accordance with their national law and consistent with international law (UNSCR 1540, operative paragraph 10).

Strengthening Security without Hurting Business Interests

Changes to national legislation will be required in many countries, and there is a real danger that steps to implement the suggested measures might be retarded or not acted upon by some governments because of other pressures and economic priorities. At first sight it might appear that facilitation of trade and the relaxation and simplification of border control procedures, which are both priorities for increasing foreign trade and inward investment, might work against the introduction of measures to strengthen security. But this view of the problem is based on a misunderstanding, because increased security does not necessarily mean reduced facilitation. On the contrary, facilitation and security should be viewed as complementary. Improvements to security through cooperative action and the exchange of information between customs administrations and between customs and business lead to more effective and efficient controls. Interventions can be carried out in advance of shipment and reduced to individual consignments that have been identified for further screening and examination at an earlier stage in the supply chain. For the business community, compliance with customs regulations can be rewarded through an authorization process that provides an authorized trader with certain trade facilitation benefits derived from simplified customs procedures and quicker clearance.

For developing countries the main pressure on governments is the collection of revenue, which can account for as much as fifty percent of their total revenues. Revenue collection at borders and the combating of commercial fraud is the principal role for many customs administrations. In the past decade the customs role in protecting society has increased in prominence, but it is still a subsidiary activity for many customs administrations. However, governments needing to comply with the binding elements of UNSCRs 1373,

1456, and 1540[11] and other Security Council resolutions must recognize security as a potential new role for customs and the consequent need in turn for this role to be recognized and developed within the overall structure of government departments.

To accelerate this process and to give assistance, the WCO and other international organizations need to demonstrate that improving security can increase the efficiency of governments' processes, including customs, and can lead to improvements in revenue yield as well as inward investment and business stability rather than impede it. If accepted, this approach should encourage governments to work toward implementing various international instruments: Security Council resolutions, the International Ship and Port Security Code of the International Maritime Organization, and the WCO's instruments and guidelines. In this regard the establishment of the regional intelligence liaison offices network can assist in the efficiency of customs' risk management process.

Empowerment and Funding

The role of protecting society against a wide variety of risks such as drug smuggling, the trafficking of endangered species, and counterfeit products has become highly professional in some countries. However, prevention and environmental activities remain subsidiary tasks in the majority of WCO member countries, especially developing countries where, as noted above, the collection of revenue and taxes at import remains the primary role of customs.

Many developing countries consider economic security as a primary concern of their societies. As a result they view physical security and antiterrorism either as not a recognized customs activity or as a subsidiary task performed mainly in support of other agencies. The greater threat is perceived as inefficiency and corruption and associated attempts by foreign and domestic traders to commit fraud against revenue collection, for example by undervaluing goods at import. Loss of tax revenue at the frontier can have serious harmful consequences on the social and economic well-being of developing countries, and for that reason governments rely on their customs services to collect and protect the revenue yield. Unfortunately, the same level of empowerment, pressure, and expectation is not applied consistently by all governments to the role of customs in preventing the smuggling of drugs, enforcing intellectual property rights, and dealing with security issues such as WMD proliferation and antiterrorism. Clearly, this has major implications for the implementation of Resolution 1540. Leadership within (developing) countries at senior administrative levels can help to redress this imbalance. An integrated government antiterrorism and anti-WMD proliferation strategy should have clarity of approach and objectives and should recognize that several agencies, including customs, can fulfill a credible and complementary role. The cooperation that is sometimes lacking between governmental agencies needs to be assured as part of a customs development policy.

To maintain effective and efficient security controls at the border, it is vital for customs to maintain a high level of integrity. Management and systems must be in place to achieve this level of professionalism, and relevant steps should be consolidated into a comprehensive strategy and action plan for integrity, based upon the individual needs of each country. Assistance in fighting against corruption can be provided by the WCO through the implementation of recommendations and guidelines set out in the WCO's Arusha Declaration.

Customs must be fully empowered to carry out this new role, and therefore appropriate and proportionate legislation and new procedures must be implemented. Partnership with legitimate business and the use of intelligent controls and technology are also vital prerequisites.

Even though capacity building efforts may take considerable time to achieve, many improvements can be accomplished without additional cost, for example the restructuring, reprioritization, and reallocation of existing resources. Programs of more comprehensive change will require full funding by governments, donor institutions, or both. This financial assistance is being provided through a close partnership between the WCO, the World Bank, and other donors. The partnership approach to capacity building is illustrated in the *Customs Modernization Handbook*, published by the World Bank, which is a useful compendium for governments and consultants wishing to carry out reform programs in customs.[12]

Capacity Building

The adoption and enforcement of laws and other measures referred to in UNSCR 1540 is a major challenge for many UN member states. Security and facilitation of the global supply chain require a high degree of professionalism and motivation from customs administrations and other governmental parties. Training customs staff to enhance and maintain the skills required for handling advance electronic information and operating intelligence-based controls will be of great importance. For this reason the UN Counter-Terrorism Committee, the World Customs Organization, and other international bodies have recognized that capacity building is a crucial activity.

The WCO's approach to compliance with security and facilitation provisions is to encourage and assist its members to improve effectiveness and efficiency through progress in building capacity. Experience has shown that building capacity requires high political will and commitment, accurate diagnosis of needs, ownership, and the participation of the recipient administration. The WCO has developed a comprehensive approach to this subject, which is now contained in its capacity building strategy (see below). In implementing the necessary measures, each country will be operating at different levels of effectiveness and efficiency. For this reason, building capacity requires a progressive, phased approach whose final objective is to achieve effective implementation of all measures required to meet the obligations established by the UN resolutions and other international standards. The implementation of Resolution 1540 is an obvious and integral part of this strategy. Each capacity building program is a unique process with its own time line based upon the needs of the recipient country and the level of funding available.

When the capacity building process begins, there must be a self-assessment or a diagnosis (or both) of the relevant needs as well as an external assessment of them. In order to assist countries to carry out the complex measures involved in capacity building, the WCO has finalized a customs capacity building strategy and associated action plan. As part of the strategy, a diagnostic framework has also been drafted that can be used by external consultants to carry out diagnostic assessments or for self-assessments of the capabilities of a customs administration. This framework contains a comprehensive section dealing with security that is designed to help administrations to assess their readiness to deal with the tasks of security and trade facilitation. It is divided into sections addressing the various elements required for successful implementation of security processes, including organization, legislation, procedures, techniques, communication, integrity, managing risk, deployment of resources, and partnership with business. The particular needs of a country can be considered for each topic, and the appropriate levels of technical assistance can be identified and built into long-term reform projects. In addition, the framework helps states to identify possible solutions and improvement options and refers to material that will assist with the reform process.

The Role of the WCO and Its Member States

It has been established that the general mission of the World Customs Organization is to improve the effectiveness and efficiency of customs administrations and thus of border controls. Promoting security and facilitating the international trade supply chain is an essential activity of the WCO and the countries of its membership. It contributes to the implementation of UNSCR 1540 by developing a number of international instruments.

Seeing the need to develop further managerial and technical guidance for security, the WCO Council adopted in 2002 by Resolution the International Task Force on Security and Facilitation of the International Trade Supply Chain (hereafter Task Force). In passing this resolution, its directors general realized that for protecting society and facilitating trade the international community would need to combine existing skills (as described in the Revised Kyoto Convention and in the Harmonized System, the latter a nomenclature for collecting duties and trade statistics) which together can be used to better identify shipments of sensitive and high-risk goods. Recognizing that close cooperation between all key players involved in international trade is essential—it is called for in both UNSCR 1373 and UNSCR 1540—the WCO secretariat and senior officials from the WCO's member administrations have established appropriate working arrangements with the International Maritime Organization, the United Nations Office on Drugs and Crime, the International Atomic Energy Agency (IAEA), the Organisation for the Prohibition of Chemical Weapons (OPCW), Interpol, and also international business organizations.

Partnerships with ocean shipping, air industry, road transport, rail, and many other organizations were also initiated by the Task Force on Security and Facilitation of the International Trade Supply Chain. This group met six times in two years and produced a range of instruments, tools, and guidelines ready for implementation by governments. These instruments, such as the Revised Kyoto Convention, the Johannesburg Convention, the WCO Model Bilateral Agreement, and various recommendations and guidelines, have significant implications for customs and businesses in terms of legal revisions, system changes, and capacity building requirements. Clearly, progress on all these fronts is a requirement for the full implementation of Resolution 1540.

In the technical area involving the trafficking of nuclear, chemical, and biological material, the WCO continues to work in partnership with other international organizations in the delivery of training courses and guidance material for border controls. The WCO cooperates with the IAEA and the Universal Postal Union in forming the Guidelines for Monitoring Radioactive Material in International Mail and it works closely with the IAEA in developing practical guidance on detecting illicit traffic. The WCO shares information on incidents of trafficking in radiological materials with the IAEA and cooperates with Europol and Interpol in joint meetings on the illicit trafficking of nuclear and radiological materials. Further, it provides technical support to the OPCW on customs matters relating to the implementation of the Chemical Weapons Convention. Technical improvements are also envisaged in complex areas such as transit and trans-shipment, where supply chain security is increasingly vulnerable.

It should be recognized, however, that although the WCO Council adopted in 2003 the measures and instruments recommended by the Task Force, very few customs administrations have implemented those measures so far. The international customs community is therefore examining and debating the implications of moving from guidelines to internationally recognized standards and how best to provide capacity to implement them and thus be observed by the majority of customs administrations and business entities.

To meet this range of challenges a high-level strategic group of directors general (HLSG) from six WCO regions was created in June 2004 by a further Resolution on Global Security and Facilitation Measures Concerning the International Trade Supply Chain. Working in close cooperation with the WCO secretariat and business representatives, the HLSG initiated the development of the international Framework of Standards to Secure and Facilitate Global Trade that was adopted by the WCO Council in June 2005. This framework is consistent with the existing WCO instruments and measures for security and facilitation. It is built around four core elements: harmonizing advance electronic manifest information, to allow risk assessment; taking a common risk management approach; using non-intrusive detection equipment to effect examinations; and defining the accrual of benefits to states' customs and business. These objectives are grouped into two "pillars" that describe arrangements for customs-to-customs and customs-to-business cooperation. The first pillar encourages cooperation among customs administrations on the basis of common and accepted standards. This covers the use of advance electronic information to identify high-risk containers and the use of smarter and more secure containers. The second customs-to-business pillar promotes the establishment of close partnership between government and business and the accreditation of businesses that conform to specified security standards. These reliable partners can then be granted the status of an authorized economic operator and receive tangible benefits.

Technical annexes and appendixes are also being developed, to enable the practical implementation of the measures contained in the 2005 Framework of Standards. Implementation requires a phased approach in accordance with each administration's capacity and legislative authority. Membership of the WCO will be invited to consider a recommendation that will bring the Framework into effect. This will initiate a process that involves members progressively applying certain standards and good practices. A phased implementation scheme with varying target dates for final implementation is being considered in order to allow all countries, regardless of their level of development, to contribute to the Framework. The intention is to secure the participation of as many countries as possible and to encourage them to enter into a process of implementing enhanced security and facilitation standards.

Conclusion: Conventions, Guidelines, and Frameworks

To facilitate compliance with UNSCR 1540, governments and their customs administrations have access to a wide range of tools, instruments, and techniques already developed by the WCO. These are summarized as follows:

—The revised Kyoto Convention provides the foundation and defines the functioning of a modern customs administration;[13]

—The Johannesburg Convention on Mutual Administrative Assistance allows the exchange of information in customs matters between administrations and is a vital step toward advance identification of high-risk consignments;[14]

—The WCO's Model Bilateral Agreement assists the establishment of the exchange of information;[15]

—The Arusha Declaration outlines the key principles for comprehensive and sustainable integrity action plans and the fight against corruption;[16]

—Integrated supply chain management guidelines describe how information can be shared and managed for security purposes, including cooperative arrangements between WCO members and the private sector; [17]

—Advance passenger information, for managing passenger movements in advance of arrival;[18]

—The unique consignment reference (UCR), a unique number that will be given to every international shipment, allowing government agencies to track and trace shipments. The UCR will enable customs to link information received from the different parties for a particular consignment and will facilitate the exchange of customs data between customs administrations;[19]

—High-security mechanical seals and electronic seals (being developed). Seal integrity programs include procedures for recording, affixing, changing, and verifying seals;

—The WCO data model provides a comprehensive set of data required to facilitate information exchange. This can assist governments in developing cooperative arrangements between customs and other government agencies involved in international trade in order to facilitate the seamless transfer of international trade data through a "single window concept." An agreed list of twenty-seven data elements, which form a subset of the data model and whose purpose is to assist risk management at both national and international levels on security and antiterrorism initiatives, is being discussed. Under this system traders electronically submit one set of information to a single designated authority, preferably customs;[20]

—Guidelines for smart and secure containers;

—Guidance on the procurement, deployment, management, and maintenance of scanning equipment;

—A databank of technological devices that is Internet-based and that enables members of the WCO to identify technology for assisting the detection of illegal consignments and contraband;

—By the implementation of risk management and risk assessment guidelines, customs can assess and manage the relative risks of goods and traders and their levels of compliance with customs law;[21]

—The WCO's Diagnostic Framework and Strategy for Capacity Building, for assessment or self-assessment of various aspects of a customs administration and for identifying capacity building needs;[22] and

—The Framework of Standards to Secure and Facilitate Global Trade, with detailed assistance for implementation.[23]

The application of these international norms, instruments, tools, and guidelines developed by the WCO in response to increased security risks and international terrorism make an important contribution to the UN Security Council's initiatives against the proliferation of nuclear, chemical, and biological weapons and their means of delivery. The WCO can contribute its many preexisting instruments and tools and assist states in complying with their obligations under UNSCR 1540 with particular reference to improvements in and enforcement of border controls.

Improving the security and facilitation of global trade is a complex and multifaceted challenge. By way of establishing a working platform, customs administrations should be encouraged to accede to the revised Kyoto Convention, the international instrument that describes how a modern customs administration should operate. Already, the World Customs Organization is inviting customs administrations to indicate their intention to adopt the Framework of Standards to Secure and Facilitate Global Trade, which, as its name suggests, integrates many of the existing security guidelines into a comprehensive framework of security and facilitation measures. Implementation of the Framework will be a major challenge owing to its scope and complexity. Many of the 166 member customs administrations are from developing countries where the priority for customs is collection of revenue. The protection of society, and particularly anti-terrorism initiatives, is viewed as a new and specialized role that is outside their current purview. For this reason, customs administrations will require strong support from within their own governments if they are to play a meaningful role in improving security at the border against terrorism. With this support guaranteed, the WCO's capacity building program can facilitate the changes and improvements required for full compliance with Resolution 1540.

Notes

1. Guidelines on controlling Free Zones in relation to Intellectual Property Rights infringements, Enforcement Committee, WCO, 24th Session, January 15, 2005, at www.wcoipr.org/wcoipr/gfx/freezones2005.doc.

2. Michel Danet, "Message of the WCO Secretary General," International Customs Day, Brussels, 26 January 2005, at www.wcoomd.org/ie/En/Past_Events/speech/ Speeches.html.

3. Operative paragraph 10 of UNSCR 1540 makes reference to international co-operation: "Further to counter that threat, *calls upon* all States, in accordance with their national legal authorities and legislation and consistent with international law, to take cooperative action to prevent illicit trafficking in nuclear, chemical or biological weapons, their means of delivery, and related materials." It thereby reconfirms paragraph 4 of UNSCR 1373: "Notes with concern the close connection between international terrorism and transnational organized crime, illicit drugs, money-laundering, illegal arms trafficking, and illegal movement of nuclear, chemical, biological and other potentially deadly materials, and in this regard emphasizes the need to enhance coordination of efforts on national, subregional, regional and international levels in order to strengthen a global response to this serious challenge and threat to international security."

4. Examples of this new approach are already found in the United States and Canada. In China, customs has retained its separate agencies but combined its investigative border enforcement capabilities within a new customs police force under the control of the director general of customs, a rank now raised to ministerial level.

5. International Convention on the Simplification and Harmonization of Customs Procedures as amended in 1999 (called the Revised Kyoto Convention), WCO, Brussels, June 1999, including the Guidelines for Implementation. See www.wcoomd.org/ie/ en/Topics_Issues/FacilitationCustomsProcedures/Kyoto_New/ Content/content.html.

6. See the Arusha Declaration Concerning Good Governance and Integrity in Customs, WCO, Arusha, Tanzania, July 1993, and revised in June 2003, at www.wcoomd. org/ie/En/Topics_Issues/CustomsModernizationIntegrity/6.%20Revised%20Arush% 20E-Print%20version.PDF.

7. International Convention on Mutual Administrative Assistance in Customs Matters (Johannesburg Convention), WCO, June 2003. See WCO News, No. 44 (June 2004), p. 2, at www.wcoomd.org/ie/EN/Magazine/OMD%20No44%20news%20EN %20-%20final.pdf#search=%22Johannesburg%20Convention%20WCO%20June% 202003.%22.

8. In this way a means is provided for countries to act according to Article 3(a) of UNSCR 1373, which "*Calls* upon all States to: Find ways of intensifying and accelerating the exchange of operational information, especially regarding actions or movements of

terrorist persons or networks; forged or falsified travel documents; traffic in arms, explosives or sensitive materials; use of communications technologies by terrorist groups; and the threat posed by the possession of weapons of mass destruction by terrorist groups."

9. WCO Model Bilateral Agreement, WCO, Brussels, June 2003.

10. Framework of Standards to Secure and Facilitate Global Trade (Framework of Standards), WCO, Brussels, June 2005. See www.wcoomd.org/ie/en/Press/WCO%20%20FRAMEWORK%20OF%20STANDARDS%20June%2021%20Final.pdf.

11. These resolutions refer to border, export, and other customs-related controls, but are most explicitly required in UNSCR 1540.

12. *Customs Modernization Handbook* (Washington, D.C.: World Bank, January 2005).

13. The Revised Kyoto Convention, WCO, 1999, including the Guidelines for Implementation. See www.wcoomd.org/ie/En/Topics_Issues/FacilitationCustoms Procedures/Kyoto_New/Content/content.html.

14. International Convention on Mutual Administrative Assistance in Customs Matters (Johannesburg Convention), WCO, June 2003. See www.wcoomd.org/ie/En/ Conventions/MAA%20Legal%20Text%20FINAL%20VERSION_publish%20E.pdf.

15. WCO Model Bilateral Agreement, WCO, June 2003.

16. The Arusha Declaration, WCO, June 2003. See www.wcoomd.org/ie/En/ Topics_Issues/CustomsModernizationIntegrity/6.%20Revised%20Arush%20E-Print %20version.PDF.

17. Customs Guidelines on integrated supply chain management (ISCM Guidelines), WCO, June 2004. See www.wcoomd.org/ie/En/Topics_Issues/Facilitation CustomsProcedures/ISCM_Guidelines_VI.pdf.

18. Recommendation concerning Adherence to Standards in Relation to Data Requirements for Advance Passenger Information (API), WCO, July 1993, revised in March 2003. See www.wcoomd.org/ie/En/Topics_Issues/FacilitationCustomsProcedures/API GuidelinesE%20.pdf.

19. WCO Recommendation on the Unique Consignment Reference (UCR), WCO, June 2004: WCO UCR Accompanying Guidelines, WCO, 2003. See www.wcoomd. org/ie/En/Topics_Issues/FacilitationCustomsProcedures/UCR_new_e.pdf.

20. WCO Customs Data Model, WCO, 2003. See www.wcoomd.org/ie/En/ AboutUs/fiche7_ang.pdf.

21. Risk Management Guide, WCO, June 2003 and Guide on Risk Assessment 2004. See www.adb.org/Documents/Events/2005/Trade-Facilitation/wco-risk-guide-eng.pdf.

22. WCO Diagnostic Framework and Strategy for Capacity Building, WCO, 2004.

23. Framework of Standards, WCO, June 2005.

SIEW GAY ONG

11

The Proliferation Security Initiative and Counter-Proliferation: A View from Asia

The terrorist attacks on the World Trade Center and the Pentagon on September 11, 2001 (9/11), raised the specter that similarly ruthless and organized terrorists equipped with weapons of mass destruction (WMD) could wreak even more horrific carnage. Thus as combating terrorism rose to the top of the international agenda in the wake of the disaster, so too did countering the proliferation of WMD, their delivery systems, and related materials and technology. This has resulted in a number of regional and global counter-proliferation and other security initiatives, including the Proliferation Security Initiative (PSI).

First launched by President George W. Bush during a visit to Krakow, Poland in May 2003, the PSI is a timely response to the growing challenges posed by the proliferation of WMD, their delivery systems, and related materials in that it reflects the need for a more dynamic approach. It envisions states working in partnership, employing their national capabilities to develop a broad range of legal, diplomatic, economic, military, and other tools to interdict illicit shipments of WMD and missile-related equipment and technologies. The emphasis of the initially eleven core group members of the PSI was on finding creative ways to fight the spread of nuclear, chemical, biological, and radiological weapons on land, in the air, and at sea in a way that conforms to the domestic legal frameworks of the participating countries and is in accordance with international law.[1]

The strength of the PSI lies partly in its loose and informal partnerships. As a senior arms control official from the U.S. State Department argued at a counter-proliferation meeting in Tokyo, in 2005, the PSI is "not diverted by disputes about candidacies for Director General, agency budgets, agendas for

153

meetings and the like."[2] Instead, it is almost entirely operational, relying primarily on the activities of law enforcement, intelligence, and other government officials. The PSI does not have a formal charter, and officials of the participating countries often comment that it is an activity, not an organization. Its character reflects the Bush administration's preference for less formal multilateral partnerships than would be practicable in, for example, the United Nations. Working within an informal structure and with like-minded governments enables Washington to act as quickly as possible on its strong political commitment to the interdiction of WMD.[3]

In line with this preference for informality, the PSI can be seen as a loose arrangement of a group of like-minded countries that share similar counter-proliferation goals and a political commitment to take concrete and practical action in pursuit of those goals. Actions are undertaken within a broad set of guiding principles, encapsulated in the PSI's Statement of Interdiction Principles adopted in Paris in September 2003,[4] with the details sorted out by legal and operational experts in each country.[5] This loose arrangement gives the participating countries a high degree of flexibility in defining the scope of their actions and pursuing their objectives.

This flexibility is a source of strength given the nature of the proliferation problem. The challenge is constantly changing and evolving as proliferators adapt to counter-proliferation measures, and governments must constantly update their approach. For instance, the original focus of the PSI was on the interdiction of illicit goods by bringing together customs officials of participating countries. Now there are indications that what is needed is strengthened cooperation among intelligence officials in response to increasingly sophisticated proliferators using trading companies and other legitimate entities as fronts for their operations. The revelations, intensively covered in the international media, about the A. Q. Khan network add weight to this requirement. It emerged that the Pakistani metallurgist A. Q. Khan had helped to provide nuclear technology to Libya, not only directly by way of his personal expertise but also by sourcing technology and components through a wide network of trading entities and companies acting as a front for his activities that spanned parts of the Middle East and Southeast Asia. B. S. A. Tahir, known as Khan's chief operating officer, was based in Malaysia. These revelations resulted from close intelligence cooperation, principally between the United States and the United Kingdom, and underscored the importance of further international cooperation between intelligence and law enforcement officials.

In this light President Bush's call to widen the scope of the PSI, from merely interdicting transfers and shipments to cooperation among intelligence, military, and law enforcement officials in order to focus on and shut down the operations of suspect middlemen, suppliers, and buyers, is a step in the right direction. His appeal was echoed by other participating countries in the PSI core group at its Lisbon plenary of March 2004, where participants "supported the call by U.S. President Bush to expand the role of the PSI to not only interdict shipments of WMD, their delivery systems and related materials, but to cooperate in preventing WMD proliferation facilitators (that is, individuals, companies, other entities) from engaging in this deadly trade."[6] The growing list of government agencies involved in meetings of PSI operational experts is testament to this changing response to the challenge.

The Threat in Asia

The PSI and the rising trends of proliferation and terrorism that it is meant to address are relevant to all countries, but particularly to the Asian region, for several reasons. First, of the four states currently outside the framework of the Nuclear Non-Proliferation Treaty (NPT), three are in Asia: the Democratic People's Republic of Korea (DPRK), Pakistan, and India. In addition, it is arguable that Israel, the fourth state outside the NPT, is part of the political dynamic of the proliferation challenge in Asia—some countries in Asia and the Middle East have long cited Israel's refusal to join the NPT as justification for their own refusal to go beyond their safeguards agreement with the International Atomic Energy Agency (IAEA) and sign and ratify subsequent additional protocols on nuclear safeguards.

Second, some of the most contentious non-compliance issues facing the IAEA arise from the alleged transgressions of the NPT by two Asian countries, the Republic of Korea (ROK) and Iran, that were brought to the Agency's attention in autumn 2004. In addition, the DPRK's withdrawal from the NPT regime in January 2003, its subsequent admission that it possesses nuclear weapons and the crisis to the Six-Party Talks that Pyongyang engendered in July 2006 have caused serious concern in Asia as well as in the rest of the international community. Third, the dangers posed by the proliferation of WMD and related materials to Asia have been recognized by Asian leaders. For instance, the former prime minister and now senior minister Goh Chok Tong of Singapore has singled out the DPRK nuclear crisis and the Pakistan–India standoff as two of the three major flashpoints that could set back economic growth in the region for several decades.[7]

To compound the problem for the region, Southeast Asia has swiftly become one of the major theaters in the global war against terrorism since the attacks of 9/11. In October 2002 the Jemaah Islamiyah (JI) masterminded a series of bombing attacks in Bali, Indonesia, that caused scores of deaths and hundreds of injuries. The JI was also behind the 2003 JW Marriott Hotel bombing in Jakarta and the 2004 suicide bombing attempt outside the Australian embassy there. According to published sources from the Singapore Ministry of Home Affairs, the JI is a transnational terrorist organization that traces its roots back to the anticolonial war in Indonesia in the 1940s. Its ultimate goal is to establish, through the use of violence, a daulah Islamiyah (Islamic state) in the region centered in Indonesia but also including Malaysia, the southern Philippines, Singapore, and Brunei. The organization shares the virulent anti-Western ideology of global jihad purveyed by Al-Qaeda.[8]

The JI is not the only terrorist group active in Southeast Asia. Similar organizations continue to pose a threat, either directly or together with operatives and "sleepers" of the Al-Qaeda global network. Nor did the region's serious encounter with terrorism begin only after September 11, 2001. Al-Qaeda had extended its reach into Southeast Asia considerably earlier, providing funding and training for various groups in the Philippines, Indonesia, and other parts of Southeast Asia. It is no wonder that the region has been recognized by international analysts as a new theater for terrorist operations by extremist groups.

This mix of global terrorism and proliferation risks has long been recognized, and the threat is felt acutely in Southeast Asia. The perpetrators of terrorist attacks in the region have inflicted considerable carnage in recent years using relatively simple techniques. The damage would have been far worse if the terrorists had obtained WMD, and the threat that they may do so is very real. Analysts have warned that terrorist procurement of relatively rudimentary WMD is no longer beyond the bounds of possibility. Regional security experts are already concerned about the rising tide of terrorism and piracy, and they are alarmed by the ability of international criminal syndicates to mount very sophisticated attacks with highly trained personnel using speedboats, modern weapons, and sophisticated communications. In the 1990s the ability of the Aum Shinrikyo to mount chemical attacks against the Tokyo subway caused consternation. It does not require much imagination to foresee a potential disaster arising from the combination of JI and Al-Qaeda's regional and international jihadist agenda and the increasing availability of WMD technology and materials.

Southeast Asia is densely populated, so the impact of a single WMD attack cannot be overemphasized. Maritime experts have pointed out that the region is straddled by narrow waterways and busy shipping lanes. This makes it a choice option for terrorists aiming to use maritime attacks to cripple the international supply chain, disrupt global commerce, and thereby make a strong political statement of their ideological goals. As Efthimios Mitropoulos, the secretary general of the International Maritime Organization (IMO), said in a lecture in October 2004:

> With Southeast Asia still, unfortunately, recording the highest number of pirate attacks globally, there is clearly a fear that terrorists could resort to pirate-style tactics, or even work in concert with pirates, to perpetrate their evil deeds. There have been suggestions that an upturn in crew abductions could signal a move by terrorists to train themselves in operating and navigating large commercial vessels—and you will recall that, in a similar vein, the 9/11 terrorists had taken the trouble to become trained pilots before hijacking the aircraft that later became their weapons of mass destruction.[9]

The PSI and Asia

The launch of the PSI has occurred against the backdrop of rising anti-American sentiments both globally and in Asia, especially given America's strong leadership role in the initiative. As in other areas of the world, anti-American political sentiments in Asia occur within the broader context of the international controversy surrounding the U.S. invasion and occupation of Iraq in 2003. Regional reactions to the PSI have been mixed. Some countries, principally Japan and nearby Australia, joined the core group of the PSI immediately, recognizing the heightened security risks posed by WMD proliferation in the post–9/11 world. But in other countries, initial suspicions of the initiative were enmeshed in vociferous arguments in academic and political circles about the U.S. role in the international order and the seeming irrelevance and ineffectiveness of the UN and the multilateral approach to international peace and security issues that it embodies. At the same time there were lamentations that America had become an arrogant imperial power, opting to abandon multilateralism for unilateral action.

It is not within the purview of this chapter to discuss the role of the United States and the United Nations in maintaining international peace and security or whether America is abandoning multilateralism in favor of a unilateral approach to international issues. Defining the relationship between the United States and the UN is a principal theme in international security in the post–9/11 world; and reaffirming the necessity of the multilateral approach while addressing the concerns of states that feel uniquely vulnerable and thus driven to take unilateral action is the major challenge faced by the international system. These issues have been and will continue to be discussed at the UN in New York as part of its members' examination over the years of Secretary General Kofi Annan's reform initiative.[10] This initiative to reform the UN, sparked by strong international criticism over its effectiveness and relevance following U.S. military actions in Iraq, culminated in the UN Secretary General's report *In Larger Freedom: Towards Development, Security and Human Rights for All*, released in March 2005, and the subsequent UN Summit in September 2005.

It is important to review the arguments made by early detractors of the PSI and see how these have been addressed. Critics have made two fundamental points in questioning whether the PSI has international legitimacy. First, they have raised the concern that the PSI, a loose collection of like-minded countries pursuing their narrow security interests rather than a comprehensive multilateral initiative by the UN or one of its relevant specialized agencies, lacks international legitimacy. Second, they question whether participating countries' actions to expedite the PSI will be taken in accordance with international law. The latter point reflects unease that the PSI resembles a group of countries banding together essentially to board vessels at will on the high seas at the slightest concern about the proliferation of WMD, with some suggesting that the initiative seems to be legitimizing piracy.

This apprehension about legality is echoed in various circles. For example, a representative of the Australian activist group Just Peace protested that "our government seems prepared to join the U.S. in vigilante attacks on the high seas," adding that "if these plans continue, we shall be seeing Australian troops committed not to the defence of Australia, but rather to international kangaroo court justice."[11] Similar worries have been raised in academic circles. Some have questioned the relationship between the PSI and the 1988 Convention for the Suppression of Unlawful Acts against the Safety of Maritime Navigation (SUA Convention) under which, at that time, countries were *not* forbidden to carry WMDs and related materials at sea. Two scholars have argued that unless the flag-state concerned permits the interception of a ship on the high seas or the grounding of an aircraft in international airspace, any interdiction would potentially amount to an act of belligerence. They have also asserted that in the absence of clarity about the exceptions to flag-state jurisdiction, the PSI conflicted with international law. Interesting legal questions such as those surrounding criminal jurisdiction over ships carrying WMD materials, innocent passage, and the freedom of navigation were involved.[12] The legality of interdiction on the high seas was clarified, however, by the October 2005 amendments to the SUA Convention, which added provisions for the potential boarding of vessels suspected of being involved with WMD and terrorism.[13] Going a step further, others have suggested that the PSI could be part of a broader strategy of the Bush administration to secure de facto agreement on the doctrine of preemptive self-defense.[14]

An additional point of concern is that the PSI seems to be directed principally at the DPRK, which could undermine ongoing diplomatic efforts within the ambit of the six-party talks (involving the United States, China, Russia, Japan, the DPRK, and the ROK) to achieve Pyongyang's dismantling of its nuclear program. This issue, owing to concern for the sensitivities of Pyongyang, has prevented China and the Republic of Korea from joining the PSI. It is as well an issue on which not every country participating in the PSI agrees. Some have been careful to stress that their participation is not aimed at the DPRK, but others have been less circumspect. For instance, Australia's office of the foreign minister Alexander Downer, in a press statement issued in the run-up to Canberra's hosting of the PSI's Lisbon plenary meeting in July 2003, explained that although "[t]he initiative is global in nature and . . . is not directed at any one country, it is relevant to the [Australian] government's concerns about North Korea including its declared nuclear weapons programme."[15]

Counterarguments to the PSI

There is some truth in the above arguments. The ideal approach would be for the entire international community to come together at the UN and discuss a comprehensive agreement on tightening the current counter-proliferation regime. This would generate much more agreement from member states. Universality remains an important goal; and the UN, however imperfect, remains the most appropriate framework. It is based on the essential principle that legitimate goals can best be attained through legitimate means.[16]

Furthermore, it has been argued that the longer-term success of the PSI depends on broad-based participation because in view of the worldwide nature of the proliferation problem, every link of the global supply chain is important in securing the movement of sensitive materials and technology.[17] And the chain is only as strong as its weakest link. That the leading countries participating in the PSI felt compelled to demonstrate the global reach they have achieved in promoting the initiative was shown by the commemorating of its first anniversary at Krakow in May 2004 with a meeting involving more than 60 countries, with numbers to have reached more than 70 by June 2006.[18]

However, formulating a comprehensive multilateral approach requires much more time. Historically, landmark international conventions that are universal in nature are seldom born overnight. Many start off as an agreement between only a handful of states that gradually gain currency in the international community over years as its relevance become more obvious in light of subsequent developments in the international situation.

In the interim, the multilateral approach should not preclude any group of countries that have immediate worries about the dangers of proliferation from taking other initiatives to counter the risks, as long as these initiatives are consistent with domestic and international law and are not targeted at a particular country. In this regard, several members of the PSI's core group have taken pains to emphasize that whatever actions they undertake under the aegis of the PSI will be consistent with their domestic law and international law and that no particular country is the target of the initiative. These principles are clearly enshrined in the PSI's Statement of Interdiction Principles, adopted at its Paris meeting of September 2003.[19]

Cooperating in the PSI necessitates that participating countries seek legal authority under domestic and international law in order to empower their actions. That they have begun to do so, for example by successfully seeking the passage of UNSC Resolution 1540 (April 2004) on counter-proliferation, by proposing amendments to the SUA Convention, and by negotiating bilateral shipboarding agreements with flag states, suggests that they have already recognized this requirement. It remains important for the United States to embark on the multilateral track, especially as it takes measures to combat proliferation. No matter how powerful the world's sole superpower may be, it will not be able to solve all its, and the world's, problems alone. In a globalized world post–9/11, taking action to counter proliferation cannot in the longer term be a challenge met by a select few. Only a multilateral approach involving all key players, one with the legitimacy accorded only by the UN system, will be able to succeed.

In this vein, the United States initiated the International Maritime Organization's amendment of the SUA Convention, in a manner to maintain the integrity of the international maritime regime while taking into account the proliferation question. States were encouraged to participate actively and constructively in this legal forum, and the maritime security regime was updated to be relevant to the challenges and realities of the twenty-first century. This meant carefully balancing the need to curb the illicit trade in WMD and related materials with the legitimate rights and interests of flag states, port states, and the shipping and trading community.[20]

The PSI and UNSCR 1540

Amending the SUA Convention is not the only way that the United States has been trying to respond to criticisms that its approach does not have the necessary legitimacy conferred by the United Nations. President Bush raised the proliferation issue at the annual debate of the United Nations General Assembly in October 2003. This was followed by efforts in the Security Council to achieve a resolution obliging UN member states to take specific steps to tighten export control measures, among other means of combating the proliferation of WMD. Negotiations were difficult in the beginning. Owing to doubts over America's political agenda underlying the PSI, the resolution was perceived as an attempt by it to gain quick and broad international legitimacy for the PSI.

Some member states also suspected that the resolution was targeted critically at them, as their own proliferation record had been the subject of much debate within counter-proliferation circles. It took months of negotiations, including interventions by other countries to nuance the language and remove direct references to the PSI, before the resolution was passed in April 2004. UNSCR 1540 calls on UN member states to, inter alia, enhance domestic controls, step up cooperation against WMD proliferation, and make timely national reports to the UNSC on their national efforts. Although it does not achieve the comprehensive approach sought by the United States, it reflects the need for compromise at the multilateral level and is a step in the right direction.[21]

The launch of the PSI predated UNSCR 1540 by almost a year. In fact, the initiative to adopt UNSCR 1540 can be viewed as an American attempt to accord legitimacy to the PSI in response to criticisms that the Bush administration was once again working outside the UN and the multilateral framework in order to achieve its foreign policy goals. But when the United States attempted to have the counter-proliferation resolution passed in the Security Council, there was strong resistance because certain member states expressed reservations about its scope. These states were also those with the strongest worries about what they perceive as America's increasing unilateralism and its inclination to use the UNSC as an instrument to impose binding legislation on all member states.

To secure the support of the dissenting states, as an expert sitting on the UNSCR 1540 Committee disclosed, the text of the Resolution was significantly moderated to omit specific mention of the PSI, though its generic function is retained through the use of the phrase "to take cooperative action to prevent illicit trafficking" (operative paragraph 10). For the same reason, the Committee gave member states very little specific direction on implementation of UNSCR 1540; and in contrast to the Counter-Terrorism Committee, which had a strong mandate and gave specific reporting formats, the UNSCR 1540 Committee initially gave only broad and sometimes ambiguous directions. Consequently, member states were given much latitude on how to report and how much to report, though the Committee eventually developed in 2005 a matrix for obtaining additional information as well as outstanding reports.

Without the PSI, there would have been no Resolution 1540. And although its text was considerably moderated, it still is a step in the right direction in that it has put counter-proliferation on the agenda of the Security Council. The Resolution's first step is necessarily a modest one: it calls on member states to refrain from providing support to non-state actors in the development and use of WMDs and to adopt effective national controls against proliferation. Member states are also required to submit national reports on what measures they have taken to achieve these objectives nationally, regionally, and internationally. But when this first step has been taken, there is always the possibility of doing more as international momentum and support gathers and there is wider acceptance of the need to combat the proliferation of WMD in a new age.

Singapore's Approach

It has been argued earlier that for practical purposes and because of the usually slower pace of a multilateral approach, states with compelling worries about proliferation ought to be able to pursue "pathfinding ways" in the meantime to deal with it without precluding a more multilateral approach in the longer term. This was how Singapore viewed the PSI and concurrent efforts to combat proliferation. This view, reflecting its general approach to most regional and international issues, combines pragmatism with an emphasis on principles, in particular the principle of the international rule of law.

First, Singapore quickly saw the clear and present dangers facing it as a small country of less than 700 square kilometers in a region where the threat of terrorism looms large. Members of Jemaah Islamiyah (JI) have made attempts to bomb diplomatic missions and key installations in Singapore, and the country remains a prime target for attacks in view of arrests of Singaporean members of JI as well as JI's stance on the second Gulf war. JI operatives capable of independently mounting operations remain at large, and the organization has taken steps to regenerate itself.[22] The country is ever mindful that the damage of a single WMD attack would be catastrophic and even spell the physical end of Singapore in the light of its small size and dense population. Even a "dirty bomb" attack by terrorists would seriously undermine and perhaps irreversibly damage investors' confidence in Singapore, crippling an economy heavily reliant on international commerce.

Second, Singapore's economy depends on shipping and maritime services to trade even more than on trade itself. These services account for the bulk of its gross domestic product. According to statistics provided by the Maritime and Port Authority of Singapore, container throughput in 2004 amounted to more than 21 million TEUs.[23] Given the large volume of container traffic, the government had long recognized that keeping its ports and waters free and safe from WMD is essential to ensuring that Singapore's economy remains secure. Singapore also saw that in time new rules and norms governing maritime security and counter-proliferation would be promulgated. It was thus in its interest as a maritime hub to be "ahead of the curve" and participate actively in the process of establishing the new norms while ensuring that its legitimate shipping interests would be safeguarded.

Third, however American policy is viewed, there is little question that the international security and counter-proliferation regime is in need of renovation. A compelling argument to this effect is made by the IAEA's director general, Mohamed ElBaradei, an Egyptian diplomat who has served with considerable distinction in Vienna for many years. Writing in the *Financial Times* in 2005, he observed that in recent years three phenomena had radically altered the security landscape: the emergence of a nuclear black market, a determined effort by more countries to acquire the technology to produce the fissile material used in nuclear weapons, and the clear desire of terrorists to acquire weapons of mass destruction.[24] This trend, ElBaradei argues, necessitates a review and strengthening of the international counter-proliferation regime.

Fourth, as a small nation-state, Singapore has always articulated an abiding interest in upholding the international rule of law as embodied in multilateral institutions, of which the UN system is the principal pillar. As enunciated by Minister of State for Foreign Affairs Zainul Abidin Rasheed in a speech in Parliament in March 2005, Singapore believes that "the UN is an important component of the international system, upholding the rule of international law and safeguarding the rights of large and small states alike."[25] Singapore's approach to counter-proliferation issues is consistent with this. It has encouraged the pursuit of the multilateral approach through discussions at the IMO during the amendment process of the SUA Convention. It regards this as the best way to address issues of international legitimacy because it does not preclude moves by like-minded countries to take immediate and effective unilateral steps to fight proliferation.

Singapore's national efforts, including enactment of the Strategic Goods (Control) Act, to combat the increasing threat of proliferation predate the launch of the PSI. Singaporean officials thus see the PSI as a natural extension of their own efforts to address the risk. One official has indicated that the PSI is seen as critically important in complementing Singapore's general strategy on counter-terrorism as well as on counter-proliferation. The Strategic Goods (Control) Act, which came into force on January 1, 2003, covers a wide array of transactions: exports, reexports, trans-shipments, transits, brokering, and intangible technology transfers. Its control list is drawn from the major international export control regimes. Most importantly, there is a "catchall" clause, which covers all other items suspected of WMD end-use. From discussions with enforcement and policy officials within the Singaporean establishment, it is understood that the export control regime is subject to constant review. Given the nature of Singapore's administrative system, the review and implementation of the export control system has been relatively smooth and is expected to be updated regularly.

In 2003, the Customs Department stopped various suspicious shipments under the catchall clause and related legislation. In April, Singapore customs, upon receiving intelligence tip-offs, investigated companies for offenses related to the import and export of sodium cyanide, a precursor linked to the production of chemical nerve agents.[26] Since then, two companies have been prosecuted and convicted of false declarations and exporting sodium cyanide without a valid export permit.

Several administrative refinements to the system have been made since the legislation was implemented, and it is understood that further refinements are not precluded in view of the probable beneficial impact on port traffic from prospective changes. The current focus is on effectively preventing WMD material from reaching its destination by using a combination of intelligence, profiling, physical enforcement, and legislation. Regular informal consultations with the shipping, trading, and logistics community have aimed to raise awareness of the export control system and gradually to ease the community into the new system. This will ensure that its legitimate interests are not jeopardized.

After carefully assessing the implications of the PSI on its domestic legal framework and on international legal norms, Singapore quickly came to the conclusion that it could and would support the PSI and its Statement of Interdiction Principles. It announced this in December 2003 and then attended the PSI's operational experts meeting in December 2003 and the U.S.-hosted exercise Sea Saber in the Arabian Sea in January 2004. Singapore subsequently joined the PSI's core group at the fifth PSI plenary meeting, in Lisbon in March 2004. Since then it has participated actively in the series of operational experts meetings held in various PSI core group countries as well as in the first global PSI meeting, held in Krakow, Poland, in June 2004. During that meeting, Russia joined the core group as a full member.

Singapore hosted its own maritime interdiction exercise in August 2005, the second such exercise to be held in Asia after exercise Team Samurai hosted by Japan in October 2004. This was a good opportunity for Singapore to test its operational capabilities in a maritime exercise, seen to be of the utmost relevance to the region. It was as well an opportunity to raise awareness of the PSI's goals in the region and to give neighboring countries firsthand experience of how an actual PSI operation might take place, thus helping to allay their concern about the initiative's legal and operational aspects and gaining their acceptance. In addition, Singapore cohosted with Canada an ASEAN Regional Forum export licensing experts' meeting in late 2005. Its purpose was to provide a platform for member countries to exchange national experiences of implementing export licensing and to identify strategies to enhance export control capacity in Asia.

Conclusion

In the wake of 9/11, countering the proliferation of WMD and related materials and technology, together with the global fight against terrorism, has risen to the top of the international agenda. The launch of the PSI is a strategic tool reinforcing these objectives. In Asia, this development has occurred against a backdrop of anti-American sentiment linked to the strong association between the United States and the PSI and to the controversies surrounding the U.S. military action in Iraq in March 2003 and since. Partly as a result of this, the initial response by some regional countries to the PSI has been negative. This is unfortunate, because the PSI and the security risks it is meant to address are particularly salient for the Asian region. There were initial concerns about the PSI's relationship with international law and about the need for a more comprehensive multilateral approach addressing the wider concerns of countries other than the U.S. But a thorough examination of these reservations, particularly in view of the October 2005 amendment of the SUA Convention, suggests that they need not hinder countries from taking immediate practical steps to combat proliferation as long as what is done is consistent with international law and domestic legal frameworks as stipulated in UNSCR 1540.

In fact, the launch of the PSI played a catalytic role in the passing of Resolution 1540: although there had previously been calls in the UNSC to intensify the fight against proliferation, the Resolution was passed less than a year after the PSI's inception. It is an attempt to counter criticisms of the PSI and to accord it legitimacy. Although the Resolution's language was moderated in order to mollify critics of the PSI, further action by the UNSC is not precluded as international support for the fight against proliferation gathers momentum. Thus the international cooperation engendered by the PSI can play a constructive role in the development of international legal instruments to address the proliferation issue in a more comprehensive, multilateral way.

Notes

1. Wade Boese, "The Proliferation Security Initiative: An Interview with John Bolton," *Arms Control Association*, December 2003, at www.armscontrol.org/act/2003_12/PSI.asp.

2. Remarks made during the Second Asian Senior-Level Talks on Non-Proliferation (ASTOP), Tokyo, February 9, 2005.

3. Andrew C. Winner, "The Proliferation Security Initiative: The New Face of Interdiction," *Washington Quarterly*, Vol. 28, No. 2 (Spring 2005), p. 132.

4. Office of the Press Secretary, "Interdiction Principles for the Proliferation Security Initiative," The White House, Washington, D.C., September 4, 2003, at www.state.gov/t/np/rls/fs/23764.htm.

5. Andreas Persbo and Ian Davis, "Sailing into Uncharted Waters? The Proliferation Security Initiative and the Law of the Sea," BASIC, June 2004, at www.basicint.org/pubs/Research/04PSI.htm.

6. Chairman's Conclusions, "Proliferation Security Initiative: Lisbon, 4–5 March 2004," fifth Plenary meeting, paragraph 4, at www.dfait-maeci.gc.ca/arms/psi2-en.asp.

7. Goh Chok Tong, Keynote Address, *Third International Institute of Strategic Studies Asia Security Conference (Shangri-La Dialogue)*, June 4, 2004, at www.mfa.gov.sg/internet/. Apart from terrorism, which was the theme of Goh's speech, he identified Kashmir, North Korea, and cross-straits tensions between Beijing and Taipei as the three major security challenges facing Asia.

8. For a genesis, ideology and methods of Jemaah Islamiyah (JI), see *The Jemaah Islamiyah Arrests and the Threat of Terrorism*, White Paper, Ministry of Home Affairs, Republic of Singapore, January 7, 2003, at www2.mha.gov.sg/mha/detailed.jsp?artid=667&type =4&root=0&parent=0&cat=0.

9. Efthimios Mitropoulos, Secretary General, International Maritime Organization, lecture at the Japan International Transport Institute, October 21, 2004, at www.imo.org/Newsroom/mainframe.asp?topic_id=847&doc_id=4402.

10. UN Secretary General Kofi Annan, speech at the UN General Assembly, September 23, 2003, at www.un.org/apps/news/story.asp?NewsID=8330&Cr=general&Cr1=assembly.

11. Nikki Todd, "Activists Hit out at PSI Plans to Stop Weapons Trade," *AAP Newsfeed*, July 9, 2003, as quoted in Rebecca Weiner, "Proliferation Security Initiative to Stem Flow of WMD Material," Centre for Non-Proliferation Studies, July 16, 2003, at http://cns.miis.edu/pubs/week/030716.htm.

12. Persbo and Davis, "Sailing into Uncharted Waters?"

13. In view of legal concerns, there was an initiative in the International Maritime Organization to amend the international convention governing unlawful acts at sea, formally the Convention for the Suppression of Unlawful Acts against the Safety of Maritime Navigation (SUA Convention), 1988. These amendments were adopted on October 14, 2005, in the form of Protocols to the SUA Convention, at www.imo.org/Conventions/mainframe.asp?topic_id=259&doc_id=686.

14. Fabrice Pothier, "The Proliferation Security Initiative: Towards a New Anti-Proliferation Consensus," BASIC, November 18, 2004, at www.basicint.org/pubs/Notes/BN041118.htm.

15. Department of Foreign Affairs and Trade website, Canberra, "Australia to Host Forum on Mass Destruction Weapons 9–10 July," June 26, 2003, BBC Monitoring.

16. Pothier, "The Proliferation Security Initiative."

17. Weiner, "Proliferation Security Initiative to Stem Flow of WMD Material."

18. Office of the Press Secretary, The White House, "President's Statement on Proliferation Security Initiative," Message delivered by Robert Joseph from U.S. President George W. Bush, The High Level Political Meeting of the Cracow Proliferation Security Initiative, Warsaw, June 23, 2006, at www.whitehouse.gov/news/releases/2006/06/20060623.html.

19. PSI Statement of Interdiction Principles also at www.dfait-maeci.gc.ca/arms/psi-en.asp.

20. Persbo and Davis, "Sailing into Uncharted Waters?"

21. Idem.

22. The arrests of members of Jemaah Islamiyah in October 2003 were of two young Singaporeans who had been trained in Pakistan and Afghanistan to be part of the next generation of JI leaders. Restriction orders under the Internal Security Act were issued on January 10, 2004, against twelve persons. Ten of them were members of JI and two were members of the Moro Islamic Liberation Front. On September 15, 2004, the orders of detention for seventeen of the nineteen persons arrested between August and September 2002 were extended, as they have had long and extensive exposure to militant ideology and have received military or terrorist training. Several of them were directly involved in terrorism-related activities, including helping to identify potential targets of terrorist attacks.

23. See www.mpa.gov.sg. In 2004 Singapore was the world's second-largest container port after Hong Kong, and the volume of its traffic was 20.9 million TEUs (twenty-foot equivalent units, a standard container size). See Judith Rehak, "Every Port in a Storm: China Is the Center of a Global Boom in an Increasingly Strategic Sector," *International Herald Tribune*, March 25–26, 2006, p. 16.

24. Mohamed ElBaradei, "Seven Steps to Raise World Security," *Financial Times*, February 2, 2005.

25. See www.mfa.gov.sg/internet/.

26. See speech by the then minister for foreign affairs Professor S. Jayakumar to the Singapore parliament, March 11, 2004, at www.mfa.gov.sg/internet/.

GERALD L. EPSTEIN

12

Law Enforcement and the Prevention of Bioterrorism: Its Impact on the U.S. Research Community

UN Security Council Resolution 1540 requires states to "adopt and enforce appropriate effective laws which prohibit any non-State actor to manufacture, acquire, possess, develop, transport, transfer or use nuclear, chemical or biological weapons and their means of delivery, in particular for terrorist purposes." Although the authority of the Security Council, acting under Chapter VII of the UN Charter, to compel states to enact domestic laws and regulations to combat bioterrorism is clear, if unprecedented, the precise nature of those legislative measures is not. Biological science and biotechnology are pervasively dual-use: practically all the materials, know-how, information, and biological organisms needed to produce biological weapons also have legitimate civilian applications. Owing to this inherent ambiguity, developing legal machinery that can impede terrorist activities without unduly burdening legitimate technically similar work is, and will remain, a challenge.

Consistent with UNSCR 1540 but predating it, legislation enacted in the United States after the 9/11 attacks has attempted to provide law enforcement with tools to prevent bioterrorism rather than just to prosecute offenders after the fact. The difficulties encountered in applying these tools in practice are shown by three cases discussed below in which this American legislation has been applied. If other countries enact similar legislation to "prohibit any non-State actor to manufacture, acquire, possess, [or] develop . . . biological weapons," as called for in operative paragraph 2 of UNSCR 1540, they may well face difficulties similar to those that the United States has encountered to date.

It is appropriate and necessary to have rules governing activities that are relevant to the production of biological weapons, but those rules have to be

168

sensible and sensibly enforced. Recent legal actions in the United States indicate that it may take some time for law enforcement officials to learn how to effectively use legal authorities of the type that are mandated by UNSCR 1540. This chapter draws upon the experience of the United States in addressing the difficulties in drafting, enacting, and implementing such provisions. It offers insights into what problems other countries may face in their future attempts to implement Resolution 1540 and also some "do's and don't's" for other countries, which will be reflected upon in the conclusion.

Statutory and Regulatory Provisions before 9/11

The United States signed the Biological and Toxin Weapons Convention (BTWC), an international treaty banning biological weapons, in 1972, the year of its inception.[1] The Convention entered into force in 1975. Recognizing that biological organisms are found in nature, that they have legitimate uses, and that the nature and extent of those uses cannot necessarily be predicted in advance, it does not attempt to specify what amounts or types of organisms would be considered as legitimate. Instead, it asserts what is known as the "general purpose criterion," which bans the development, production, stockpiling, acquisition, or retention of "microbial or other biological agents, or toxins" that are "of types and in quantities that have no justification for prophylactic, protective or other peaceful purposes."[2]

The BTWC's obligations are legally binding upon the United States government and upon the governments of other signatory states upon ratification. The Convention does not by itself regulate the activities of citizens, businesses, and other nongovernmental entities in the United States or domestically in other states with similar legal systems that are party to the treaty—until the ratification or accession legislation has been passed to implement its prohibitions domestically and to establish details such as penalties for violation. The United States did not enact this legislation until fourteen years after the BTWC entered into force, when the Biological Weapons Antiterrorism Act of 1989 was passed.[3] This legislation bans biological agents, toxins, or delivery systems "for use as a weapon," where "use as a weapon" is defined as not including "prophylactic, protective, or other peaceful purposes."

Concerned that ambiguity about the acceptable use of biological agents could put legitimate biological research in jeopardy, the American Society for Microbiology (ASM), the professional society for the country's microbiologists, worked with the drafters of this legislation to ensure that it did not restrict legitimate microbiological research. Language was added in the section describing the bill's purpose and intent to make clear that "nothing in the

Act is intended to restrain or restrict peaceful scientific research or development." The Senate Judiciary Committee's report accompanying this legislation recognized that scientists conduct research with potentially dangerous biological agents and toxins, and it stated that the bill would not interfere with this activity.[4] When a draft of the legislation proposed to give federal authorities the ability to seize biological agents that researchers could not prove were for a legitimate purpose, the ASM helped legislators to introduce an amendment that put the burden of proof justifying a seizure on the government. As enacted, the law requires the government to obtain a warrant "in the same manner as provided for a search warrant" before conducting a seizure, although a provision exists to seize materials upon probable cause "in exigent circumstances" without a warrant. In any prosecution under this act, the government must prove "beyond any reasonable doubt" that an individual did not intend to use biological agents for a peaceful purpose—a requirement that would be extremely difficult to fulfill against a scientist or researcher who had a plausible justification for his or her use of biological agents.[5]

The Centers for Disease Control and Prevention (CDC), an agency of the U.S. Department of Health and Human Services, is the main body regulating the interstate shipment of infectious substances. Several other government agencies, including the U.S. Postal Service, the Department of Transportation, and the Occupational Health and Safety Administration, also have some jurisdiction over the packaging, shipment, and handling of biological substances. The CDC's responsibilities focus on minimizing the public health and environmental consequences of shipping infectious agents, as well as on assuring that its experience with these agents would be available should packages containing such agents be damaged.[6]

In May 1995 an incident demonstrated the limitations of the controls on the use and possession of biological agents that were in effect at the time. Larry Wayne Harris, who was a member of the white supremacist group Aryan Nation, ordered three vials of *Yersinia pestis*, the bacterium responsible for bubonic plague, from the American Type Culture Collection (ATCC). The ATCC was established in 1925 as a central microorganism repository to serve scientists around the world.[7] When Harris impatiently telephoned the ATCC to ask why his shipment had not arrived, an employee became suspicious that he might not be an appropriate recipient and contacted law enforcement authorities. The police raided Harris's home, recovered the vials (which had been en route at the time of his call) from the glove compartment of his car, and arrested him.[8]

Harris claimed to be a microbiologist who was writing a training manual on defense against biological weapons. However, law enforcement officials stated that he did not have the facility or the training to handle this material safely. Even so, he had broken no law in possessing the agent or in keeping it in his glove compartment. The prohibition in the U.S. Biological Weapons Antiterrorism Act against possession or development of biological weapons required the authorities to prove that Harris intended to use his cultures *as a weapon*, for which there was no evidence. Nor was the possession of bubonic plague otherwise regulated. Instead, Harris was convicted of wire fraud for misusing a laboratory registration number in the letterhead he created to assure the ATCC that he maintained a laboratory suitable for studying *Yersinia pestis*. Facing a maximum possible sentence of six months in jail and a $25,000 fine, Harris was sentenced to eighteen months' probation, 200 hours of community service during the first twelve months of that probation, and a $50 fee. He was also enjoined from conducting experiments or obtaining disease agents except at approved laboratories and in connection with verified employment.[9]

Select Agent Regulations

Largely in response to this incident, the U.S. Congress tightened regulations on biological agents by adding a provision to a major piece of legislation that was being drafted in response to the April 19, 1995, Oklahoma City bombing. The Antiterrorism and Effective Death Penalty Act of 1996 augmented the existing regulatory structure for transporting biological agents by assigning to the federal government a new mission of "prevent[ing] access to [dangerous biological] agents for use in domestic or international terrorism or for any other criminal purpose."[10] The Act directed the U.S. secretary of health and human services to maintain a list of biological agents that have "the potential to pose a severe threat to public health and safety" or "select agents."[11] It also directed the secretary to establish and enforce procedures for shipping such agents safely, to ensure that laboratory facilities can appropriately handle, contain, and dispose of them, and to provide safeguards against access to them for adverse use. At the same time, it directed the secretary to provide for the "appropriate availability of biological agents for research, education, and other legitimate purposes."[12]

The CDC's regulations under this new authority went into effect on April 15, 1997.[13] For the first time, facilities that wished to send or receive select agents, as designated by the secretary, were required to register with the federal government. Registration could be denied if the secretary had "evidence that the facility has or intends to use covered agents in a manner harmful to the health of humans." In addition, the regulations authorize inspections of registered facilities, either at random or for cause, in order to ensure compliance.

Under these regulations, any institution, company, or individual that wishes to ship a select agent must check that the receiving facility is registered and must file a notification of the shipment with the registering authority. Receipt of the shipment must also be acknowledged. If the shipper suspects that the agent might not be used for the requested purpose, it must notify the CDC.

As a public health agency, the CDC assumed these regulatory responsibilities reluctantly. Its effectiveness depends on free and open interaction between its own expert research and medical staffers and their counterparts in the state and local medical, public health, and clinical laboratory communities. It feared that these interactions might be impaired if new regulatory or law enforcement responsibilities were to put it in an adversarial rather than collaborative position with these constituencies. Nevertheless, these regulations have been implemented. By September 2001 about 250 institutions had registered under the regulations governing the transfer of select agents.[14]

The American Society for Microbiology helped the CDC to arrive at regulations that would not unduly constrain legitimate scientific research and medical activities. Based in part on an e-mail survey of 11,000 members, the ASM worked to develop a list of select agents that focused on those with the highest potential for use as biological weapons.[15] In addition, the final regulation exempted clinical laboratories if they used select agents only for diagnostic, reference, verification, or proficiency testing purposes. This exemption ensured that medical diagnostic procedures were not impaired and prevented the system from being utterly overwhelmed by routine diagnostic shipments to and from the nation's 150,000 clinical labs.

Regulating Select Agent Possession

The select agent regulations described above do not require registration or other regulation of those who possess select agents, only of those who ship them from one facility to another. In 1998, Attorney General Janet Reno expressed her concern before Congress that the "mere possession of a biological agent is not a crime under federal law unless there is proof of its intended use as a weapon, notwithstanding the existence of factors, such as lack of scientific training, felony record, or mental instability, which raise significant questions concerning the individual's ultimate reason for possessing the agent."[16] In addition to the Harris case, law enforcement officials cited cases involving the toxin ricin that also illustrated the complications of requiring proof of use as a weapon.[17] To tighten restrictions in federal law on the possession and handling of biological agents, the Department of Justice drafted legislation in late 1998. However, a number of the provisions of this proposed legislation proved to be controversial when circulated for interagency review before submission to Congress.

On May 12, 1999, President Clinton announced that his crime bill, the "21st Century Law Enforcement and Public Safety Act," would include provisions that "prohibit certain possession and unsafe handling of biological agents and toxins and make it more difficult for these agents to fall into the hands of terrorists."[18] However, disputes over the final wording of this legislation had not been resolved, and in fact would not be resolved for many months. Although agencies agreed on the need to regulate the possession of dangerous biological agents, the "careful balance" that the attorney general had acknowledged needed to be struck between public safety and legitimate scientific research was very difficult to arrive at in practice.[19]

Part of the difficulty concerned the inability of government officials, pending resolution of interagency disagreements, to discuss these provisions with members of the scientific community who would be significantly affected by them. Ronald Atlas, the cochairman of the ASM's Task Force on Biological Weapons Control, had testified before Congress that the ASM "supports measures to prohibit possession of listed biological agents, unless they are held for purposes that are in the public interest . . . and . . . are maintained under appropriate biosafety conditions."[20] However, the ASM was not directly involved in interagency discussions on the details of the proposed legislation during this period.

Controlling Biological Agents: Controversial Issues

Several provisions of the draft legislation illustrate the difficulty in criminalizing the inappropriate use of biological agents while allowing legitimate activity. These controversial issues illustrate the difficulties that implementation of Resolution 1540 will encounter in other countries as well. Among these provisions were:

—Unlawful possession. At the heart of this legislation was a provision that made it illegal to knowingly possess "any biological agent, toxin, or delivery system of a type or in a quantity that, under the circumstances, is not reasonably justified by a prophylactic, protective, or other peaceful purpose." This language alone, however, failed to account for the fact that biological agents exist naturally in the environment. As a result, an early draft of this legislation might have made a criminal of anyone with a piece of moldy bread in the kitchen—or even anyone who had contracted an infectious disease. Therefore, this language was subsequently augmented by the qualification that for the purposes of that provision, "the terms 'biological agent' and 'toxin' do not encompass any biological agent or toxin that is in its naturally occurring environment, if such agent or toxin has not been cultivated, collected, or otherwise extracted from its natural source."

—Unsafe handling. Another provision of the 1999 legislation would have made it a crime to handle a biological agent "with conscious disregard of an unreasonable risk to public health and safety" in a manner that "grossly deviates from accepted norms." Although the motivation for this provision was understandable, considerable negotiation went into its exact wording. Law enforcement officials wanted to set a standard that could be upheld in a criminal prosecution. By contrast, scientists were wary of legislating on the practice of science and potentially criminalizing innovative research methods. Government agencies were able to agree to final wording that met both interests, but the language included in the draft legislation had not been reviewed more widely by the law enforcement and the research communities or by industry.

—Unreported possession of select agents. In addition to the ban on the unjustifiable possession of any type of biological agent, the draft bill would require reporting the possession of any amount of a select agent. This provision would extend to possession the existing registration requirement that applies to anyone shipping select agents. In 1999 the ASM estimated that about 300 institutions were in possession of select agents, not including the clinical laboratories that are exempt from registering under the existing regulations.[21]

—Possession of select agents by "restricted individuals." Associated with the reporting requirement for select agents was the most controversial section of the 1999 legislation: the specification of several categories of "restricted individuals" who would be prohibited from possessing select agents without a waiver. In the earliest drafts of this bill, the set of "restricted individuals" was taken from those categories of individuals who cannot legally purchase firearms or ammunition under federal law.[22] Forbidden from having access to select agents would be those who are under indictment for, or who have been convicted of, a crime punishable by imprisonment for a term exceeding one year; those discharged dishonorably from the armed forces; those who are fugitives from justice or who have renounced U.S. citizenship; unlawful users of or addicts to any controlled substances; those who have been adjudicated as a mental defective or who had been committed to a mental institution; aliens who are in the United States illegally or under a temporary visa; those who are subject to restraining orders regarding potential domestic violence; or those who have been convicted of domestic violence misdemeanors.

These early drafts of the legislation also provided provisions for waiving some of these exclusions under certain conditions, with waivers in most cases to be issued by the employing institution.

Debate over these provisions was largely responsible for the delay in submitting the bill to Congress. Law enforcement officials supported these provisions in the hope of preventing biological terrorism by excluding categories of individuals deemed untrustworthy from gaining access to dangerous pathogens. However, other participants in these discussions questioned how relevant some of these conditions would be for identifying individuals likely to misuse biological agents. In addition, they were worried about the chilling effect that such restrictions would have on legitimate research if they were not clearly justified on security grounds. For example, some participants in these discussions questioned the propriety of excluding individuals who have been indicted but not convicted of a crime or who are addicted to lawfully prescribed medication. Concern was expressed that this provision would require employers to inquire about, or even to investigate, the mental health and medical history of their employees, raising questions of civil liberties. Further questions were raised as to whether institutions that issue waivers permitting otherwise restricted individuals to work with select agents would incur liability should those individuals later commit criminal acts.

Given the heavy participation of foreign nationals in the U.S. scientific workforce and the importance of international engagement in science, the Office of Science and Technology Policy (OSTP) was particularly anxious about excluding foreign nationals with temporary visas from working with select agents. Moreover, the OSTP pointed out that this restriction would have little effect on preventing foreign states from acquiring biological agents for weapons because those states would have the ability and the resources to obtain practically any of them from natural sources. Moreover, concentrating on foreign nationals would not necessarily have much effect in preventing terrorism, which the Oklahoma City bombing showed could be perpetrated by U.S. citizens too.

Extensive discussion whittled down the final set of "restricted individual" categories from that contained in the earlier drafts. The ultimate list of categories in the Clinton administration's final draft covered, as noted above, individuals who had been indicted or convicted of crimes with sentences of more than one year, unlawful users of controlled substances, fugitives from justice, and those who had received a dishonorable discharge from the military. The only foreign nationals who remained on the "restricted individuals" list were illegal aliens or those in the United States on a temporary visa from countries designated by the secretary of state as having repeatedly supported acts of international terrorism. Gone were the restrictions on those addicted to controlled substances, those under restraining orders or misdemeanor convictions for domestic violence, those judged mentally incompetent or who had been committed to mental institutions, and those who have renounced U.S. citizenship.

The interests of researchers differed from the interests of their employing institutions when considering who should have the authority to grant waivers to restricted individuals. Researchers wanted this authority to be vested in the hands of their employing institutions, whose officials would know them and their research. The institutions, on the other hand, wanted to avoid the liability that might accrue from having issued waivers, and they sought to vest the waiver authority with the government. Officials from the U.S. Department of Health and Human Services (HHS), which funds the vast majority of the federal government's biomedical research, considered these waivers to be a law enforcement and security matter and thus that they should be issued by the Justice Department. Officials from other departments, however, wanted waivers to be issued by an agency, such as the HHS, that understands the scientific research that those seeking waivers would be conducting. The final draft bill established conditions under which waivers would be allowed but it did not resolve who would issue them. Instead, it provided that the president would designate who would provide waivers sometime after the bill was passed.

During the course of 1999, agencies reached (or were instructed to reach) agreement on the wording of this legislation, and the result was informally transmitted to Congressional staff late in 1999. But it was not introduced as legislation until June 2000, when Senator Leahy, the senior Democrat on the Senate Judiciary Committee, introduced comprehensive anticrime legislation containing language on biological agents that was very similar to the administration's 1999 draft.[23] This bill was referred to the Judiciary Committee but received no legislative attention. Four months later, Senator Biden reintroduced the biological agent portion of this legislation with some minor changes.[24] He acknowledged that not enough time remained in the Congressional session for the bill to be considered but offered it for review and comment as an "initial draft that is a work in progress."[25]

9/11: Impact on U.S. Statutory and Regulatory Provisions

In the wake of the 9/11 terrorist attacks in the United States, the Bush administration proposed broad anti-terrorism legislation that returned to the issue of establishing additional controls over biological agents. This legislation took on new urgency with the death of a Florida man from inhalational anthrax and the discovery that his employer, a media organization, and several other media and also government offices had been attacked with anthrax through the U.S. mail system. The proposed legislation would:

—criminalize the possession of biological agents that had no justifiable purpose (described in the preceding section as "unlawful possession");

—ban the possession of select agents by "restricted individuals," who were defined in much the same way as they had been in the Clinton administration's draft legislation, with the reinsertion of the mental health provision and with the important exception that no waivers were provided at all; and

—establish a subset of the select agent list for which possession, use, and transfer would be regulated for national security purposes.

Legislation containing the first two of these provisions, but not the regulation of possession, use, and transfer, passed both houses of Congress on October 25, 2001, as part of the U.S. PATRIOT Act and was signed into law the next day.[26] Other provisions, such as a ban on the "unsafe handling" of biological agents, were introduced and, in some cases, passed by one house of Congress or the other, but these provisions did not become law.

Representatives of the scientific community had engaged in dialogue with Congressional staff members in both the House and the Senate during the consideration of these pieces of legislation, and they were instrumental in having the phrase "bona fide research" inserted into the list of legitimate purposes (along with prophylactic, protective, or other peaceful purposes) that the final law stated could justify the possession or use of biological agents.[27] But no hearings were held on these provisions before the bill's passage, and the urgency with which the issue was handled did not lend itself to the kind of deliberation and consideration that helps for reaching an appropriate balance between competing interests.

As a follow-up to the U.S. PATRIOT Act, the Public Health Security and Bioterrorism Preparedness and Response Act was passed on June 12, 2002. It contains a requirement to register the possession, use, or transfer of select biological agents and requires the secretary of health and human services to ensure that anyone seeking such registration has a lawful purpose to possess, use, or transfer them.[28] This legislation also establishes safeguards and security requirements for registered persons and creates criminal penalties for knowingly possessing unregistered select agents or for transferring select agents to persons who are not registered to possess or use them. Equivalent requirements are established, under the jurisdiction of the secretary of agriculture, for agricultural pathogens determined to have "the potential to pose a severe threat to animal or plant health, or to animal or plant products."[29] In addition, the Public Health Security and Bioterrorism Preparedness and Response Act requires background checks to be made on all seeking access to select agents to ensure that they are not prohibited from having such access, that they are not "reasonably suspected" of committing terrorism-related crimes or having "knowing involvement" in terrorist groups, and that they are not agents of a foreign power.[30] This legislation also restricts access to select agents to only those with a legitimate need for them. Regulations implementing the Health and Human Services and the Agriculture Department's responsibilities went into effect in February 2003.[31]

The Law Enforcement and the Scientific Communities: Differing Perspectives

The process of developing legislation to tighten controls on the possession, use, and transfer of biological agents illustrates the different motivations and perspectives of the scientific and the law enforcement communities and the tensions that these differences can generate.

The law enforcement community sought to achieve two fundamental objectives in tightening up biosecurity laws and regulations. First, it hoped to be able to prevent bioterrorism by placing those who are allowed access to dangerous pathogens under greater scrutiny; by tightening up physical access controls over those materials so as to make it more difficult for unauthorized individuals to obtain them; and by preventing untrustworthy or unreliable people (as defined by the "restricted individual" provisions) from gaining access to them. These provisions also provided a legal basis to prosecute individuals who are cultivating biological agents without a reasonable justification, whether or not the intent to use those agents as a weapon can be proven.

The law enforcement community had a second objective in pursuing this legislation, which may have been even more important. Widened controls over biological agents also extend the legal basis under which law enforcement officials can conduct investigations because investigations have to be tied to crimes. If intent to use a biological agent as a weapon must be proved before there is a crime, then police must have reason to believe that there is intent to use a biological agent as a weapon before they can even open an investigation. Conversely, without the requirement to prove intent to use biological agents as weapons, police are able to use their investigatory powers in situations where they suspect that biological agents are being amassed without legitimate purpose—even if there is no evidence of any intent to use those agents as weapons.

To reassure scientists worried that these new legal tools threaten to criminalize legitimate activity, law enforcement officials pointed out that securing convictions in the American legal system requires proving criminal violations beyond a reasonable doubt. Thus, the law enforcement community could argue, the scientific community should not worry about its freedom to operate under the new legal provisions. Bona fide research is explicitly mentioned as providing a legitimate reason to use biological agents, even though it could be argued that research is already included under protective, prophylactic, or other peaceful purposes. Therefore, according to the law enforcement community, no scientist whose activities could plausibly be described as research need fear unwarranted conviction. On the contrary, regulations tightening up controls over select biological agents are justified as a matter of community safety. They should not prevent any scientist or laboratory willing to comply with the new regulations from conducting any research they might like to do.

Leaders of the scientific community have acknowledged that institutions and individuals should be prohibited from possessing select biological agents unless they observe the appropriate biosafety and biosecurity conditions.[32] At the same time, it is recognized that "the biological community would be negligent to forgo measures that reasonably protect those pathogens and toxins that would cause the greatest consequences for society if used as weapons."[33] And the scientific community is well aware too that the ability to continue working with, and transferring, select biological agents depends on public confidence that health and safety will indeed be protected.[34] However, scientists are concerned that recently enacted measures may go too far and hinder research. Moreover, scientists and research administrators worry that the financial and administrative burdens and time delays associated with these new regulations will harm productivity and could even drive researchers and institutions out of the field, threatening the nation's ability to respond to bioterrorism and infectious disease.

In addition, as discussed above about the possession of select agents by "restricted individuals," the scientific community is concerned that the restrictions on foreign nationals and other restricted persons may not be sufficiently justified on security grounds, particularly as they are categorical bans with no waiver possible. A Massachusetts Institute of Technology (MIT) faculty committee concluded that the restricted person provisions "are not consistent with MIT's principles" and that "at some point, MIT may rightfully decide that on-campus research in areas governed by these regulations is no longer in its interest."[35] If scientists do not believe that security regulations and procedures actually contribute to security, they are not likely to implement those procedures and regulations effectively.

Finally, even for a scientist with no desire at all to pursue anything other than legitimate research with biological agents, the existence of criminal penalties casts a shadow that can impede creative research. Whether an innocent violation of regulations, a laboratory accident, or even innovative research warrants triggering an investigation or a prosecution ultimately depends on the prosecutor's discretion and judgment. Although the law enforcement community can claim that the burden of proof in a prosecution lies with the government and that any legitimate scientist should be able to raise the reasonable doubt that would prevent him or her from being convicted of a crime, the picture looks different from the perspective of someone facing prosecution. Winning an indictment or mounting an investigation faces a much lower threshold than securing a conviction, and a scientist forced to defend him/herself in the course of such an investigation can pay a tremendous price in terms of personal disruption and legal bills, even if the scientist ultimately "wins."

The tension between the law enforcement community's desire to criminalize illegitimate activity with biological agents and the scientific community's desire to ensure that legitimate research should not be impeded will be mirrored in any other country that enacts similar biosecurity legislation in compliance with UNSCR 1540's mandate. In view of the inherent dual-use nature of bioscience and biotechnology, this tension will be difficult to resolve in any country's legal system. On the one hand, these difficulties increase the value in sharing approaches that work. When the legal and the scientific communities in any country succeed in striking an acceptable balance between these competing objectives, other countries seeking to implement UNSCR 1540 by drafting similar biosecurity legislation can seek to emulate that success. On the other hand, to the extent that each state's legal system or constitutional context shapes the resulting balance—for example if striking an acceptable balance in the United States depends on the "beyond a reasonable doubt" standard that prosecutors must reach in order to attain criminal convictions—states must apply lessons learned from other states with care.

Applying the New Biosecurity Laws: Three Case Studies

As hard as these laws have been to devise, they have proven even harder to apply. There have been three notable cases in the United States in which these new laws have been exercised or at least considered. Unfortunately, the record of their application to date does not inspire confidence that the law enforcement community knows how and when to use them effectively. Whether or not the difficulty in implementing these laws is inherent in the ambiguity of science and technology and whether this difficulty will be overcome in time as additional experience is gained remains to be seen.

Tomas Foral

In July 2002 Tomas Foral, a graduate student of the University of Connecticut at Storrs' College of Agriculture and Natural Resources, became the first person to be charged under the biosecurity provision of the U.S. PATRIOT Act.[36] In late October 2001 Foral found a container labeled anthrax in a malfunctioning freezer he had been asked by a professor to clear out. The container held about half a dozen vials of cow tissue collected in the 1960s. Interpreting clear out to mean save what you can use and destroy the rest, he moved two vials to another freezer. However, the professor assumed that he had destroyed all the samples.[37]

One month later, as law enforcement authorities were investigating the anthrax death of Ottilie Lundgren, a 94-year-old woman who had lived about seventy miles away, they received an anonymous tip about Foral's vials and came searching for them. Foral turned them over on November 27, at which time the laboratory building was closed for a week. The frozen samples posed no threat to human health, although they could have enabled someone to cultivate anthrax. FBI agents investigated Foral and searched his home and his university office.

On July 22, 2002, Foral was charged with possessing a biological agent, *Bacillus anthracis* (anthrax), that was not "reasonably justified" by a peaceful, prophylactic, bona fide research, or protective purpose. Despite the efforts of his supervisors to explain that retaining samples was an accepted laboratory practice, the U.S. Attorney's office denied that he had a legitimate, bona fide research purpose in keeping them. "He wasn't authorized to save it," said a spokesman from the U.S. Attorney's office. "He had never done any research with anthrax, and he had no plans to do so." Foral faced a maximum sentence of ten years in jail and a $250,000 fine.[38]

Foral avoided prosecution by cooperating with the FBI, by agreeing to community service, and by accepting a letter in his Reserve Officers' Training Corps file attesting to his "illegal activities." He felt that he had no choice. "Lawyers are too expensive, and I'm in the midst of applying to medical schools."[39]

Thomas Butler

On January 13, 2003, Thomas Butler, a renowned researcher of plague at Texas Tech University, reported to university authorities the disappearance of thirty tubes of *Yersinia pestis* (bubonic plague). The next day, university officials informed the local health department and the police, who in turn contacted the FBI.[40] The FBI informed the White House and deployed sixty agents, which was what one report has called the largest single deployment of FBI personnel since the 9/11 attacks.[41]

After extensive interrogation, Butler signed a statement admitting that he had accidentally destroyed the vials himself and that he had then fabricated the story about the tubes' disappearance in order to account for the fact that he had not properly documented their destruction. He was subsequently arrested for lying to the FBI, a charge with a sentence of up to five years in jail.[42] In April he was indicted on eleven felony counts associated with the illegal import, export, or transport of plague cultures, for three felonies associated with lying to investigators and to the university (causing a false federal filing), and for one felony charge of tax evasion associated with a consulting agreement Butler had with a pharmaceutical firm to conduct a clinical trial.[43]

When he rejected a plea bargain in which prosecutors offered him a sentence of six months in jail and a fine if he pleaded guilty to several charges, Butler was indicted in August on sixty-nine felony counts.[44] In addition to the initial charges relating to the handling of plague cultures, he was indicted for a number of fraud and tax evasion charges stemming from his involvement in clinical trials. Since early 2001 he and the university had disputed issues associated both with the protection of human subjects during clinical trials and with the method in which he was recompensed. If convicted on all counts, he faced 469 years in jail and a $17 million fine.[45]

Butler went to trial in November 2003, with prosecutors alleging that he had fabricated the story about the theft of the plague vials so as to distract attention from his financial difficulties with the university and the Internal Revenue Service. On December 1 the jury returned a curious combination of convictions and acquittals. He was acquitted of the initial charge of lying to the FBI, of lying to the university, and of lying on his tax returns and also of fifteen of eighteen charges associated with the illegal handling of plague. On the other hand, he was convicted of forty-four of the fifty-four fraud counts, and there were also three convictions associated with an export of plague cultures to Tanzania in 2002. With a maximum sentence of 240 years in jail and millions of dollars of potential fines and with sentencing guidelines suggesting a nine-year term, Butler was sentenced to two years in prison. He also repaid Texas Tech University $250,000, resigned his post at the university, and gave up his medical license.[46] Butler appealed, but his conviction was upheld in October 2005 and the Supreme Court refused to hear his case. After serving twenty months of his sentence, he was released in December 2005.[47]

Steven Kurtz

On May 11, 2004, Steven Kurtz, an art professor at the State University of New York at Buffalo, awoke to find that his wife had passed away in the night. He called paramedics, who, upon responding, noticed test tubes, Petri dishes, and other biological laboratory apparatus in his home and contacted the Buffalo police. FBI agents later arrived on the scene, confiscated the laboratory material, and searched the house for two days before determining that the premises were safe and announcing that Kurtz's wife had died of natural causes.[48] Materials seized from Kurtz's home included samples of *Serratia marcescens,* a brilliant red bacterial strain typically used as an indicator, and *Bacillus atrophaeus,* a bacterial strain used as an anthrax simulant. Neither organism is on the select agent list, and both are considered harmless, although *Serratia marcescens* can cause a pneumonia-like illness, particularly in weakened patients.[49] The authorities also found a nonpathogenic strain of *E. coli.*[50]

Kurtz was a founding member of the Critical Arts Ensemble (CAE), a group of artists that uses human DNA and other biological materials to draw attention to political and social issues, including the use of biotechnology.[51] Law enforcement authorities continued their investigation, convening a grand jury in June. Eight of Kurtz's CAE colleagues were subpoenaed to appear before a grand jury in an investigation that they believed was being mounted under the bioterrorism provision of the U.S. PATRIOT Act.[52] However, when indictments were handed down at the end of June, the bioterrorism statute was not involved. Instead, Kurtz and a collaborator, Robert Ferrell, the chairman of the University of Pittsburgh's human genetics department, were each indicted on two counts of mail fraud and two counts of wire fraud, charges stemming from the manner in which the authorities alleged that Kurtz had obtained two of his microorganism cultures.

According to the indictment, Ferrell obtained the agents from the American Type Culture Collection under the terms of a material transfer agreement that precluded him from passing them to Kurtz, which he is alleged to have done.[53] Kurtz and Ferrell each face a maximum sentence of eighty years in prison and a $1,000,000 fine. By February 2005 Kurtz's attorneys had countersued, seeking the dismissal of the case and challenging the basis on which the search warrants were initially issued,[54] but as of May 2006, the case was still proceeding.[55]

Conclusion: Implementing UNSCR 1540

If there is a unifying theme to the three cases discussed above, it is that none of them were associated with terrorism—and yet law enforcement officials seemed determined to use them to send a message to the scientific community. Their approach seems to be one of making very public examples of alleged errant scientists, with the expectation that eventually their colleagues will understand that biosecurity regulations are to be taken seriously.

In the Foral case, it is questionable whether any violation of law occurred at all. In the Butler case, the preponderance of economic charges, coupled with a history of controversy between Butler and Texas Tech University, gives the appearance that the biosecurity criminal laws were being used to settle old scores—an impression strengthened by the fact that the jury failed to return convictions on the biosecurity charges that were most directly related to the original impetus for prosecution. Those charges, if proven, would have indicated a serious lack of commitment to appropriate biosecurity and biosafety procedures. However, they appear to have been uncovered rather serendipitously by an investigation originally motivated by the allegations of missing plague. And although the authorities in the Kurtz case acted appropriately when first confronting a fatality amid a collection of biological paraphernalia, the continued pursuit of criminal charges in the absence of any evidence of terrorist conduct or threats to public health or safety raises serious questions regarding prosecutorial discretion.

Law enforcement authorities are within their rights to demand compliance with the law, particularly when they need to call attention to changes in the law that may not be commanding community respect. But there may be better ways to gain respect for the new laws besides making public examples of a few scientists and hoping that all the others will fear they are next.

Perhaps it should not be surprising that the first few cases brought under the new laws have been weak. As time passes, it can be hoped that the law enforcement community will apply these new laws more effectively and also that a culture of responsibility may have developed further among the scientific research community. However, maladroit application of these laws and regulations has the potential to drive a wedge between the scientific and the law enforcement communities, creating tensions between communities that must work in partnership. More effective than forcing grudging compliance would be developing a culture of responsibility in which scientists believe the rules to be useful and work to implement them as a partner with, not an adversary of, the law enforcement community. Whether such a partnership can be successfully established may depend on how the next several such cases are handled.

Taking these experiences into account, one can conclude only that the record in the United States of drafting, enacting, and implementing biosecurity legislation has mixed implications for UNSCR 1540. It was difficult to draft legislation to criminalize various activities associated with bioterrorism, a difficulty compounded by the rush to enact legislation in the immediate aftermath of the 9/11 attacks and the October 2001 anthrax mailings. But that did not unduly impede research and other legitimate activities with biological agents. Nevertheless, the legislation that was enacted had at least the ostensible support of both the law enforcement and the scientific communities, offering a positive model for other countries pursuing similar legislation in accordance with UNSCR 1540.

Whether or not this new U.S. legislation actually provides American law enforcement authorities with useful tools that can frustrate bioterrorists without harming legitimate research remains to be seen. It is not yet clear whether or not legislation enacted pursuant to UNSCR 1540 actually serves to support the objectives and purposes of that resolution when implemented in practice. The prosecutions that have been pursued in the United States do not appear to have been aimed at anyone with malicious intent, although they may well have been motivated in part to show the scientific community that the new biosecurity regulations and laws must be taken seriously. However, this approach risks damaging legitimate scientific research, and in particular it threatens to disrupt the sense of cooperation and common purpose that must be fostered between the law enforcement and the technical communities in order to maximize the nation's ability to counter bioterrorism. Given the idiosyncrasies of every country's legal system and the culture of its law enforcement and scientific communities, it is not clear how these efforts will play out in other countries pursuing biosecurity legislation in accordance with UNSCR 1540.

Notes

1. This section draws on Gerald L. Epstein, "Controlling Biological Warfare Threats: Resolving Potential Tensions among the Research Community, Industry, and the National Security Community," *Critical Reviews of Microbiology*, Vol. 27, No. 4 (2001), pp. 321–54 (but especially pp. 321–35).

2. Convention on the Prohibition of the Development, Production and Stockpiling of Bacteriological (Biological) and Toxin Weapons and on Their Destruction, Article 1(1).

3. Public Law 101-298, May 22, 1990. This was enacted in the U.S. Code as 18 USC, sections 175–78.

4. Senate Report 101-210 accompanying S. 993, as described in Ronald M. Atlas, Kenneth I. Berns, Gail Cassell, and Janet Shoemaker, "Preventing the Misuse of Micro-organisms: The Role of the American Society for Microbiology in Protecting against Biological Weapons," *American Society for Microbiology*, at www.asm.org/Policy/index. asp?bid=3009.

5. James Ferguson, "Biological Weapons and U.S. Law," in Joshua Lederberg (ed.), *Biological Weapons: Limiting the Threat* (Cambridge, Mass.: MIT Press, 1999), p. 86.

6. "Packaging and Handling of Infectious Substances and Select Agents," Proposed Rule, *Federal Register*, Vol. 64, No. 208 (October 28, 1999), p. 58023.

7. See American Type Culture Collection, at www.lgcpromochem.com/atcc/.

8. Jessica Eve Stern, "Larry Wayne Harris," in Jonathan B. Tucker (ed.), *Toxic Terror: Assessing Terrorist Use of Chemical and Biological Weapons* (Cambridge, Mass.: MIT Press, 2000), pp. 234–35.

9. Ibid., p. 238.

10. Antiterrorism and Effective Death Penalty Act of 1996 (Public Law 104-132, April 24, 1996), section 511(e)(2).

11. Ibid., section 511(d)(1)(A).

12. Ibid., section 511(e)(4).

13. "Additional Requirements for Facilities Transferring or Receiving Select Agents; Final Rule," *Federal Register*, October 24, 1996, 61 FR 55189. This notice added sections 72.6 (Additional requirements for facilities transferring or receiving select agents), 72.7 (Penalties), and Appendix A (Select Agents) to the existing Part 72, Title 42 (Interstate Shipment of Etiologic Agents) of the Code of Federal Regulations.

14. Steve Ostroff, private communication, Centers for Disease Control and Prevention, September 14, 2001.

15. Atlas and others, "Preventing the Misuse of Microorganisms."

16. Testimony before the Senate Select Committee on Intelligence and the Subcommittee on Technology, Terrorism, and Government Information of the Senate Judiciary Committee, April 22, 1998, as quoted in testimony by Ronald Atlas, American Society for Microbiology, in prepared testimony before the House Energy and Commerce Committee, Subcommittee on Oversight and Investigations, Hearing on "Threat of Bioterrorism in America: Assessing the Adequacy of Federal Law Relating to Dangerous Biological Agents," May 20, 1999 (referred to below as Biological Agents Hearing), at http://frwebgate.access.gpo.gov/cgi-bin/getdoc.cgi?dbname=106_house_hearings&docid=f:57449.pdf, p. 51.

17. Testimony of Robert Burnham, Federal Bureau of Investigation, testimony in Biological Agents Hearing, at http://frwebgate.access.gpo.gov/cgi-bin/getdoc.cgi?dbname=106_house_hearings&docid=f:57449.pdf, p. 19.

18. "President Clinton and Vice President Gore: Reaching a Milestone in Law Enforcement and Public Safety," White House Fact Sheet, May 12, 1999, at http://clinton4.nara.gov/textonly/WH/Work/051299.html.

19. The attorney general raised this point in her April 22, 1998, testimony, as quoted in the testimony of James Reynolds, Department of Justice. See Biological Agents Hearing, at http://frwebgate.access.gpo.gov/cgi-bin/getdoc.cgi?dbname=106_house_hearings&docid=f:57449.pdf, p. 15.

20. Testimony of Ronald Atlas, American Society for Microbiology, at Biological Agents Hearing, p. 48.

21. Ibid., p. 49.

22. United States Code, Title 18, Section 922(g).

23. Section 3121 (Expansion of the Biological Weapons Statute) of S. 2783, a comprehensive bill entitled the "21st Century Law Enforcement and Public Safety Act."

24. S. 3202, the Dangerous Biological Agent and Toxin Control Act of 2000, introduced on October 21, 2000. The only significant difference between S. 3202 and the

earlier Leahy language (section 3121 of S. 2783) was the deletion in the former of the death penalty as a possible sentence for the development of biological agents as weapons when death results from the offense.

25. Senator Joe Biden, remarks in the *Congressional Record*, October 12, 2000, p. S10421.

26. Uniting and Strengthening America by Providing Appropriate Tools Required to Intercept and Obstruct Terrorism Act of 2001 (U.S. PATRIOT Act), Public Law 107-56, October 26, 2001.

27. Section 817 of the U.S. PATRIOT Act, amending and renumbering section 175(c) of Title 10 of the US Code.

28. Public Law 107-188, section 201(a), inserting a new section 351A into the Public Health Service Act. The registration requirement is specified in paragraph (d)(1) of the new section.

29. Public Law 107-188, section 212(a)(1).

30. Paragraph (e)(3)(B) of the new section 351A inserted into the Public Health Service Act by Public Law 107-188, section 201(a). As implemented by the Federal Bureau of Investigation, these background checks are repeated whenever a scientist seeking access to select agents changes employers, even though the background being checked will hardly have changed in the interim and would not have merited reinvestigation had the researcher remained at his or her original job.

31. See reference material on select agent regulations maintained by the American Society for Microbiology, at www.asm.org/Policy/index.asp?bid=6330.

32. "The ASM . . . continues to believe . . . that the law should prohibit institutions and individuals from possessing cultures of select agents unless such institutions or individuals maintain the agents under appropriate biosafety and biosecurity conditions." Testimony of the American Society for Microbiology before the Senate Judiciary Subcommittee on Technology, Terrorism and Government Information, presented by Ronald Atlas, President-elect, American Society for Microbiology and cochair, ASM Task Force on Biological Weapons, November 6, 2001, at www.yale.edu/lawweb/avalon/sept_11/atlas_001.htm.

33. Jennifer Gaudioso and Reynolds M. Salerno, "Biosecurity and Research: Minimizing Adverse Impacts," *Science*, Vol. 304, April 30, 2004, p. 687e.

34. As an example, the development of and compliance with shipping and packaging regulations on the part of the scientific community was necessary to convince the aviation industry that shipments of pathogens, including clinical samples, could be carried safely on airliners. In the absence of these regulations, there was the threat that airlines would refuse to carry biological samples. Personal communication, Dr. Ronald Atlas (who participated in negotiations on this topic with the aviation industry), February 15, 2005.

35. Report of the Ad Hoc Faculty Committee on Access to and Disclosure of Scientific Information, Sheila Widnall (chair), "In the Public Interest," Massachusetts Institute of Technology, June 12, 2002, p. iii, at http://web.mit.edu/faculty/reports/publicinterest.pdf.

36. Except as noted, the material in this section is from David Malakoff, "Student Charged with Possessing Anthrax," *Science*, Vol. 297, August 2, 2002, p. 751. Paul Zielbauer (compiled by Anthony Ramirez), "Metro Briefing Connecticut: New Haven: Anthrax Possession Charge," *New York Times*, July 23, 2002, p. B-6.

37. Jessica Snyder Sachs, "Will Terror Laws Give Science a Chill?" *Popular Science*, Vol. 262, No. 4 (April 2003), p. 30.

38. Idem.

39. Idem.

40. Martin Enserink and David Malakoff, "The Trials of Thomas Butler," *Science*, Vol. 302, December 19, 2003, p. 2059.

41. "A Poisonous Kind of Justice," *Belfast Telegraph*, August 31, 2004, at www.humanitarian.net/law/biodefense/sat_9404.html.

42. David Malakoff, "Plague of Lies Lands Texas Scientist in Jail," *Science*, Vol. 299, January 24, 2003, p. 490.

43. Indictment of Thomas Campbell Butler, United States District Court for the Northern District of Texas, Lubbock Division, Criminal Case 5-03CR0037-C, at http://fas.org/butler/indict.pdf.

44. Enserink and Malakoff, "The Trials of Thomas Butler," p. 2061.

45. Idem.

46. David Malakoff and Kelly Drennan, "Butler Gets 2 Years for Mishandling Plague Samples," *Science*, Vol. 303, March 19, 2004, p. 1743.

47. John Dudley Miller, "Supreme Court Won't Hear Butler Case," *Scientist*, June 2, 2006, at www.the-scientist.com/news/display/23453/.

48. David Staba, *New York Times* (late edition (East Coast)), June 7, 2004. p. B-5.

49. Jennifer Couzin, "U.S. Prosecutes Professors for Shipping Microbes," *Science*, Vol. 305, July 9, 2004, pp. 159–60.

50. Margaret Kosal, "Art or Bioterrorism? The Implications of the Kurtz Case," *CNS Research Story*, July 27, 2004, at http://cns.miis.edu/pubs/week/040727.htm #fnB6.

51. "Artist Resuming Work after Terrorism Probe," *Associated Press*, September 24, 2005.

52. Celeste Biever, "Bioterror Grand Jury Trial Begins for Professor," *NewScientist.com News Service*, June 15, 2004, at www.newscientist.com/article.ns?id= dn5109.

53. Joe Fahy, "Pitt Professor Indicted on Fraud Charge," *Pittsburgh Post-Gazette*, June 30, 2004, at www.post-gazette.com/pg/04182/339526.stm, and Press Release, U.S. Department of Justice, United States Attorney, Western District of New York, June 29, 2004, at http://buffalo.fbi.gov/dojpressrel/pressrel04/474.htm.

54. Carolyn Thompson, "Artist's Attorney Seeks Dismissal of Case," *Associated Press*, February 2, 2005, at www.16beavergroup.org/mtarchive/archives/001438.php.

55. Carolyn Thompson, "Trial, and Book Launch, of Indicted Artist Move Forward," *Associated Press*, May 18, 2006, at www.caedefensefund.org/press/AP_ 31806.pdf.

ROELOF JAN MANSCHOT

13

Prosecuting Violations of Non-Proliferation Legislation

Violations of legislation for the non-proliferation of weapons of mass destruction (WMD) confront prosecutors with a variety of obstacles to obtaining a conviction. This chapter describes some of these problems from a prosecutor's perspective and provides examples of cases that have or are due to come to trial in the Netherlands, the seat of several international courts in its capital, The Hague. The Netherlands is among the most densely populated countries in the world, and in 2004, the Dutch port at Rotterdam was Europe's largest (and the world's sixth largest) container port.[1] These factors suggest the challenges that confront European exporting, importing or transit countries in ensuring the safe and secure movement of goods, particularly when these are dual-use nuclear, chemical, and biological materials and delivery systems.

Issues Arising in Obtaining Convictions

The first problem concerns prosecutions aimed at averting the use of WMD. Although normally a prosecution takes place after an offense has been committed, it is manifestly important not to delay criminal investigation and prosecution in this instance until after the weapon has been used. Therefore the prosecutor has to look for a clear opportunity to act at an early stage in

The author would like to thank Professor Gerard A. M. Strijards of the University of Groningen and Mrs. Jacalyn Birk and Mrs. Christine McAlear of EUROJUST for their assistance with this chapter.

189

order to stop the sale, transfer, and storage of WMD, including their precursors, and also the transfer of technical knowledge, for example about how to build these weapons or to construct the necessary facilities to produce them. To this end, international criminal law has developed several legal grounds for establishing criminal accountability, such as "conspiracy"—acts at a very early stage of pursuing the criminal goal—that offer the prosecutor the chance to use his penal enforcement powers pre-emptively. Nevertheless, the probative problem remains: how to prove the subjective, that is psychological, elements or intent of the alleged crime before sufficient overt action has taken place.

In any country that upholds the rule of law, criminal investigation can be started when there is reasonable suspicion that a criminal offense has been or is about to be committed. A principal difficulty is knowing when this situation has arisen. Those who transfer the materials or the technical knowledge for creating WMD for economic or political reasons will not publicize their actions, and the recipients will want the process to be kept as secret as possible until the recently obtained or developed WMD are tested or used. The problem is how to collect the necessary evidence. In many legal systems, the relevant information from intelligence services, which traditionally "own" matters concerning WMD, cannot be used as evidence in a trial, and may only provide the grounds to start a criminal investigation.

Countries may of course use political pressure and diplomacy in order to try to stop other countries' WMD programs, as currently in the cases of North Korea and Iran, but this is not within prosecutorial competence. It would be unwise for a prosecutor to take a case to court when there is clearly insufficient evidence for a conviction. If states are accused of having WMD or related programs but this cannot be proved, embarrassing or counterproductive international situations could ensue. Meanwhile, if the accusations are true and steps are not taken to dissuade or otherwise prevent the proscribed activities, this constitutes a signal that the perpetrators can carry on their proliferation activities undeterred and possibly with greater ease. When non-state actors such as companies or individuals are being prosecuted, dismissal of the case by the court would have the same effect and could lead to the payment of damages to the former suspect.

Thus the prosecutor will have to choose the moment for issuing an indictment very carefully, so as to avoid either the failure of a dismissal or a delay during which proliferation takes place or, even worse, the weapons are used. Quite often this means that cases are not brought to court because of insufficient evidence, and the only action prosecutors can take is to inform their governments in confidence about the results of the investigation.

The Dual-Use Nature of Technology

A second problem for the prosecutor is the dual-use, civil–military nature of biological, chemical, and nuclear technology.[2] United Nations Security Council Resolution (UNSCR) 1540 mandates states to prevent non-state actors from proliferating not only WMD but also related materials. The latter are defined in a footnote to the Resolution as "materials, equipment and technology covered by relevant multilateral treaties and arrangements, or included on national control lists, which could be used for the design, development, production or use of nuclear, chemical and biological weapons and their means of delivery."

Many of the relevant precursors, as well as much of the equipment for making WMD, are freely available internationally, along with the necessary technical knowledge. Research laboratories, whether in private industry or universities, cannot be prevented from conducting peaceful research. Also, countries obtain nuclear technology in order to generate the necessary energy to develop their economies, and they conduct peaceful research in areas of biology and chemistry in the interest of public health, of great importance in view of the feared avian flu pandemic.

Legislators normally take this dual nature into account, as exemplified by UNSCR 1540, which states that "prevention of proliferation of nuclear, chemical and biological weapons should not hamper international cooperation in materials, equipment and technology for peaceful purposes while goals of peaceful utilization should not be used as a cover for proliferation." However, prosecutors are faced with the difficult prospect of having to prove at what point the peaceful development of a dual-use technology served as a cover for clandestine weapons programs or was involved with some other proscribed proliferation activity under the legislation required by UNSCR 1540.

How is a prosecutor going to prove that a seemingly innocent activity was a front for obtaining dual-use material or expertise for proscribed purposes before matters have progressed to a point where it is (almost) too late? A prosecutor planning to take a case to court wants clear evidence that an illegal act has occurred or that a criminal offense is going to be committed. In other words, he will have to prove the intent of the suspect. Gerald Epstein in chapter 12 of this volume provides examples of recent court cases in the United States the majority of which ended successfully because of plea bargaining, a practice that does not exist in most countries' civil and criminal law systems.[3] A different process exists in Japan, where the leader and members of the Aum Shinrikyo cult were successfully prosecuted for, among other things, using sarin gas in the Tokyo metro in 1995, because the juridical culture is one in which most successful convictions are a result of confession.

When goods or technology move across a border, the situation favors the prosecution more, particularly when legislation exists that forbids this transfer without an official government export license. In the past this legislation varied greatly between countries; but the adoption of UNSCR 1540 now means that all states should have such legislation, and also reinforced border and export controls, so that there are fewer safe havens, and legislation exists on the basis of which indictments and court cases may be heard.

Dr. A. Q. Khan was prosecuted in the Netherlands in the early 1980s for taking classified information (blueprints from Urenco's facility relating to the production of highly enriched uranium by means of ultra-centrifugation) and some small components without applying for a license, which he would never have obtained. A list of strategic goods and technology requiring an import and export license has been drawn up by the Dutch government, and special import and export licenses for specific strategic technology and equipment destined for export are issued on the basis of that list.[4] Lacking the necessary license constitutes a violation of this import and export law.

Maintaining Up-to-Date Control Lists and Trans-Shipments

A third, related issue that can affect prosecutions pertains to export controls, including the status of the technology in question on the annually updated list of strategic goods and technology. For example, goods such as computers or floppy disks were included on strategic export and import control lists in the 1960s and 1970s, when these items were relatively uncommon, but many of them were removed in the 1990s when they were no longer considered to have strategic defense value. Therefore, a prosecutor cannot bring a case regarding exportation without a license if the item was, at the time of prosecution, no longer on the list of prohibited goods or technology.

In accordance with Dutch criminal procedural law, the suspect may benefit from a change in the law taking place after the alleged offense was committed when this results from a change in opinion about what should be regarded as a criminal offense. But in the case of "S" discussed below, the Dutch Supreme Court ruled that it was not so much a change of opinion as a new evaluation of technology that caused the list to be updated. At the time of the export, the equipment and the technology were on the export control list, and it was clear that the intention of the suspect was to export without the necessary government license. For the time being, this problem has been solved in the Netherlands.

A more complex related issue concerns the reshipment of goods, whether as trans-shipments or in transit. Goods or technical knowledge on the strategic control list may be exported to, for instance, an ally or another NATO partner with the necessary export license. From there, the blueprints or the equipment could be forwarded to a third country to which the country of origin would not have granted an export license. This is because, as is often the case, the authorities of an intermediary or transit country do not have the information that would lead them to suspect the recipient state. The authorities of the country of origin sometimes ask for a declaration that the initial recipient country will not forward the equipment or the technical knowledge to a third country, but experience has shown that quite often such end-user documents are falsified for the equipment after arriving in an intermediary country. If the goods are a trans-shipment, they are repackaged into new containers (or into other means of transport to internal destinations), and thus they are more likely to be subject to inspection before being reexported. However, goods in transit often remain in their container under customs control while in an intermediary country before moving on to the next country, and the authorities may not be aware of a breach of declaration. A suspect may say that he knew only that the items were going to the country for which the license was given and that he was unaware that they were going to be forwarded. It is for the prosecutor to prove otherwise.

Jurisdiction

The fifth problem for the prosecutor concerns jurisdiction. Most countries must prove, via their criminal procedural legislation, that the offense being prosecuted has been committed within the territory of the prosecuting authority (the territorial principle). This burden of proof often poses a problem if a suspected non-state actor argues that there was no criminal intention or that the real offense has been committed elsewhere. Especially in the age of cybercrime, it may not always be easy to determine when and where classified, legally prohibited, or treaty-proscribed knowledge, particularly in electronic form, was actually transferred to an unauthorized party.

There are many dogmatic constructions, such as the theory of constructive presence, for "territorializing" acts that were physically committed abroad. But jurisprudence, be it at the national or international level, shows reluctance to accept these kinds of fiction, which are considered as startling or confusing metaphors. Some countries must also prove that a suspect is a citizen of the country initiating the prosecution, and he may then be prosecuted for any criminal offense he commits anywhere in the world (the principle of personality). Few countries claim the right to prosecute non-citizens committing criminal offenses outside their territory (the principle of universality), although there are an increasing number of offenses that may be prosecuted all over the world, for example hijacking and certain terrorist acts. In this context, the International Criminal Court (ICC) in The Hague was created specially to deal with genocide and war crimes, but the ICC has complementary jurisdiction only in regard to those states that have ratified the Statute of Rome of July 17, 1998, the treaty that established the ICC. The Statute of Rome came into force after the ratification by the sixtieth country on July 1, 2002.[5]

Several of the most important countries in the world, notably the United States and some potentially more aggressive nations, do not participate in the ICC's activities, thus allowing many atrocities to go unpunished if they are not dealt with in other courts or in other ways.

The Prosecution and Intelligence Trade-off

Even when a proliferation offense can be proved and jurisdiction can be established, a prosecution still might not take place, for intelligence reasons. Again the case of Dr. Khan is relevant, this time, however, for the proliferation of nuclear technology not to his home country, Pakistan, but to other countries, for example Libya, North Korea, and the Islamic Republic of Iran.[6]

The strategic position of Pakistan, first in relation to Afghanistan and later in the global war against terrorism, kept the United States in particular, at least since 1991, from making strong representations to the Pakistani government about the details, supplied by intelligence sources from various countries, of the apparently ongoing proliferation by the Khan network.[7] This proliferation was probably with the consent, if not the full cooperation, of successive Pakistani governments or at least of army leaders. Political pressure was put on the Pakistani government to change its attitude, but there was apparently no will to force the issue. When the Khan network's activities came more fully to light with Libya's declaration that it would stop its nuclear weapons development and reveal its sources of nuclear technology, the Pakistani government reacted quickly. It publicly shamed Dr. Khan, but it also granted him a general pardon after he promised to stop his proliferation activities. He was placed under house arrest, and remains in confinement as of July 2006. It is not convincing that since its nuclear test in 1998 Pakistan's development of nuclear facilities serves only peaceful purposes, even though it is not a signatory to the 1968 Nuclear Non-Proliferation Treaty.[8]

No prosecutor felt able to start a criminal investigation against the Khan network and other involved persons, even in those countries where the prosecution service is quite independent of its government, despite the fact that some jurisdictions have competence to prosecute or to try a suspect *in absentia*. It is not suggested that such a prosecution would have been an easy exercise, but there have been examples of prosecutors or investigating magistrates applying the principle of universality. Apparently, the more important goal of keeping Pakistan in the antiterrorism camp justified taking no prosecutorial action.

This does not mean that the prosecution of offenses against non-proliferation does not stand a good chance of success. As discussed below, analysis of an earlier conviction in the Netherlands and reference to a number of ongoing prosecutions and investigations demonstrates that there is no reason for pessimism, although patience, perseverance, and relevant expertise are required. The last is difficult to find in the average prosecutor, and it is important to ensure that the government is willing to supply the necessary cooperation both at home and at the international level in order to generate the vital evidence for a court conviction.

Successful WMD Prosecutions

In a case in 1985 in the district court of Alkmaar in the Netherlands, "S", a former acquaintance of Dr. Khan and also a metallurgical engineer, was accused of having exported, among other goods, either alone or through his limited company (of which he was the responsible CEO), a cathode-beamed oscilloscope without the necessary government license.[9] The final destination of the equipment was Pakistan, with the main component shipped through the port of Sharjah in the United Arab Emirates and some small components shipped directly. "S" was convicted by the district court on July 2, 1985, of a violation of the Import and Export Law in relation to the Export Decision on Strategic Goods. He was given a conditional prison sentence of six months and fined 20,000 guilders. Additionally, the seized equipment, worth approximately 100,000 guilders, was confiscated. This offense fell within the remit of Dutch economic criminal law, and thus the verdict was given by the economic chamber of the first instance court.

It should be mentioned here that although the Nuclear Non-Proliferation Treaty addresses states' nuclear weapons programs, a country's ratification (or accession) after signature of the Treaty means that its international obligations become part of domestic law and thus apply to individuals and other non-state actors of that state. UNSCR 1540 reinforces the obligations of states under the Treaty but it also goes further, requiring stronger export, physical protection, border, and financial controls and their enforcement, with a particular focus on non-state actors.

Although "S" admitted the offense, he appealed against the sentence at the Amsterdam Court of Appeal. The Court of Appeal, Economic Chamber, sentenced him on July 3, 1986, for the same offense and imposed the same sentences as before, although with a slightly different motivation.

"S" then appealed to the Supreme Court, and made the three arguments in his defense. First, the indictment was neither clear nor consequent because it did not clarify the relation between the mainframe of the oscilloscope and the other parts. Were there one or more violations of the Import and Export Law? On the one hand, the indictment stated that the radio emission part of the oscilloscope should have a band reach of no more than 100 MHz; but on the other hand, it indicates that this is a separate part. Therefore, the indictment should be declared null and void and the prosecution should restart the whole procedure because the defendant could not defend himself properly against an unclear indictment.

Second, the annually updated list of strategic goods for which a government import or export license is required is a law and not an addendum to a law. Under Netherlands law the defendant may benefit from a change in the law after the alleged crime if the change is in his favor. In this case, the accepted band reach of the radio emission part was, at the time of the export, limited to 100 MHz; but at the time of the trial the limit had been raised to 250 MHz. As the average reach in this case was around 180 MHz, this would mean that there was no longer a criminal offense.

At the time of this case in the 1980s, the list was updated every year after consultation with state members of CoCom (the Coordinating Committee for Multilateral Export Controls). The decision in this instance was that equipment with a band reach of over 100 MHz but less than 250 MHz was no longer regarded as technology that had to be protected for strategic reasons and that the parts themselves did not constitute a danger. Some goods are "permanently" on the list, although the technology is no longer a secret, and can provide a basis for monitoring their trade in the event of a future strategically adverse or destabilizing accumulation. An example is gunpowder: it has civilian uses but can be undesirable to export without a license when it will clearly be used for military purposes. Computers are another example. They were originally on the CoCom export control list; but most types had become so ubiquitous that when the Wassenaar Arrangement succeeded CoCom in 1996, many were taken off the list.

Third, the confiscation of the goods is too severe a penalty in relation to the financial situation of the defendant. The Court of Appeal did not explain why such a measure was justified.

The Supreme Court ruled on the three arguments as follows.[10] On the first one, the Court of Appeal did not give a clear decision on the defendant's assertion of a lack of clarity in the indictment concerning whether the strategic control list is the law itself or an addendum to it. The Court of Appeal stated that the indictment did make it clear that the list was the law itself, but it did not indicate why this was the case in its view. However, because at some time during the procedure the counsel for the defense had said that "in his view the indictment had not been sufficiently specific, but that he thought that he understood what its meaning was," there was no need to nullify the verdict, as this point was no longer of interest for the defendant. It seems to this author that the Supreme Court tried to save the case from a reopened trial.

On the second argument, the Court of Appeal had said that updating the strategic control list did not signify legislators' change of view about the necessity to exert control over the export of strategic goods as such. The list had been updated only in view of advanced technical developments, to make it clear to citizens which requirements still had to be met in case of import or export. Thus, the changes had significance *ad nunc* (at present/now) and not *ad tunc* (then).

On the third argument, the Supreme Court ruled that the Court of Appeal had not duly demonstrated why the goods had to be confiscated in relation to the defendant's financial situation, and so the case was referred to another court of appeal, but only on this point. The Court of Appeal, Economic Chamber, at The Hague rendered a verdict on June 17, 1988.[11] It stated that the defendant was motivated by financial profit and deliberately took the risk of exporting strategic goods without a government license and that therefore, in order to prevent similar acts in the future and taking into consideration the seriousness of the offense, confiscation was necessary and appropriate. The Court also considered the defendant's indication that in the meantime he had paid off the loan he had earlier needed in order to purchase the goods.

A further appeal to the Supreme Court failed because no reasons for the appeal were brought to its attention in time. The case ended on December 13, 1988, three-and-a-half years after the first instance court verdict and more than five years after the offense had been committed.[12]

A Similar Case

A similar case concerning illegal export of grenade shells (Supreme Court case number: 99.763 E) ended with a successful prosecution against the Company

"E" and one of its employees. The shells were exported without a license through Austria to Iran. In this case, the defense used similar and further arguments to those used by "S." The first argument was that the procedure had taken too long in relation to article 6 of the European Treaty on Human Rights. The alleged offenses had been committed in 1986 and 1987. The first instance court at Haarlem gave a verdict on December 21, 1990; the verdict of the Amsterdam Court of Appeal was given on December 11, 1992; and the Supreme Court's session took place on January 24, 1995. In the Netherlands the "reasonable time" mentioned in article 6 should normally not exceed two years from the formal beginning of the prosecution, and the period between the different instances also should not normally exceed two years. However, there may be exceptions, owing, for example, to the complexity of the case, to delay in part by the defendant and his counsel during the investigation, and to various court procedures. If these factors complicate the progress of the case unnecessarily, prolonging the "reasonable time" might be justified. The consequences of exceeding "reasonable time" can be either loss of the right to prosecute or a significant reduction in sentence, depending on the amount of time in excess.

The second argument was that in the indictment, the first reference to the destination of the goods, in this case shells for certain types of grenade, was not to the final destination (Iran). It is considered better to mention all the countries through which the goods have passed before reaching their final destination, but the Supreme Court ruled that it was enough if the facts made clear that in the end the goods went to a country for which an export license was necessary but not requested by the exporter.

The third argument by the defense was that the intention of the defendant to export the goods to Iran could not be proved because he had a license to export the goods to Austria and did not know that a portion of the goods were destined for Iran. It was not his responsibility to investigate whether the goods were going to be exported from Austria to another country. However, the evidence showed that the defendant had asked during the export process whether the goods were going elsewhere but had failed to wait for the answer. This was, in the view of the Court of Appeal, enough to establish that "the suspect thus wilfully took the fair risk that the goods mentioned in the indictment were not going to the Austrian Army but elsewhere." This principle is known in the jurisprudence of the Netherlands as the "conditional intention," which is enough to fulfill the judicial requirement for the intentional committing of a criminal offense.

A further argument was that there was no proof that a portion of the goods had actually reached Iran. It is up to the first instance courts and the courts of appeal to establish the facts. The Supreme Court only checks whether the reasoning in establishing the facts is sound; it does not examine the facts themselves. But it is clear that this situation may create a problem for the prosecutor. He has to prove that the goods reached their (prohibited) destination or, at least, that they did not get there because of circumstances that the defendant could not influence. Thus in a case where the goods did not reach their destination, the defendant might still be convicted for illegal export or for a criminal attempt to export. However, neither the perpetrator nor the country of final destination would be likely to inform the authorities that the goods had arrived.

So as in the case of Dr. Khan and Pakistan, it almost needs evidence such as a nuclear test explosion (which took place there) in order to demonstrate that the technology and the equipment are obviously in a particular country for the investigative process to be triggered of establishing and reconstructing how, when, and from where they came. It is not an easy task for the prosecutor when such evidence is not obviously available, as few people will be ready to enlighten him.

"S" Revisited

"S" did not learn much from his conviction. As of July 2005 an official criminal investigation against him had begun concerning the illegal export to Pakistan of equipment and a precursor through one or more companies of which he was the CEO or by "S" and these companies in concert.

"S" was convicted by the first instance Court of Alkmaar in December 2005 to six months' imprisonment, of which three months were suspended, and a fine of €20.000. Both the prosecutor and "S" appealed at the High Court of Amsterdam. The appeal is still pending.

The Prosecution against "A"

There is also an interesting case against "A," a Dutch national who is accused of willfully supplying Saddam Hussein's Iraq with precursors for the production of mustard gas and nerve gas and of willfully having given advice to the regime on how to produce chemical weapons. The chemicals were actually used with the intent to destroy national or ethnic groups totally or partly, and they killed members of these groups or inflicted heavy physical or mental damage on them in, among other places, Halabja and Goptata. This is a criminal offense according to articles 1 and 2 of the Implementation Law of the Genocide Convention in relation to articles 1 and 2 of the Convention on

Torture or, if this cannot be proved, a violation of article 8 of the Law on War Crimes. Of interest here is that the Chemical Weapons Convention of January 13, 1993, which forbids the development, production, storage, and use of chemical weapons and which was incorporated into Dutch law on June 8, 1995, could not be applied because the period of the offenses ended before the law came into effect.[13] In any event, this law is part of the law on economic crimes, which has much lower maximum penalties than the law on genocide, torture, and war crimes.

"A" is being prosecuted for being a willful accessory to crimes committed by persons in the former Iraqi regime. The *locus delicti* (place of the offense) is not a problem in this case because "A" has Dutch nationality and thus can be prosecuted in accordance with the previously mentioned personality principle, irrespective of where his alleged crimes took place.

"A" was convicted by the first instance Court of The Hague to fifteen years' imprisonment in December 2005 for war crimes. Both the prosecutor and "A" appealed at the High Court of The Hague. The prosecutor's view is that the conviction should have been for genocide. The appeal is still pending.

Conclusion

Several challenges and problems for prosecutors in securing a conviction have been identified. They cannot wait until WMD have been used, with high levels of casualties and injuries, if action can be taken to prevent use. But this action reduces their chance of gathering the necessary evidence, which is a problem in the first place. This is because most of the initial information about WMD normally comes from the intelligence services and, in many legal systems, may not be used as evidence.

Many WMD-related materials and precursors are of a dual nature, and as their peaceful use is a possibility, the prosecution will have to prove convincingly that the objective was to produce weapons. The rapid progress and dissemination of scientific and technological knowledge means that expertise and materials that are initially classified soon become common knowledge in the public domain.

Jurisdiction can be complicated to establish. There are differences in legal systems; the goods often pass through a number of countries before they reach their final destination; and the suspects may consist of a chain of legal or natural persons in several countries. Political and intelligence considerations may weigh against encouraging the prosecution service to do its job, and there is the additional problem that the judiciary has insufficient expertise in the technology of WMD and their related materials.

The investigations are therefore complicated and time-consuming, which may cause problems in relation to the "reasonable time" of article 6 of the European Treaty on Human Rights. The Netherlands' experience so far has been that the majority of the procedural obstacles are due to the difficulties in gathering evidence, to the dual-use nature of the materials and technology concerned, and to establishing the final destination of the goods. However, most of these difficulties can be tackled successfully. Moreover, the (international) legislation on WMD has been expanded significantly during the 1990s, thus providing the prosecutor more alternatives for drafting indictments. UNSCR 1540, adopted on April 28, 2004, is helpful in this respect. In its operative paragraph 2 it is foreseen that "all States, in accordance with their national procedures, shall adopt and enforce appropriate effective laws which prohibit any non-State actor to manufacture, acquire, possess, develop, transport, transfer or use nuclear, chemical or biological weapons and their means of delivery, in particular for terrorist purposes, as well as attempts to engage in any of the foregoing activities, participate in them as an accomplice, assist or finance them."

If all states live up to this obligation, it will be easier for prosecutors to draft indictments because legislation will be in place in all countries as a result of UNSCR 1540's universal mandate. Nonetheless one cannot be overoptimistic because there is no real sanction mechanism in place for those states that (deliberately) do not fulfill this obligation and use the cover of dual-use technology to conceal a clandestine WMD development program. However, the Resolution's adoption is a step in the direction of enforcing states' existing obligations under the main WMD treaties for which ratification and enforcement remain outstanding. UN member states still have much to do to comply fully with the Resolution and to incorporate its contents into their national law.

As criminal proliferation activities are rarely of a purely national character, there is a growing need for international cooperation in order to bring suspects to trial successfully, before WMD have been used, and as early as possible in the process of proliferating technology, precursors, and equipment. UNSCR 1540 calls on all states to "promote dialogue and cooperation on non-proliferation" (operative paragraph 9) or "take cooperative action" (operative paragraph 10) to combat proliferation of nuclear, chemical, and biological weapons, related materials and delivery means. In this respect, EUROJUST, the European judicial cooperation unit, can play an important role. The unit's core purpose is the coordination of investigations and prosecutions of serious cross-border crime. It can also initiate investigations and prosecutions, gather all the competent authorities concerned to analyze a case, coordinate the efforts of all the participants, and set up arrangements between the parties on further procedures and on establishing a working plan covering the allocation of roles, both leading and support.

This may even be done through the creation of a joint investigation team, in which two or more European member states participate. Non-member states may be invited to participate in the deliberations, which is already the practice, for example, in countering terrorism. So instead of individual, often splintered, investigations and prosecutions by one country, it is now possible for different jurisdictions to join forces for more effective action through combining the available evidence and coordinating subsequent investigations and prosecutions on a European Union level.

As stated earlier, there is no reason to despair. Often action will be taken too late, and that gives cause for concern. When proliferation is evident, a prosecution will still not be easy (but a prosecutor's job is not supposed to be easy). However, it is not an impossible mission. A well-prepared prosecution stands a good chance of succeeding with a conviction, and the prosecutor must be prepared to take a risk—and in this field probably a higher risk than usual—because the interest of society in bringing a suspect of these kinds of crimes to trial is far more important—even if the end is an acquittal—than not bringing that person to trial at all.

Notes

1. Judith Rehak, "Every Port in a Storm: China Is the Center of a Global Boom in an Increasingly Strategic Sector," *International Herald Tribune*, March 25–26, 2006, p. 16.

2. See Gerald L. Epstein, "Controlling Biological Warfare Threats: Resolving Potential Tensions among the Research Community, Industry and the National Security Community," *Reviews of Microbiology*, Vol. 27, No. 4 (2001), pp. 321–54.

3. Ibid.

4. *Uitvoerbesluit Strategische Goederen* [Export Resolution on Strategic Goods], 1963.

5. The jurisdiction of the International Criminal Court is restricted in the sense that it is competent only in the states that ratified the statute. Moreover the court has a complementary function: it can only act when the authorities of the states involved cannot or do not want to prosecute the case. The ICC prosecutor can only investigate on the territory of a state with the consent of that state. The jurisdiction of the court is limited to the crime of genocide, crimes against humanity, war crimes, and the crime of aggression.

6. Gaurav Kampani, "Proliferation Unbound: Nuclear Tales from Pakistan," CNS Research Story, Center for Nonproliferation Studies, Monterey Institute of Interna-

tional Studies, February 23, 2004, at http://cns.miis.edu/pubs/week/040223.htm, and Leon Weiss, "Turning a Blind Eye Again? The Khan Network's History and Lessons for U.S. Policy," *Arms Control Today*, Vol. 35, No. 2 (March 2005), at www.armscontrol.org/act/2005_03/Weiss.asp.

7. Krishnadev Calamur, "Dutch Say CIA Resisted Khan Arrest," ISN Security Watch, August 12, 2005, at www.isn.ethz.ch/news/sw/details.cfm?ID=12443.

8. Mohamed ElBaradei, "In Search of Security: Finding An Alternative to Nuclear Deterrence," presentation at CISAC, Stanford University, November 4, 2004.

9. In the Netherlands, the use of a suspect's or a convict's full name is generally not permitted.

10. Supreme Court of the Netherlands, HR 24 November 1987, nr. 81.744 E.

11. Gerechtshof te 's-Gravenhage [Court of Appeal of The Hague], vijfde Kamer [5th Chamber], rechtdoende in economische strafzaken [For economic criminal cases], rolnummer [reference number] 2200243287.

12. Supreme Court of the Netherlands, HR 13 December 1988, nr.84.960 E.

13. Uitvoeringswet Verdrag Chemische Wapens, Trb. 1995, nr. 338.

PART IV

UNSCR 1540 and Effective Global Governance

OLIVIA BOSCH *and* PETER VAN HAM

14

UNSCR 1540:
Its Future and Contribution to Global
Non-Proliferation and Counter-Terrorism

Until 9/11 the United Nations was, in terms of effectiveness, a marginal actor in dealing with international terrorism. But since the "war on terror" took preeminence in the security agenda of the United States, the UN has had little choice other than to prove its relevance in a vastly changed strategic environment. In his speech to the UN General Assembly on September 12, 2002, President Bush argued, "All the world now faces a test, and the United Nations a difficult and defining moment. . . . Will the United Nations serve the purpose of its founding, or will it be irrelevant? . . . We cannot stand by and do nothing while dangers gather."[1] The president's important message was that the UN could become obsolete if it did not act forcefully and effectively to fight the new threat of terrorism, seen as "catastrophic" in view of the potential use of nuclear, chemical, and biological weapons. UN Secretary General Kofi Annan's subsequent speeches and reform proposals as well as UNSCR 1540 (April 2004) were aimed to address these challenges.

Together with the Counter-Terrorism Committee (CTC) that resulted from UNSCR 1373, the 1540 Committee has become the principal instrument whereby the UN can "prove its relevance" in dealing effectively to keep WMD out of the hands of terrorists. In taking these steps, the UN has become the prime mover in extending existing WMD proliferation norms to non-state actors as diverse as terrorists, academic researchers, the industrial sector, and individuals.[2] The UN has sought to fill gaps in international law by applying to non-state actors prohibitions similar to those states already face, primarily by way of the three main WMD treaties.[3]

Over the decades the UN has codified more than a dozen global conventions related to terrorism in its many different forms. However, these conventions were hardly monitored and implemented, which made them de facto dead letters and limited the UN's practical contribution against terrorism. According to Martha Crenshaw, this lack of follow-up was mainly because "there appeared to be no penalties for non-compliance. Nor were there concrete rewards for cooperation."[4] This changed altogether when, in the wake of 9/11, UNSCR 1373 put into place mandatory requirements that all states report on the status of their counter-terrorism legislation. Where legislation was lacking, or where the numerous conventions had yet to be signed and ratified, laws and enforcement measures had to be put into place.[5]

UNSCR 1540 followed in the footsteps of 1373. One of its key objectives is to oblige all states to penalize WMD proliferation within their national legal systems and jurisdictions. Thus UNSCR 1540 also has the effect of prohibiting states from outsourcing to non-state actors the procurement of WMD technologies, as in the case of Iran's use of the illicit A. Q. Khan trafficking network for proscribed nuclear technology.[6]

Since the UN lacks the capability to monitor, verify, and implement these new obligations, it needs the active cooperation of states and international organizations as well as of relevant actors within states. Although Resolution 1540's global application focuses on the proliferation behavior of non-state actors, states themselves must adopt legislation and a variety of controls and enforce them against these non-state entities in accordance with domestic and international law. The essential requirements for states are outlined in operative paragraphs 1–3, with operative paragraph 8(d) being a longer-term and far-reaching objective that the authors of this chapter draw attention to as it more closely involves the work of industry and academia which have the technical expertise and related materials that can be of interest to traffickers and terrorists. States in effect comply with the Resolution when they implement and enforce a range of measures by generally undertaking the following:

—ratification (or accession) of, not just signing, the main WMD treaties. The emphasis is on setting national legislation, not the treaties per se, in accordance with operative paragraphs 1–3;

—increased physical protection of sensitive dual-use materials and also new border, customs, and financial controls,

—strengthening existing export controls, and

—new ways to work with industry and academia, such as science codes of conduct, so that they fulfill their legal obligations under the Resolution (operative paragraph 8d).

Although national legislation is the basis for the criminalization and control of WMD proliferation, actual implementation requires the full support of all relevant actors. This book has examined in depth how states and relevant international organizations are, and will continue to be, incorporated further in any strategy aimed at keeping WMD proliferation at bay. Adopting a Resolution at the UN Security Council will not by itself deal with the nexus of proliferation and terrorism. Without UNSCR 1540, however, no formal, normative and enforcement framework would exist to provide legitimacy for this global agenda. For the first time the Security Council has affirmed by a Chapter VII resolution the proliferation of nuclear, chemical, and biological weapons *and* their means of delivery as a threat to international peace and security; and, uniquely, it has identified the illicit trafficking of these weapons, related materials and means of delivery as a threat too.

This chapter offers an interim assessment of UNSCR 1540 within the larger context of global governance issues concerning non-proliferation and counter-terrorism efforts. The chapter provides an overview of the work of the 1540 Committee and examines insights obtained from states' implementation of the Resolution as a way to assess how successful it has been in contributing to global non-proliferation. Finally, it draws conclusions from the two and a half years of the Resolution's existence concerning the type of global governance arrangement that can deal effectively with the dangerous nexus between WMD proliferation and terrorism.

The 1540 Committee

On April 27, 2006, the UN Security Council adopted Resolution 1673, renewing the work of the 1540 Committee for another two-year period.[7] UNSCR 1540 had limited the committee's initial mandate to no more than two years to end with a report to the Security Council on how well states had implemented the Resolution's objectives.[8] In preparing for this report, the first two years of the work of the committee, and of the group of experts appointed to support it, focused on obtaining reports from states on what steps they had taken or intend to take to comply with the Resolution, setting up a global legislative database and creating a matrix of the types of legislative and control measure that a country might adopt in order to comply with UNSCR 1540. The legislative database provides information on states' national legislation and measures related to the Resolution. In the interest of transparency, it includes original texts of laws, decrees, and other decisions concerning the Resolution that are publicly available, including from the Internet. The database has proved to be useful as a tool in assisting states to update their initial reports and as a resource for those states that still have to submit their first report.

Most states' reports clearly spell out what kind of legislation, programs, and initiatives are in place for dealing with WMD proliferation on the national level. They provide information on the country's membership in a variety of WMD-related treaties, informal arrangements, organizations, and export control regimes. Some reports are rudimentary, merely indicating that the country is not involved in the export or import of WMD and that there is no direct and pressing need for further legal action. It is here that the 1540 Committee becomes involved, because many national laws and regulations, export and border controls, and other elements of a national non-proliferation system have gaps and loopholes.

Implementing the requirements of UNSCR 1540 implies that several government departments must be involved, ranging from the ministries of foreign affairs and defense to trade. The 1540 experts group realized the need for this wider cooperation, and from its realization arose the creation of the legislative database.[9] The experts group's examination of legislation reveals gaps, so that states can request assistance to further develop their legislation and other controls to implement it. The matrix developed by the committee was an essential measure that in turn has become a means by which future assistance can be facilitated, in accordance with operative paragraph 7. The 1540 Committee acts as a clearing house for such offers and requests. If asked, it will channel requests to states as well as to international organizations that have relevant training programs, such as the Organisation for the Prohibition of Chemical Weapons (OPCW) and the International Atomic Energy Agency (IAEA).

The next phase of the committee's work will be to continue with these tasks, as well as with obtaining reports from states that have yet to submit their initial report. Following a new detailed "program of work,"[10] regional meetings and outreach activities will continue to take place so as to raise awareness of the Resolution among the 62 states that (as of April 2006) have not submitted first reports, 55 of which are in three geographical areas: Africa, the Caribbean, and the South Pacific. The committee's work will therefore focus on the outreach and dialogue activities, trying to encourage first-time reporting as well as to foster additional, subsequent reporting. The fifth work program also includes examination, not just compilation, of states' reports to facilitate implementation of the Resolution. Additionally, the work program reinforces UNSCR 1673's operative paragraph 5b for the 1540 Committee to explore making a catalogue of "best practices," drawn from national practices as well as international, regional and sub-regional organizations, thus offering concrete guidelines to states on how to implement the Resolution's requirements.

Measures of Success: A Positive Scorecard

Given the Chapter VII nature of UNSCR 1540, which means that its requirements are legally binding and implies a route to sanctions for non-compliance,
it is politically pertinent to assess critically the Resolution's practical contribution to halting, or managing, WMD proliferation. However, measuring success
in dealing with security issues is not straightforward. First, it is assumed that
proliferation remains a security issue. Thus while the initial priority is to monitor proliferation and to establish institutions both to prevent incidents and to
mitigate adverse effects when prevention fails, counter-proliferation is a management process rather than a final product or a fixed end point. Second, it is
difficult to measure success in preventing security problems. In view of the
often discrete nature of operations for thwarting proliferation, one cannot
always advertise their success without compromising the means and methods
of the intelligence community, the traditional domain of counter-proliferation.
Third, many of the technologies underlying nuclear, chemical, and biological
weapons are now universally available, in varying degrees, for perfectly legitimate purposes. There have been few cases in which terrorist groups have used
such dual-use technologies to develop non-conventional weapons; but even so,
constant alertness remains essential. In light of these caveats, this section will
examine some indicators that can be used to assess how effective UNSCR 1540
has been in forging a more robust and effective global non-proliferation
regime.

Reporting

The first step toward the Resolution's success is states' initial reports to the
1540 Committee, which should have been submitted by October 28, 2004.
These reports are in themselves an important indicator of states' awareness of
the WMD proliferation threat. Although there was some criticism that no
standards were set for the nature and quality of first reports, the variety of submissions made without established criteria was valuable as a baseline indicator of what states understood or perceived as the threats identified and the
issues posed by 1540.

The initial reading of these reports by the 1540 Committee and its experts
group led to the subsequent devising of a standardized matrix format for future
reporting to help the experts and states identify remaining gaps in legislation
and other controls. The matrix has approximately 380 data elements, such as
a country's status on its export controls, its legislation for dealing with each of
the three WMD treaties, and what measures it has taken to protect sensitive
materials. But states do not need to provide all these or to follow a standard

procedure. For example, states that lack relevant industrial or scientific assets may decide to take advantage of a "catchall" approach and cover all nuclear, biological, and chemical weapons and delivery systems in one piece of legislation. The committee's fifth program of work will enable the committee to explore further the Resolution's definitions including what is to be considered "dual use," as well as stimulate tailored dialogue and offer technical assistance to encourage further reporting. These questions have been prompted by calls for standards for reporting and legislation to which the matrix will have contributed much toward achieving.

The 1540 Committee's April 2006 report to the Security Council gives a general impression of how states have implemented the Resolution, but the 62 non-submissions make a full assessment difficult. According to the report, "The reasons for not submitting national reports as well as for the gaps in national implementation result from insufficient understanding, lack of capacity, and different national priorities."[11] A country's lack of capacity or awareness that its territory may be part of a trafficking route or a front company location for illicit networks (akin to that of A. Q. Khan) is the most likely reason for not satisfying the Resolution's requirements. Still, that 129 states submitted reports by April 2006 is a sign of UNSCR 1540's initial success. And although submitting reports is easier than putting in place the national legislation and the wide spectrum of controls required, the process of preparing a report has enhanced the awareness of government officials across departments in many states of the variety of issues arising from Resolution 1540. This is an intangible but important part of its success.

Intelligence Sharing

Another measure of success is the level of effectiveness of intelligence and information sharing. The Resolution calls on "all States to promote dialogue and cooperation on non-proliferation" (operative paragraph 9), and when taking action to prevent the illicit trafficking of related materials, to do so in a "cooperative" manner (operative paragraph 10). Clearly, such activities require at least some degree of intelligence sharing. It is especially important now to encourage the sharing of data, information, and intelligence because terrorist groups such as Al-Qaeda are widely reported to be interested in obtaining a nuclear capability[12] and to have tested aspects of a chemical weapons capability.

The need for effective intelligence was raised pointedly by the U.S. director of national intelligence, John D. Negroponte[13] when commenting on the crucial role that intelligence sharing has played in strengthening counter-terrorism efforts in the aftermath of 9/11. Shortcomings in the intelligence and law enforcement communities' capacities for sharing intelligence in the run-up to

9/11 were widely reported, and Negroponte and others have tried to address this problem over the past five years. One result was the sharing of U.S. and Pakistani intelligence so as to assist the United Kingdom in thwarting the alleged terrorist airline plot in August 2006. The importance of an improved approach to information sharing becomes even more noticeable when dealing with intelligence on WMD, one of the traditional domains of the intelligence community. This is the new challenge set by UNSCR 1540, and the United States has tried to meet it by situating its National Counterterrorism Center next to the newly created National Counterproliferation Center and by creating a WMD division within the Federal Bureau of Investigation in an effort to boost domestic counter-terrorism know-how and efforts. In the spirit of 1540's challenge to states to inform and work with industry and the public (operative paragraph 8(d)) to prevent the misuse or otherwise malicious or ill-intentioned use of WMD, related materials, and delivery means, the United States has also created a WMD Innovation Fund for the intelligence community's collection, analysis, and science and technology projects.[14]

One of the main achievements of UNSCR 1540 is that it provides a framework within which states can inquire about each other's actions or intentions when there are developments that could suggest the acquisition or potential use of WMD. Assessments of intent are essential in the context of increased attention to the acquisition of weapons or component parts. They require good intelligence in order to inform decisions "to act against such emerging threats [of WMD proliferation by terrorist groups and rogue states] before they are fully formed."[15]

Enforcement and Prosecution

Submitting reports and information and enacting legislation are only the first steps toward UNSCR 1540 achieving success. Enforcement of that legislation and accompanying regulations is also required. Unlike traditional treaty regimes, the Resolution imposes obligations on all states that, in light of Chapter VII of the UN Charter, are urgent and mandatory and imply sanctions for non-compliance. In this discussion, the most relevant development is that if states do not comply with UNSCR 1540, other countries can now ask questions about what they are doing to contain suspect proliferation activity on their territory in the spirit of operative paragraph 9. States can no longer avoid answering such questions without arousing suspicion. If suspicions remain unaddressed, then issues of non-compliance could arise.

The Proliferation Security Initiative (PSI) is seen as one of the main tools by which "coalitions of the willing" can take cooperative action on enforcement.[16] In accordance with the Resolution's operative paragraph 10, such action could include "interdiction" as practiced by the PSI's participating states, even though that word was deleted from a draft of Resolution 1540 during its negotiation. One measure of success might thus be in terms of the number of PSI-like interdictions, of which about three dozen had been reported by June 2006.[17] Bare numbers, however, do not indicate much about the degree to which these interdictions hamper proliferation, as intelligence successes are shy of publicity and it is difficult to measure illicit activities not undertaken. It remains unknown whether prosecutions have taken place as a result of these interdictions. The levels of funding, staffing, training, and exercises for undertaking interdictions are also often reported as measures of success,[18] but these types of input too indicate little about the outcome achieved.

The implications of enforcing Resolution 1540 are therefore especially significant for those states that have no watertight national legal framework in place to satisfy the new UN requirements. These are substantial, and meeting them demands effort and commitment. But there is no clarity as to how those states should proceed. It remains unclear as to who will decide when a state is not complying with the demands of the Resolution, and if they are not, what will happen. Despite the fact that UN member states have a collective security responsibility, this lack of clarity reflects concern about state sovereignty and non-interference in states' internal affairs. Although all states are now obliged to control and monitor what happens on their territory more closely, a state may still be unaware of illicit trafficking associated with proliferation. Resolution 1540, in effect, requires states to take more responsibility for countering WMD proliferation with respect to non-state actors.

The mandatory character of Resolution 1540 implies that both military and non-military sanctions could be pursued in accordance with further decisions by the Security Council. However, debates before the adoption of the Resolution indicated that resort to military force as a preventive enforcement tool is not yet an accepted option in the range of counter-proliferation measures.[19] The potential use of preventive force was hotly debated in the summer of 2006 against the backdrop of deliberations in the Security Council over the status and intent of Iran's nuclear technology research and development activities, which suggested that it was seeking a nuclear weapons capability.[20] When the UNSC can or will impose sanctions on states that are in breach of Resolution 1540's obligations, and whether this requires another UNSC resolution, remains to be determined. This issue is addressed in operative paragraphs 11 and 12 of the Resolution.

Another measure of Resolution 1540's success is prosecution under the relevant legislation, which makes all forms of proliferation a criminal or civil offense. This highlights the Resolution's emphasis on enforcement, which is lacking in existing WMD treaties and in many export control agreements. Prosecutions not only may deter all but the most determined potential terrorists but also show that states have both the political determination and the juridical capacity to prosecute. Even so, there is a security trade-off between prosecuting and refraining from doing so if instead more intelligence might be acquired for valuable leads for interdicting and thwarting the actual use of WMD.[21]

The Centrality of Technical Engagement

Controlling the transnational trade in WMD and related materials, technologies, and knowledge is key to dealing effectively with the threat of terrorism. But as determined terrorists are unlikely to seek an export license for the materials they require, toughening customs and export control standards is only part of the job at hand. Strengthening fences is an important part of the nonproliferation effort. But, as this book has indicated, the very nature of the challenge requires broad societal support based on a "culture of responsibility."

Perhaps among the strongest reasons for UNSCR 1540 was to fill the gap still left in the management of bioweapons proliferation. This is also the reason why this book has paid much attention to the impact of UNSCR 1540's requirements for biotechnology and bioweapons. In sharp contrast to the nuclear and chemical fields, in which the NPT/IAEA and the CWC/OPCW play a central role, the management and control of bioweapons lack strong and effective treaties and verification regimes. Since bioweapons may be relatively easy to produce to devastate economies or unsettle societies, they may well become more of a weapon of choice of terrorists, fanatics, and lunatics in the future. Resolution 1540's efforts to fill the gaps that exist in national legislation in the area of bioweapons were discussed at the Sixth Review Conference of the BWC at the end of 2006.[22]

The lessons learned from the engagement of scientists and technicians who have worked in former state WMD programs contribute to fostering a nonproliferation culture worldwide. The law enforcement and intelligence communities are concerned with ascertaining the intent not only of traffickers and terrorists but also of scientists and engineers with knowledge of WMD weaponization or dual-use technology processes who might be compromised and forced to aid terrorist or other criminal purposes. This expertise would be found among the technicians, scientists, engineers, and military personnel who were associated with former WMD programs in states such as the former Soviet Union, apartheid South Africa, Libya, and Iraq. Numerous international programs, including the work of the International Science and Technology Centers, and G-8 action plans have been established in order to deal with anxieties about the potential use of their skills in countries of proliferation concern. Many of the programs also instill non-proliferation norms into the redirected work or over-hauled education systems of these scientists and academics.[23]

These efforts can be seen to fall within the objectives of the Resolution's operative paragraph 8(d), according to which states are to work with and inform industry and the public about their obligations in helping to achieve non-proliferation. Operative paragraph 8(d) is vague, but any number of activities can contribute to states' efforts in effectively implementing this part of UNSCR 1540. They would include free and open interaction between the expert industry and the academic research community, on the one hand, and their counterparts in the medical, public health, and clinical laboratories in each country, on the other hand. The United States alone has more than 150,000 clinical laboratories, which cannot be monitored effectively without their full and voluntary cooperation in complying with biosafety and bio-security measures. The American Society for Microbiology has estimated that within the United States, some 300 institutions (excluding the clinical labo-ratories that are exempt from registering under the existing regulations) are in possession of "select agents."[24] This implies that if the scientific and tech-nical community—in effect every individual researcher—does not believe that the security regulations and procedures imposed on it contribute effec-tively to societal security, the implementation of these regulations will be extremely difficult. It could be done only at a high cost, and at the expense of scientific innovation and output.

Some of the case studies presented in this book—on the Tomas Foral, Thomas Butler, and Steven Kurtz prosecutions—indicate that law enforce-ment authorities (in these examples, in the United States) may use borderline cases to call attention to changes in the law that may not yet command the respect of the research community.[25] While there may well be more effective methods with which to gain respect and attention for these new laws, there might also be a backlash against them. The maladroit application of these new laws and regulations, many of them falling within the scope of responsi-bility of Resolution 1540, could drive a wedge between law enforcement authorities and the scientific community, as indicated in the American case studies.

More effective than grudging compliance, however, would be to develop a "culture of responsibility" in which scientists and other practitioners actually believe the rules to be useful and effective. If this belief is internalized and the non-proliferation norm is established within the relevant communities, implementing UNSCR 1540 would be much helped. The U.S. post–9/11 examples may be a positive model for other countries to emulate in pursuing similar legislation in the context of Resolution 1540. But given the idiosyncrasies of each country's legal system and the very different cultures and structures of law enforcement and scientific communities, it remains unclear how the American model of (voluntary) cooperation will play out across the world. More success might be made instead of the "good practice" that the large biotechnology industry leaders might instill across the globe.[26]

Because biotechnology is integrated into a large number of products, the criteria for determining which individuals, companies, and materials require "proliferation oversight" in the context of Resolution 1540 are blurred. Moreover, the dual-use nature of many advances in the biological sciences may result in undue impediments if the regulatory net is cast too wide. This implies that it will at times be difficult to strike a balance between competing security requirements.[27]

New dilemmas arise as naturally occurring diseases, now killing more people than the malicious use of bioweapons has in the past three decades, require bolstered public health services to diagnose, treat, and vaccinate a large number of people around the world. This requires crucial and increased cooperation among bioscientists and public health specialists. But these new relationships carry the increased risk of transferring knowledge, know-how, and materials with bioweapons and illicit trafficking potential. Shipping vaccines, viruses, cell cultures, and the tissues of patients, all of which are required to make a concerted research effort possible as well as improve response capabilities, is highly complicated in an environment that restricts these interchanges for classical security reasons (as embodied in Resolution 1540). The Sixth Review Conference of the BWC also reinforced these issues, highlighting the number of regional and international organizations involved, including those concerning plant and animal disease, and the need for continued information exchanges, such as through confidence-building measures and codes of conduct for scientists.

Requiring scientists, institutions, and even experiments to be licensed could have a chilling impact on biomedical research. A measure that avoids this possibility could be found in a strict process of self-regulation, which is already in line with existing ethical requirements to prevent the destructive uses of biology. As any effort to keep good science out of the hands of ill-intentioned people must be international if it is to be effective, Resolution 1540 is a long overdue and much-needed tool to help achieve this objective, but the legitimate requirements of the scientific community should be taken into account so as to avoid jeopardizing scientific and technological innovation. Existing bodies such as the World Health Organization (WHO) and the International Air Transport Association provide international guidelines on the clear identification, labeling, and appropriate physical containment of biological materials in order to avoid spillage or leakage during transport. Concurrent with pressure from Resolution 1540, the February 2005 amendments to the International Health Regulations mean the WHO could act regardless of the cause of an outbreak.

For Resolution 1540 to be effective, it must be regarded as both legitimate and a means to shore up the biolife science sector rather than as a new and onerous tool creating regulatory burdens. And this must happen without the imposition of a one-size-fits-all standard that will hamper technological and scientific development and innovation, especially in fledgling biotechnology sectors in developing countries. The Resolution is not intended to stifle technological advance but to improve states' capacity to enforce the appropriate legislation and prevent the (mis)use of bioscience by terrorists and other non-state actors.

Universality and Norm Building

UNSCR 1540 calls upon all states "to promote the universal adoption . . . of multilateral treaties to which they are parties, whose aim is to prevent the proliferation of nuclear, biological or chemical weapons" (operative paragraph 8(a)). All but three states are states party to the 1968 NPT,[28] but many remain outside the BWC and the CWC. Thus, there is a push, with the help of UNSCR 1540, for universal adoption of these treaties, especially as the technologies related to biological and chemical weapons are much more accessible than those related to nuclear weapons.

Table 14-1 lists all the countries that as of April 2004 have either not signed or signed but not ratified the BWC or the CWC. Shown alongside are indications of whether they had submitted reports to the 1540 Committee, those not having done so on the premise of lacking awareness of requirements or capacity to implement. As the capacity of these states can be improved through the assistance provisions of Resolution 1540, they would be able to develop legislation that in turn would also improve their ability to become parties to the BWC and CWC.

Table 14-1 shows that just about half (33) of the states not party to the BWC and CWC treaties as at April 2004 have not yet submitted reports to the 1540 Committee, although 11 of these became treaty parties since the Resolution's adoption. If these states are willing to comply with its reporting requirement, and to enact appropriate national legislation for purposes of Resolution 1540, the prospects for dealing with capacity issues is promising. The assistance provision (operative paragraph 7) in 1540, which UNSCR 1673 and the fifth program of work heavily endorse,[29] means that these states can receive assistance to submit reports and take steps to draft legislation, perhaps by the time the 1540 Committee reports formally to the Security Council at the end of its mandate in April 2008. As mentioned earlier, states will have gone a long way toward complying with the Resolution if they have ratified the main WMD treaties. But the reverse is also possible for purposes of attaining universality: if states go through all the processes of putting into place national legislation for meeting the requirements of UNSCR 1540, they could become party to the BWC and CWC without too much additional effort. The afore-mentioned 11 states perhaps found it even easier to do so, initially, than to compile the broader range of legislation for reports.

Thus UNSCR 1540 contributes to treaty universality, as do the promotional efforts under other regimes. But ultimately the stimulus for creating national legislation and improving states' capacity to do so should not make a difference if objectives are met. For example, the OPCW's Executive Council adopted the Action Plan for the Universality of the Chemical Weapons Convention in October 2003, with one analysis indicating "that the action plan had the desired effect: the number of states which had neither signed nor ratified the CWC fell from 40 in October 2003 to 16 by the end of February 2006."[30] However, the timing was such that the adoption of UNSCR 1540 and the outreach efforts of the 1540 Committee and the experts group probably contributed to this reduction. Further research can examine this question more closely.

In addition, it is important to note that the Resolution's operative paragraph 8(a), while calling on state parties to promote universality, does not require non-parties that have not signed a WMD treaty (such as Israel, India, and Pakistan with respect to the NPT) to join the WMD treaties.[31] Significantly, all three countries mentioned have nevertheless passed legislation for UNSCR 1540's purposes. This may seem a nuance, but it was a factor in achieving the Resolution's universal adoption.

The Future of UNSCR 1540

The United Nations has clearly placed itself at the centre of the international fight to try to halt WMD proliferation and terrorism. The UN is prepared to take responsibility to set out new rules and initiate a global regime that goes beyond existing treaties. Still, it remains to be seen how the UNSCR 1540 system will develop. Like the requirements of Resolution 1373, implementing it involves the development of, and often a change to, administrative and regulatory systems, as well as the purchase and installation of technical equipment, especially in the area of export controls—capabilities beyond many states (particularly in the developing world) needing to improve their law enforcing and

Table 14-1. States Not Party to the Biological Weapons Convention (BWC) or the Chemical Weapons Convention (CWC) That Have Not Submitted Reports to the 1540 Committee

State	BWC[a] Not a signatory	BWC[a] Signatory, not ratified	CWC[a] Not a signatory	CWC[a] Signatory, not ratified	Report(s) submitted to the 1540 Committee[b]	BWC/CWC[c] date of treaty ratification (or accession [a])	Possible assistance for: x = full reports, y = full reports and treaty legislation
Andorra	x				10/27/04,10/31/05		
Angola	x		x		10/27/04		
Antigua and Barbuda			x		none	CWC 08/29/05 [a]	y
Bahamas				x	10/28/04		x
Barbados			x		none		x
Bhutan				x	none	CWC 08/18/05	y
Burundi		x			none		x
Cambodia				x	03/21/05	CWC 07/19/05	
Cameroon	x				none		x
Central African Republic		x			none	CWC 09/20/06	y
Chad	x			x	none		x
Congo				x	none		x
Comoros	x			x	none		x
Cook Islands (not UN)	x				none		x
Côte d'Ivoire		x			none		x
Democratic People's Republic of Korea			x		none		x
Democratic Republic of Congo					none		x
Djibouti	x			x	03/17/05	CWC 10/12/05	y
Dominican Republic				x	none	CWC 01/25/06	x

Egypt		x	10/28/04,03/17/06		
Eritrea	x		06/22/06		
Gabon	x		none		x
Grenada			09/26/05	CWC 06/03/05	
Guinea	x		none		x
Guinea-Bissau	x		none		x
Guyana	x		11/11/04		
Haiti	x		none		
Honduras	x		06/20/06	CWC 08/29/05	x
Israel	x		11/27/04		
Kazakhstan	x		11/03/04,12/01/05		
Kiribati	x		09/20/05		
Kyrgyzstan	x		12/14/04,02/15/06	BWC 10/12/04 [a]	
Lebanon		x	10/20/04,06/19/06		
Liberia	x		none	CWC 02/23/06	y
Madagascar	x		none	CWC 10/20/04	y
Malawi	x		none		x
Marshall Islands	x		11/23/04	CWC 05/19/04	
Mauritania	x		none		x
Micronesia	x		none		x
Mozambique	x		none		x
Myanmar		x	05/06/05		
Namibia	x		10/26/04,04/27/06		
Nauru	x		none		x
Nepal	x		03/17/06		
Niue (not UN)	x		none	CWC 04/21/05 [a]	y
Republic of Moldova	x		12/17/04, 11/21/05	BWC 01/28/05	
Saint Kitts and Nevis		x	none	CWC 05/21/04	y

(continued)

Table 14-1. **States Not Party to the Biological Weapons Convention (BWC) or the Chemical Weapons Convention (CWC) That Have Not Submitted Reports to the 1540 Committee** (*Continued*)

State	BWC[a] Not a signatory	BWC[a] Signatory, not ratified	CWC[a] Not a signatory	CWC[a] Signatory, not ratified	Report(s) submitted to the 1540 Committee[b]	BWC/CWC[c] date of treaty ratification (or accession [a])	Possible assistance for: x = full reports, y = full reports and treaty legislation
Samoa	x				05/13/06		
Serbia and Montenegro	x				01/05/05, 01/20/06		
Sierra Leone				x	none	CWC 09/30/04	y
Solomon Islands		x	x		none	CWC 09/23/04 [a]	y
Somalia	x		x		none		x
Syrian Arab Republic		x	x		10/14/04,08/26/05, 09/29/05,11/07/05		
Tajikistan		x			01/11/05,12/28/05	BWC 06/27/05	
Trinidad and Tobago	x				05/07/06		
Tuvalu	x				none		x
United Arab Emirates		x			12/09/04		
United Republic of Tanzania		x			08/29/05		
Vanuatu			x		none	CWC 09/16/05 [a]	y
Zambia	x				none		x
Total	26[a]	17[a]	12[a]	19[a]	33 non-reporting states	19 new parties of which 11 are non-reporting states	x = 22, y = 11

Sources: UN and OPCW.

a. As of April 28, 2004, 60 states were not parties, 14 of which were not party to both BWC and CWC.

b. As from October 28, 2004, to November 28, 2006.

c. As of October 2006.

export control systems. The drafters of UNSCRs 1373 and 1540 foresaw and provided for both technical and administrative assistance to such states.

Building state and global institutional capacity is one of the key challenges ahead as debate continues on the extent to which there is need for more clarity of Resolution 1540's substantive obligations and criteria concerning what constitutes adequate compliance. The Resolution contributes to a global governance framework enabling states to become more aware of the underlying issues it addresses and fostering a more coordinated international approach to averting or mitigating proliferation incidents in the future.

This approach has been reinforced by the United Nations Global Counter-Terrorism Strategy and its Plan of Action, adopted unanimously by the General Assembly on September 8, 2006. Although not referring directly to UNSCR 1540, it makes more specific recommendations that would advance some of the Resolution's objectives. In particular, it "note[s] the importance of the proposal of the Secretary General to bring together, within the framework of the United Nations, the major biotechnology stakeholders, including industry, the scientific community, civil society and governments, into a common program aimed at ensuring that biotechnology's advances are not used for terrorist or other criminal purposes but for the public good."[32] Efforts to coordinate international action in response to this initiative and to build capacity are specified in additional items in the Plan of Action's sections II and III. So just as UNSCR 1540 arose from paragraphs in UNSCR 1373, it may in due course return beneath the umbrella of an increasingly institutionalized process of counter-terrorism at the global level. Thus, a more permanent structure for the 1540 Committee along the same lines as the UN Counter-Terrorism Committee's Counter-Terrorism Executive Directorate—with a secretariat and resources and the control and monitoring mechanisms that could accompany them—might not ensue. By April 2008, when the renewed mandate of the 1540 Committee expires again, all states may have in place plans for the requisite counter-proliferation legislation, operational coalitions, and other international cooperative machinery that will minimize bureaucracy and the duplication of reporting efforts. Counter-terrorism is the focus because terrorism is a tactic that can be pursued using any weapon, whether conventional explosives or nuclear, chemical, or biological weapons, but the last group warrants extra attention given the potentially graver consequences of its use.

Although the jury remains out regarding UNSCR 1540's impact on halting, or at least managing, WMD proliferation by and to non-state actors, it is clear that a stronger role for the UN in dealing with this strategic challenge has been long overdue. A global approach to countering the WMD proliferation threat by strengthening national legal frameworks and by increasing public and industry awareness, information sharing, and cooperative international mechanisms is a public good of unquestionable importance, and a major step toward a more robust system of global governance.

Notes

1. President George W. Bush, "Remarks by the President in Address to the United Nations General Assembly," Office of the Press Secretary, The White House, September 12, 2002, at www.whitehouse.gov/news/releases/2002/09/20020912-1.html.

2. Given the absence of a firm definition of terrorism, Resolution 1540 intentionally does not refer to terrorists, traffickers, or other types of non-state actor. In a footnote it defines "non-state actor" simply, and thus comprehensively, as an "individual or entity, not acting under the lawful authority of any State in conducting activities which come within the scope of this resolution." The resolution does not use the term "WMD."

3. These are the 1968 Nuclear Non-Proliferation Treaty (NPT), the 1972 Biological (and Toxin) Weapons Convention (BWC), and the 1993 Chemical Weapons Convention (CWC).

4. Quoted in Edward C. Luck, "The U.S., Counterterrorism, and the Prospects for a Multilateral Alternative," in Jane Boulden and Thomas G. Weiss (eds.), *Terrorism and the UN: Before and After September 11* (Indiana University Press, 2004).

5. See chapter 2 by Thomas J. Biersteker in this volume. It outlines the role of UNSCR 1373 and its CTC in putting into place effective counter-terrorism measures and legislation at the global level.

6. Olivia Bosch, "Weapons Proliferation and Resolution 1540: Iran and the Traffickers," *The World Today*, May 2006, pp. 6–8.

7. The text of Resolution 1673 is available at www.un.org/Docs/sc/unsc_resolutions06.htm, and as Appendix 2.

8. See the 1540 Committee chairman's report to the Security Council, April 25, 2006, at http://disarmament2.un.org/Committee1540/chairreport.html.

9. The legislative database is available on the 1540 Committee website, at http://disarmament2.un.org/Committee1540/legalDB.html.

10. Program of Work of the Security Council Committee Established Pursuant to Resolution 1540 (2004), October 1, 2006–September 30, 2007, fifth program of work, at http://disarmament2.un.org/Committee1540/programmeofwork.html. The decision to extend the work program from three to four months to one year was initially set out in paragraph 136 of the 1540 Committee chairman's report to the Security Council, April 25, 2006, at http://disarmament2.un.org/Committee1540/chair report.html.

11. Report to the Security Council by the Committee Established Pursuant to Resolution 1540 (2004), April 28, 2004, Summary – Assistance, p. 2, at http://disarmament 2.un.org/committee1540.

12. Peter D. Zimmerman and Jeffrey G. Lewis, "The Bomb in the Backyard," *Foreign Policy*, No. 157, November–December 2006, p. 33.

13. John D. Negroponte, "Yes, We Are Better Prepared," *Washington Post*, September 10, 2006.

14. Idem.

15. The White House, *The National Security Strategy of the United States of America* (Washington: The White House, September 17, 2002), at www.whitehouse.gov/nsc/nss.html.

16. See chapter 11 by Siew Gay Ong in this volume.

17. This calculation is made from two official statements: "11 successful efforts" during a period of nine months prior to the statement by Condoleezza Rice, "Remarks on the Second Anniversary of the Proliferation Security Initiative," U.S. Department of State, May 31, 2005, at www.state.gov/secretary/rm/2005/46951.htm, and "roughly two dozen separate occasions to prevent transfers" between April 2005 and April 2006, stated by Robert G. Joseph, Under Secretary for Arms Control and International Security, "Broadening and Deepening Our Proliferation Security Initiative Cooperation," U.S. Department of State, June 23, 2006, at www.state.gov/t/us/rm/68269.htm.

18. "Proliferation Security Initiative Logs Varied Activities in Two Years," U.S. State Department, USINFO information sheet, May 2, 2005, at http://usinfo.state.gov/is/Archive/2005/May/03-764392.html.

19. Peter Dombrowski and Rodger A. Payne, "The Emerging Consensus for Preventive War," *Survival*, Vol. 48, No. 2 (Summer 2006), pp. 129–31.

20. Seymour Hersch, "Last Stand: The Military's Problem with the President's Iran Policy," *The New Yorker*, July 2006, at www.newyorker.com/fact/content/articles/060710fa_fact.

21. See chapter 13 by Roelof Manschot in this volume regarding factors affecting decisions about the prosecution of A. Q. Khan in the early 1980s.

22. Sixth Review Conference of the States Parties to the BTWC, Draft Final Document, Part II: Final Declaration, regarding Article 4, paragraph 17, p. 12, as adopted on December 8, 2006, available from www.unog.ch.

23. Rose Gottemoeller, "Cooperative Threat Reduction beyond Russia," *The Washington Quarterly*, Vol. 28, No. 2 (Spring 2005), p. 153; and "Biological Weapons Convention Expert Meeting Concludes: Experts Exchange Ideas on Content, Promulgation, Adoption of Codes of Conduct for Scientists," UN Press Release DC/2973, June 25, 2005 at www.un.org/News/Press/docs/2005/dc2973.doc.htm.

24. See, for example, the ASM's "Sentinel Laboratory Guidelines for Suspected Agents of Bioterrorism," August 2006, at www.asm.org/ASM/files/LeftMarginHeaderList/DOWNLOADFILENAME/000000001206/BTtemplateRevised8-10-6.doc.

25. See chapter 12 by Gerald L. Epstein in this volume.

26. See, in particular, chapter 9 by Jeffrey Almond in this volume.

27. See chapter 3 by Elizabeth M. Prescott in this volume.

28. North Korea acceded to the NPT in 1985 and in 2003 stated its intention to withdraw.

29. There are some states party to the BWC or CWC, such as Afghanistan, that have not submitted reports to the 1540 Committee, but this is not viewed as an act of non-compliance with 1540 because intentions are evident or temporary difficulties have been explained.

30. Daniel Feakes, "Practical Steps for Accelerating BWC Universality," *Disarmament Diplomacy*, No. 82, Spring 2006, at www.acronym.org.uk/dd/dd82/82df.htm.

31. It is also problematic, however, that the NPT does not have a provision for the so-called nuclear weapons states of India, Israel, and Pakistan to join the treaty without renegotiation of the treaty itself. The prospects of this are unlikely without renegotiating other treaty provisions.

32. United Nations General Assembly, The United Nations Global Counter-Terrorism Strategy, A/RES/60/288, Sixtieth Session General Assembly, Plenary, 99th Meeting, September 8, 2006, Plan of Action, Section II, item 11, at www.un.org/Depts/dhl/resguide/r60.htm.

Text of UN Security Council Resolution 1540 (2004)

Adopted by the Security Council at its 4956th meeting, on 28 April 2004

The Security Council,

Affirming that proliferation of nuclear, chemical and biological weapons, as well as their means of delivery,* constitutes a threat to international peace and security,

Reaffirming, in this context, the Statement of its President adopted at the Council's meeting at the level of Heads of State and Government on 31 January 1992 (S/23500), including the need for all Member States to fulfil [sic] their obligations in relation to arms control and disarmament and to prevent proliferation in all its aspects of all weapons of mass destruction,

Recalling also that the Statement underlined the need for all Member States to resolve peacefully in accordance with the Charter any problems in that context threatening or disrupting the maintenance of regional and global stability,

Affirming its resolve to take appropriate and effective actions against any threat to international peace and security caused by the proliferation of

---

* Definitions for the purpose of this resolution only:

Means of delivery: missiles, rockets and other unmanned systems capable of delivering nuclear, chemical, or biological weapons, that are specially designed for such use.

Non-State actor: individual or entity, not acting under the lawful authority of any State in conducting activities which come within the scope of this resolution.

Related materials: materials, equipment and technology covered by relevant multilateral treaties and arrangements, or included on national control lists, which could be used for the design, development, production or use of nuclear, chemical and biological weapons and their means of delivery.

nuclear, chemical and biological weapons and their means of delivery, in conformity with its primary responsibilities, as provided for in the United Nations Charter,

Affirming its support for the multilateral treaties whose aim is to eliminate or prevent the proliferation of nuclear, chemical or biological weapons and the importance for all States parties to these treaties to implement them fully in order to promote international stability,

Welcoming efforts in this context by multilateral arrangements which contribute to non-proliferation,

Affirming that prevention of proliferation of nuclear, chemical and biological weapons should not hamper international cooperation in materials, equipment and technology for peaceful purposes while goals of peaceful utilization should not be used as a cover for proliferation,

Gravely concerned by the threat of terrorism and the risk that non-State actors* such as those identified in the United Nations list established and maintained by the Committee established under Security Council resolution 1267 and those to whom resolution 1373 applies, may acquire, develop, traffic in or use nuclear, chemical and biological weapons and their means of delivery,

Gravely concerned by the threat of illicit trafficking in nuclear, chemical, or biological weapons and their means of delivery, and related materials,* which adds a new dimension to the issue of proliferation of such weapons and also poses a threat to international peace and security,

Recognizing the need to enhance coordination of efforts on national, subregional, regional and international levels in order to strengthen a global response to this serious challenge and threat to international security,

Recognizing that most States have undertaken binding legal obligations under treaties to which they are parties, or have made other commitments aimed at preventing the proliferation of nuclear, chemical or biological weapons, and have taken effective measures to account for, secure and physically protect sensitive materials, such as those required by the Convention on the Physical Protection of Nuclear Materials and those recommended by the IAEA Code of Conduct on the Safety and Security of Radioactive Sources,

Recognizing further the urgent need for all States to take additional effective measures to prevent the proliferation of nuclear, chemical or biological weapons and their means of delivery,

Encouraging all Member States to implement fully the disarmament treaties and agreements to which they are party,

Reaffirming the need to combat by all means, in accordance with the Charter of the United Nations, threats to international peace and security caused by terrorist acts,

Determined to facilitate henceforth an effective response to global threats in the area of non-proliferation,

Acting under Chapter VII of the Charter of the United Nations,

1. *Decides that* all States shall refrain from providing any form of support to non-State actors that attempt to develop, acquire, manufacture, possess, transport, transfer or use nuclear, chemical or biological weapons and their means of delivery;

2. *Decides also* that all States, in accordance with their national procedures, shall adopt and enforce appropriate effective laws which prohibit any non-State actor to manufacture, acquire, possess, develop, transport, transfer or use nuclear, chemical or biological weapons and their means of delivery, in particular for terrorist purposes, as well as attempts to engage in any of the foregoing activities, participate in them as an accomplice, assist or finance them;

3. *Decides also* that all States shall take and enforce effective measures to establish domestic controls to prevent the proliferation of nuclear, chemical, or biological weapons and their means of delivery, including by establishing appropriate controls over related materials and to this end shall:

(a) Develop and maintain appropriate effective measures to account for and secure such items in production, use, storage or transport;

(b) Develop and maintain appropriate effective physical protection measures;

(c) Develop and maintain appropriate effective border controls and law enforcement efforts to detect, deter, prevent and combat, including through international cooperation when necessary, the illicit trafficking and brokering in such items in accordance with their national legal authorities and legislation and consistent with international law;

(d) Establish, develop, review and maintain appropriate effective national export and trans-shipment controls over such items, including appropriate laws and regulations to control export, transit, trans-shipment and re-export and controls on providing funds and services related to such export and trans-shipment such as financing, and transporting that would contribute to proliferation, as well as establishing end-user controls; and establishing and enforcing appropriate criminal or civil penalties for violations of such export control laws and regulations;

4. *Decides* to establish, in accordance with rule 28 of its provisional rules of procedure, for a period of no longer than two years, a Committee of the

Security Council, consisting of all members of the Council, which will, calling as appropriate on other expertise, report to the Security Council for its examination, on the implementation of this resolution, and to this end calls upon States to present a first report no later than six months from the adoption of this resolution to the Committee on steps they have taken or intend to take to implement this resolution;

5. *Decides* that none of the obligations set forth in this resolution shall be interpreted so as to conflict with or alter the rights and obligations of State Parties to the Nuclear Non-Proliferation Treaty, the Chemical Weapons Convention and the Biological and Toxin Weapons Convention or alter the responsibilities of the International Atomic Energy Agency or the Organization for the Prohibition of Chemical Weapons;

6. *Recognizes* the utility in implementing this resolution of effective national control lists and calls upon all Member States, when necessary, to pursue at the earliest opportunity the development of such lists;

7. *Recognizes* that some States may require assistance in implementing the provisions of this resolution within their territories and invites States in a position to do so to offer assistance as appropriate in response to specific requests to the States lacking the legal and regulatory infrastructure, implementation experience and/or resources for fulfilling the above provisions;

8. *Calls upon* all States:

(a) To promote the universal adoption and full implementation, and, where necessary, strengthening of multilateral treaties to which they are parties, whose aim is to prevent the proliferation of nuclear, biological or chemical weapons;

(b) To adopt national rules and regulations, where it has not yet been done, to ensure compliance with their commitments under the key multilateral nonproliferation treaties;

(c) To renew and fulfil their commitment to multilateral cooperation, in particular within the framework of the International Atomic Energy Agency, the Organization for the Prohibition of Chemical Weapons and the Biological and Toxin Weapons Convention, as important means of pursuing and achieving their common objectives in the area of non-proliferation and of promoting international cooperation for peaceful purposes;

(d) To develop appropriate ways to work with and inform industry and the public regarding their obligations under such laws;

9. *Calls upon* all States to promote dialogue and cooperation on nonproliferation so as to address the threat posed by proliferation of nuclear, chemical, or biological weapons, and their means of delivery;

10. Further to counter that threat, *calls upon* all States, in accordance with their national legal authorities and legislation and consistent with international law, to take cooperative action to prevent illicit trafficking in nuclear, chemical or biological weapons, their means of delivery, and related materials;

11. *Expresses* its intention to monitor closely the implementation of this resolution and, at the appropriate level, to take further decisions which may be required to this end;

12. *Decides* to remain seized of the matter.

Text of UN Security Council Resolution 1673 (2006)

Adopted by the Security Council at its 5429th meeting, on 27 April 2006

The Security Council,

Having considered the report of the Security Council Committee established pursuant to resolution 1540 (2004), hereafter the 1540 Committee (S/2006/257), and reaffirming its resolution 1540 (2004) of 28 April 2004,

Reaffirming that proliferation of nuclear, chemical and biological weapons, as well as their means of delivery, constitutes a threat to international peace and security,

Endorsing the work already carried out by the 1540 Committee, particularly in its consideration of the national reports submitted by States pursuant to resolution 1540 (2004),

Recalling that not all States have presented to the 1540 Committee their reports on the steps they have taken or intend to take to implement resolution 1540 (2004),

Reaffirming its decision that none of the obligations in resolution 1540 (2004) shall be interpreted so as to conflict with or alter the rights and obligations of State Parties to the Nuclear Non-Proliferation Treaty, the Chemical Weapons Convention and the Biological and Toxin Weapons Convention or alter the responsibilities of the International Atomic Energy Agency or the Organization for the Prohibition of Chemical Weapons,

Noting that the full implementation of resolution 1540 (2004) by all States, including the adoption of national laws and measures to ensure the implementation of these laws, is a long-term task that will require continuous efforts at national, regional and international levels,

Acting under Chapter VII of the Charter of the United Nations,

1. *Reiterates* its decisions in and the requirements of resolution 1540 (2004) and *emphasizes* the importance for all States to implement fully that resolution;

2. *Calls upon* all States that have not yet presented a first report on steps they have taken or intend to take to implement resolution 1540 (2004) to submit such a report to the 1540 Committee without delay;

3. *Encourages* all States that have submitted such reports to provide, at any time or upon the request of the 1540 Committee, additional information on their implementation of resolution 1540 (2004);

4. *Decides* to extend the mandate of the 1540 Committee for a period of two years, with the continued assistance of experts, until 27 April 2008;

5. *Decides* that the 1540 Committee shall intensify its efforts to promote the full implementation by all States of resolution 1540 (2004) through a work programme which shall include the compilation of information on the status of States' implementation of all aspects of resolution 1540 (2004), outreach, dialogue, assistance and cooperation, and which shall address in particular all aspects of paragraphs 1 and 2 of that resolution, as well as of paragraph 3 which encompasses (a) accountability, (b) physical protection, (c) border controls and law enforcement efforts and (d) national export and trans-shipment controls including controls on providing funds and services such as financing to such export and trans-shipment, and in that regard:

(a) *encourages* the pursuit of the ongoing dialogue between the 1540 Committee and States on the full implementation of resolution 1540 (2004), including on further actions needed from States to that end and on technical assistance needed and offered;

(b) *invites* the 1540 Committee to explore with States and international, regional and subregional organizations experience-sharing and lessons learned in the areas covered by resolution 1540 (2004), and the availability of programmes which might facilitate the implementation of resolution 1540 (2004);

6. *Decides* that the 1540 Committee will submit to the Security Council a report no later than 27 April 2008 on compliance with resolution 1540 (2004) through the achievement of the implementation of its requirements;

7. *Decides* to remain seized of the matter.

Guidelines for Work of the 1540 Committee

Security Council Committee Established Pursuant to Resolution 1540 (2004) Guidelines for the Conduct of its Work

1. 1540 Committee

(a). The Committee of the Security Council established pursuant to paragraph 4 of Security Council resolution 1540 (2004) of 28 April 2004 will be known as the 1540 Committee.

(b). The Committee is a subsidiary body of the Security Council.

2. Mandate of the Committee

(a). The Committee is established in accordance with rule 28 of the Security Council provisional rules of procedure for a period of no longer than two years.

(b). The Committee will, calling as appropriate on other expertise, report to the Security Council for its examination on the implementation of resolution 1540 (2004).

(c). The Committee will receive and examine the national reports of Member States, a first report submitted no later than six months from the adoption of resolution 1540 (2004), on steps they have taken or intend to take to implement the resolution.

(d). The Committee may decide to establish, as necessary, arrangements to cooperate with the International Atomic Energy Agency (IAEA) and the Organisation for the Prohibition of Chemical Weapons (OPCW). If it deems appropriate, the Committee may also establish arrangements to cooperate with other relevant international, regional, sub-regional bodies and relevant committees established under the Security Council, which it decides can contribute to the work of the Committee.

(e). The Committee will submit regular reports, including recommendations as necessary, to the Security Council on the implementation of resolution 1540 (2004).

(f). The Committee recognizes that some States may require assistance in implementing the provisions of resolution 1540(2004) within their territories and will continue to invite States in a position to do so to offer assistance as appropriate in response to specific requests to the States lacking the legal and regulatory infrastructure, implementation experience and/or resources for fulfilling the above provisions.

(g). The Committee reaffirms that none of the obligations set forth in resolution 1540(2004) shall be interpreted so as to conflict with or alter the rights and obligations of States Parties to the Nuclear Non-Proliferation Treaty, the Chemical Weapons Convention and the Biological and Toxin Weapons Convention or alter the responsibilities of the IAEA or the OPCW.

3. Composition of the Committee

(a). The Committee will consist of all Members of the Security Council.

(b). The Chairman of the Committee will be appointed by the Security Council. The Chairman of the Committee will be assisted by Vice-Chairmen, who will be appointed by the Security Council.

(c). The Chairman will chair the meetings of the Committee. When he/she is unable to chair a meeting, he/she will nominate a Vice-Chairman to act on his/her behalf.

(d). The Secretariat of the Committee will be provided by the Secretariat of the United Nations.

(e). For the fulfillment of its mandate, the Committee will consider and approve the recruitment of experts. Such experts will be proposed by UN Member States as well as by the Secretariat, taking into account recommendations by UN Member States.

4. Meetings of the Committee

(a). Meetings of the Committee will be convened at any time the Chairman deems necessary, or at the request of a Member of the Committee. At least 48 hours' notice will normally be given for any meeting of the Committee, unless otherwise decided by the Members of the Committee.

(b). The Committee will meet in closed session, unless it decides otherwise.

(c). The Committee may invite any Member of the United Nations to participate in the discussion of any question brought before the Committee in which the interests of that Member are specifically affected.

(d). The Chairman may invite experts of the Committee to attend meetings as appropriate.

(e). The Committee, as appropriate, may invite members of the Secretariat, or other persons whom it considers competent, for the purpose of providing appropriate expertise or information or of providing other assistance in examining matters within its competence.

5. Documentation and Agenda

(a). The Chairman, in conjunction with the Secretariat, will circulate a provisional agenda and related documents at least 48 hours before a meeting of the Committee.

(b). The Chairman, in conjunction with the Secretariat, will circulate other relevant documents and papers to members of the Committee.

6. Information supplied to the Committee

(a). The Committee may consider information it deems relevant to its work received from those bodies referred to in paragraph 2(d).

(b). The information received by the Committee will be kept confidential if the provider so requests or if the Committee so decides.

7. Reports

Reports submitted by Member States pursuant to paragraph 4 of resolution 1540 (2004) will be circulated as documents of the Security Council.

8. Decision-making

(a). The Committee will take decisions by consensus of its Members. If consensus cannot be reached on a particular issue, the Chairman will undertake such further consultations as may facilitate agreement. If, after such consultations, consensus still cannot be reached, the matter will be submitted to the Security Council for its consideration.

(b). In cases where the Committee so agrees, decisions may be taken by a written procedure. In such cases the Chairman will circulate to all Members of the Committee the proposed decision of the Committee, and will request Members of the Committee to indicate their objection to the proposed decision within 96 hours or, in urgent situations, within a shorter period, but no less than 48 hours, to be determined by the Chairman. If no objection is received within the stated period, the decision will be considered adopted.

9. *Transparency*

(a). The Committee will undertake its tasks with utmost transparency.

(b). The Chairman, and the Vice-Chairmen, as appropriate, in consultation with the Committee, will hold regular briefings for interested Member States, relevant international bodies and the media, to explain the work of the Committee.

(c). The Committee will, as appropriate, issue press releases on its activities.

About the Authors

Jeffrey Almond is a senior vice president at one of the world's largest manufacturers of vaccines where he leads discovery research and is responsible for identifying and managing external collaborations relevant to vaccine R&D. Before joining the company in 1999, he was professor of microbiology at the University of Reading, UK, where he currently is visiting professor, and held external offices including chairman of the Virology Division of the International Union of Microbiological Societies, International Secretary for the Society of General Microbiology, and was a member of the UK government's Spongiform Encephalopathies Advisory Committee.

Thomas J. Biersteker is Henry R. Luce Professor of Transnational Organizations at Brown University, Rhode Island. The author or editor of nine books, including *State Sovereignty as Social Construct, The Emergence of Private Authority in Global Governance,* and *Countering the Financing of Global Terrorism,* his recent activities include work with the UN Secretariat on targeting sanctions. He received his Ph.D. and M.S. from the Massachusetts Institute of Technology and his B.A. from the University of Chicago.

Olivia Bosch is associate fellow, previously senior research fellow at the time of writing, International Security Programme, Chatham House, London. Among her previous work, Dr. Bosch served as a UN inspector in Iraq; senior fellow, Center for Global Security Research, Lawrence Livermore National Laboratory, on a joint project with the International Institute for Strategic Studies on the Year 2000 (Y2K) experience and critical infrastructure protection; and director of the Council for Arms Control, London. Recent publications include "Weapons Proliferation and Resolution 1540: Iran and the

Traffickers," *World Today*, May 2006, and "UNSCR 1540: Terrorism and WMD—Relevance for the Gulf States," *Security and Terrorism Research Bulletin*, Gulf Research Center, October 2005.

Gerald L. Epstein is senior fellow for science and security, Homeland Security Program, Center for Strategic and International Studies, and teaches in the Security Studies Program at Georgetown University. He previously worked at the Congressional Office of Technology Assessment, Harvard University's Kennedy School of Government, and the White House Office of Science and Technology Policy, where he served both as assistant director for national security and senior director for science and technology on the National Security Council staff.

Chandré Gould, senior researcher at the Institute for Security Studies, was global network co-ordinator for the Bio Weapons Prevention Project at the time of writing. She is a former investigator for South Africa's Truth and Reconciliation Commission, co-author with Peter Folb of an official United Nations study on *Project Coast: Apartheid's Chemical and Biological Warfare Programme* (2002) and co-author with Marlene Burger of *Secrets and Lies: Wouter Basson and South Africa's Chemical and Biological Warfare Programme* (2002).

Jan Lodding is a senior policy officer for verification and security policy coordination at the International Atomic Energy Agency in Vienna. He previously served with the IAEA's Department of Technical Cooperation and with the Swedish Foreign Ministry.

Ron G. Manley, OBE, is a chemical weapons defense specialist. He joined the Organisation for the Prohibition of Chemical Weapons (OPCW) in 1993 and served with the organization until his retirement from the post of director of the Verification Division at the end of 2001. He is currently a visiting professor at the Defence Academy, Cranfield University, UK.

Roelof Jan Manschot is vice president, Eurojust, and its National Member for the Netherlands. He was advocate general at the Court of Appeal in Amsterdam from 1985 where he worked specifically on organized and financial crime. He was appointed chief prosecutor in 1995 and joined Eurojust in 2001. He is a member of the Administrative Council of the European Institute for Law Enforcement Co-operation (EULEC) and of the International Association of Prosecutors.

Sarah Meek, who died tragically during the production of this book, was the head of policy and development at the Institute for Security Studies in South Africa. At the time of writing, she was leading ISS's Arms Management Programme, where she returned in January 2002 after a three-year break. She previously had served with the ISS as senior researcher from 1996 to 1999. Between 1999 and 2002 she was manager of the security and peace-building program at International Alert in London. She also worked at the United Nations Department for Disarmament Affairs in New York and the Center for Nonproliferation Studies in Monterey, California. She had published widely on issues related to arms control, illicit arms trafficking, and conflict prevention in Africa.

Siew Gay Ong is deputy director of the Protocol Directorate, previously having been the senior assistant director of the International Organizations Directorate at the Singapore Ministry of Foreign Affairs. Then, he was in charge of UN-related matters and various multilateral issues, including counter-proliferation. He has been with the Foreign Ministry for nine years and was posted to the Singapore Embassy in Beijing from 1999 to 2002.

Elizabeth M. Prescott was an AAAS Congressional Fellow working with the U.S. Senate Committee for Health, Education, Labor, and Pensions. She received her D.Phil. in molecular biology from Balliol College, Oxford, and degrees in molecular biology and economics from the University of California–Berkeley. She is currently a term member in the Council on Foreign Relations and a principal of the Truman National Security Project.

Tariq Rauf is head of verification and security policy coordination at the International Atomic Energy Agency in Vienna. He was expert adviser to the Delegation of Canada to the NPT Review Conferences (1990–2000) and expert consultant to the Canberra Commission for the Elimination of Nuclear Weapons.

Will Robinson was the policy adviser on security and facilitation for the World Customs Organization at the time of writing. He was responsible for management of a number of WCO enforcement initiatives, including coordination of initiatives in the field of anti-terrorism and security of the international trade supply chain; the WCO Business Partnership; and its global intelligence strategy. He has over twenty-five years' experience with policy and operational customs work, including at the UK's HM Customs and Excise National Intelligence Division.

Peter van Ham is director of the Global Governance Programme at the Netherlands Institute of International Relations, "Clingendael," in The Hague and professor at the College of Europe in Bruges, Belgium. He was professor of West European politics at the George C. Marshall European Center for Security Studies, Garmisch-Partenkirchen (1996–2001). He has held research positions at the EU Institute for Security Studies (Paris), the Royal Institute of International Affairs (London), Columbia University (New York), and COPRI (Denmark). He is a member of the Advisory Council on International Affairs to the Dutch Government (Peace and Security Committee) and of the editorial board of Security Dialogue (PRIO/Oslo). His recent books include *Mapping European Security after Kosovo* (Manchester University Press, 2002), *European Integration and the Postmodern Condition* (Routledge, 2001), and *A Critical Approach to European Security* (Pinter, 1999). He has also published in *The National Interest, Foreign Affairs, Washington Quarterly, Security Dialogue, European Security,* and *Millennium.*

Ted Whiteside is head of the Weapons of Mass Destruction Centre at NATO. Previously, he was a counselor in the Canadian delegation to NATO, responsible for a wide range of political and defense issues, including theatre ballistic missile defense. After that he became deputy head of the disarmament, arms control, and cooperative security section in the political affairs division at NATO from where he moved to his present position.

Angela Woodward is deputy director at VERTIC (Verification Research, Training and Information Centre), London. She is an expert in verification and national implementation of arms control and disarmament agreements. Her work currently focuses on national implementing legislation to comply with the 1972 Biological Weapons Convention and UNSC Resolution 1540 (2004) and the UN's role in verification. She holds B.A. (Hons., political science), LL.B., and LL.M. degrees.

Index